BREAKFAST IN
Bridgetown

THE DEFINITIVE GUIDE
TO PORTLAND'S
FAVORITE MEAL

BY

PAUL GERALD

Bacon and Eggs Press
0650 SW Lowell St. #409
Portland, OR 97239-4465
breakfastinbridgetown.com

Printed in the United States of America
ISBN: 978-0-9797350-4-2
Library of Congress Control Number: 2010915011

Cover by Alan Dubinsky
Interior by Vinnie Kinsella
Photos by Paul Gerald

As it always will be, this book is dedicated, with immense admiration and gratitude, to everybody who grows it, delivers it, preps it, cooks it, brings it out, and cleans it up.

CONTENTS

THE RESTAURANTS

CONTENTS

CONTENTS

CONTENTS

HELPFUL LISTS

CONTENTS

ACKNOWLEDGMENTS

Writing and publishing your own book is all groovy and independent and empowering—and also expensive and scary and a ton of work. Thank goodness the world is full of helpful, kind, and patient people who will assist with such things. I am sure I have forgotten some of them here, because I'm often not good at such details, but whoever you are, know that I am eternally grateful to you for your help, support, and advice.

First, to my fellow authors, upon whose shoulders I've cried and upon whose advice and support I depend the most in this respect: Cindy Anderson of the *Portland Happy Hour Guidebook*, Jen Stevenson of *100 Best Places to Stuff Your Faces*, Liz Crain of *Food Lover's Guide to Portland*, Kelly Melillo of *The Best Places to Pee*, Laura Foster of various great walking guides, and Hanna Neuschwander of *Left Coast Roast*. Mike Jones from Menasha Ridge Press must go here, as well.

Many bloggers and writers have also been helpful, whether through good information, advice or company, and I particularly thank Brett Burmeister of foodcartsportland.com, The Food Dude of portlandfood anddrink.com, the whole crew at pdx.eater.com, Amy Burglehaus of eatingmywaythruportland.com, and all the posters at portlandfood.org. Thanks again to Martha Wagner (marthawagner.com) for educating me on gluten-free dining and writing that section of this book. Clark Haass has offered a lot of education on the art of hash (the breakfast kind!) and contributed a couple of pages on *Hashcapades*; look for the *Hashcapade* watermarks on his favorite places. Also thanks to the good people at portlandhikers.org for reminding me to hike all this off.

Of course, I have much love for my Breakfast Crew, that motley lot who responds to my invitation emails and puts up with me always being the last to show up. They are Joan Frank, Jon Bell, Cheryl Juetten, Kerry Jeffrey, Sharon Streeter, Al Zimmerman, Tom and Leslie Eggers, Jeannette Lyons, Jerry Martin, Shari Melton, Michelle Boyle, Bob Malone, Judy Olivier, Jenny Boyce, Ryan and Amy Burglehaus, Curtis Chen, DeeAnn Sole, Sidnee Snell, Maria Liotta-Shindler, Jeff Macey, Ilene Ferrell, Hollie Lindauer, Debi Danielson, Anna Long, Jean Tuller, Mick Mortlock, Al and Cate Zimmerman, and Phil Wentz.

ACKNOWLEDGMENTS

On the production end, I thank all the folks at Indigo Editing & Publications for making my words into an attractive book: Ali McCart, Susan DeFreitas, and Vinnie Kinsela. Same to Alan Dubinsky for doing the cover. Bob Smith lined up the print job. Thanks, also, to Chris Alley and Tony Forsyth at Ampersand Productions for making me look half respectable in my Indiegogo video.

Thanks to Liz Feldman and Lara Damon at Portland State for all their business advice, as well as my grad student team of Klesti Brameta, Jackie Chan and Jessica Estrelle for the marketing campaign they created for me.

And finally, thanks as always to Kurt Swensen, Bill Wilson, Hank Wesselman, my Breitenbush journey friends, and the Monday Meditators for helping me stay reasonably sane and on course.

SPECIAL THANKS

I helped finance this book by running a campaign on Indiegogo (indiegogo.com), and these fine folks pitched in on the effort. I'm pretty sure the old saying, "I couldn't have done it without you" applies here!

They are Alethea Smartt, Amy Burglehaus, Andy Davis, Anne Marie Moss, Barbara Lawson, Becky Schreiber, Bill and Nancy Meyer, Bob Malone, Bob Seitz, Bob Vreeland, Buddy Cushman, Caleb Winter, Cheryl McDowell & David Snyder, Chip Shields, Chris Alley, Chris Angelus, Cindy Anderson, Cindy McElroy, Clark Haass, Cory Collins, Daniel Stultz, David Cohen, Don Pearson, Eliza McEmrys, Eric Miller, Gale Frank, Geralyn Simpson, Hollie Lindauer, Ilene Ferrell, Janet Oppe, Jeannette Lyons, Jeff Feiffer, Jeff Macey, Jeff Siegel, Jennifer Omner, Jenny Boyce, Jesse Lowe, Jim Pastene, John Talley, Kathleen Dopheide, Katie Clarkson, Kelley Roy, Ken Bibb, Kennedy Somerset, Larry Klatt, Laura Foster, Les Konrad, Leslie Eggers, Loren Skogland, Lucy Cook, Lynne Siegel, Marion Fox, Mark Bruce, Marty Williams, Nicholas Dekker, Noelle Savatta, Patrick Donaldson, Paul Gerhards, Regis Krug, Renata Chmielowski, Reuel Kurzet, Richard Crimi, River Ledgerwood, Robb Wijnhausen, Roger Livingston, Ron Shenker, Sally Turk, Shari Melton, Sharon Stern and Steve Rallison, Sharon Streeter, Sidnee Snell, Sidra Jeffries, Stan Ruckman, Steve Terrill, Su Smith, Susan Cushman, Suzie Baunsgard, Tom Healy, Tom Kloster, Tom Mahler, Tom Nelson, Peggie Schwarz, Valarie Smith, Veronica Vichit-Vadakan, Wendy Bumgardner, and Wolfkiss.

INTRODUCTION

I had no idea what I was getting into with this book.

It started with a simple idea: Describe all the breakfast places in Portland. That quaint notion was shattered as I came to realize how many such places there are. It's insane—and they keep opening! So I decided to keep it to places within the city limits that serve an honest-to-goodness breakfast. So, no coffee shops or donut shops or local taverns with an egg sandwich special.

The seed of this idea lies in my 16-year career as a travel writer for the *Memphis Flyer*, where I used to be a staffer. In the process of writing some 300 articles, a theme developed: describe a place by describing a meal eaten there, usually breakfast, which I did for Las Vegas, an Amtrak train, Hong Kong, Santa Barbara, Skykomish, and so on. To read how that seed took root in my brain, read the chapter on Beaterville Cafe.

The basic idea is to describe Portland by how and where it eats breakfast—kind of a breakfast tour of the city—while also giving folks a whole mess of options to check out. And yes, I've eaten in every one of the restaurants described. And yes, I weigh more than I used to.

For this edition, I am throwing in a collection of out-of-town places, as well as an attempted survey of breakfast carts. And I've brought on an expert, Martha Wagner, to tell us all about gluten-free breakfasts.

WHERE'S MY FAVORITE (OR THAT NEW) PLACE?

Though I try, I can't get them all. I'm sure many of you have a favorite you won't see here, and all I can say is sorry. It may be that they opened too late to make it in this time.

Another thing that happens, sad to say, is that I go to a place, forget to take notes or photos, then kind of forget I went there, then get on a deadline, go crazy, and suddenly think, "Wait, did I eat there?" In other words, you know that dream where it's the last week of the semester and you forgot a course you were supposed to be attending? That happens to me, for real, with breakfast places.

Or maybe I'm just an idiot. Either way, between carts and out-of-town places and real Portland restaurants, there's, like, 150 places in here to eat breakfast. If that isn't enough for you, I don't know what to tell you!

WHAT THIS BOOK ISN'T (OR, WHY NO STARS?)

I am neither a critic nor a foodie, and I don't have a sophisticated palate or any inside scoop on what's happening behind the scenes—mainly because I am lazy, unsophisticated, and don't care about such things. I do have this going for me: I am certain I've eaten breakfast in more Portland restaurants than any other human being. I'm just not sure how I feel about that.

Anyway, no ratings. I honestly believe that my opinion of a place, which is based on my preferences and perhaps only one visit, almost certainly has no connection to your opinion of a place. Some of these places I don't care for, some I love, but I think they're all interesting in some way, so that's what I shoot for. Besides, how do you have the same rating system for, say, the Stepping Stone and Ataula? If you really care, I listed my 12 favorites in the back.

I should let you know that with very few exceptions (when I was doing an interview for my podcast) my experiences were not influenced by restaurant staff; none knew I was writing a book when I visited, and none paid for my meals.

MY CRY FOR HELP

I still find out about breakfast places every week, and I'm usually not happy about it, because I could work on this %^!&$#! book forever! But I do want to know about them, and also how I can make the book better and more suited to your needs. What ideas do you have for organization, information, and presentation? Do you have any news tips I should know about? Is something out of date or just plain wrong?

Even if you just want to bitch at me, you are strongly encouraged to get in touch. I'm blogging regularly at breakfastinbridgetown.com, my email address is portlandbreakfast@gmail.com, and I look forward to hearing from you.

I'll see you at breakfast.

Paul Gerald

DISCLAIMER

All the facts in this book—addresses, phone numbers, prices, and so on—were confirmed with the restaurants, to the best of our ability, in early 2014.

We strongly suggest a call to your chosen place before you go to make sure it is still around, that the wait has not gotten out of control, or that it still serves that certain something you read about and must have.

I keep a list of updates and corrections on this book's website, breakfastinbridgetown.com. In fact, if you find a mistake or have an update—or if you have a suggestion of any kind—please contact the author via the website or at portlandbreakfast@gmail.com.

Happy dining!

In addition to location and category (see pages 16 and 18), I give you a little more info on each place. Here's a quick guide.

Feel (in italics): If I had to quickly summarize its essence, this is what I'd say.

Price range: Average price range for a typical meal consisting of a main dish, non-alcoholic beverage, and about a 20 percent tip.

Website: Many places are also on Facebook and Twitter; there's a list of links at breakfastinbridgetown.com under "Breakfast Places Online."

Wait: Not a science, of course, but a good guess based on what I've seen and heard from customers and staff.

Large groups: How staff will handle a group of six or more. There's a list of best bets on page 292. If they take reservations, I've tried to note that.

Other Drinks: Espresso? Fresh juices? Cocktails? Smoothies? Anything special?

Feel-goods: Free range, grass fed, shade grown, local, organic, etc.

Health options: Vegan/vegetarian options, egg substitutes, allergy-sensitive dishes.

Wifi: Not that *anyone* would want to bring a computer to breakfast, of course…

CATEGORIES

I've created categories to give you a quick take on what kind of place each restaurant is. I have also put places into more than one category, some of which probably make no sense. To try to explain things a little, here's what I'm thinking when I assign each category:

New doesn't mean it recently opened. The category is more like "New Portland" and refers to a place that has the hippie/yuppie/foodie feel to it, serves Asiago cheese and whatnot, and generally represents the changes Portland's food scene has undergone in the last, say, 20 years. Examples: Simpatica, Tasty n Sons, Tin Shed.

Old School places have generally been around a while. A lot of folks would call them diners, but that's too narrow for my purposes. When an Old School place says cheese and coffee, it probably means Tillamook cheddar and Farmer Brothers. Examples: Pattie's Home Plate, Fat City, Original Pancake House.

Mom and Pop places are often Old School as well. But where the Original Pancake House is clearly Old School, you're not likely to meet the owner when you're there, and the food wasn't cooked by Dad and brought out by Mom. *That's* a Mom and Pop place. Examples: Beaterville, John's Café, Hollywood Burger Bar.

Classy doesn't necessarily mean crazily expensive, though these places do run more expensive than average. At the very least, Classy means a place has tablecloths, the staff is in black and white, candles or flowers are on the tables, and an omelet may be $12 or more. Examples: Cafe du Berry, Aquariva, Jamison.

Hip probably sounds like I'm stereotyping. But Hip means it's the kind of place where you can chill for a while and the people generally known as hipsters often eat there—a hipster being identified by the trademark thick-rimmed glasses, vintage clothing, upturned pants, sideburns, sneakers, and late-rising hour. And if you're offended by that description, you're probably a hipster. Examples: Junior's, Cricket Cafe, Stepping Stone.

Weekend means breakfast (many call it brunch) is served only on weekends. Or, in some cases, a Weekend designation means breakfast is served all week but the place does something special on weekends— usually just a bigger menu or more griddle items. Examples: Screen Door, Petite Provence, Accanto.

Kiddie means the place goes out of its way to accommodate kids. I can't think of a place that *doesn't* want kids (or will admit it if they don't), but these places have a play area or extensive kids' menus or just generally a kid-friendly vibe about them. Examples: Old Wives' Tales, New Deal Cafe, Slappy Cakes.

Veggie, as you might imagine, means the place is particularly friendly to nonmeat-eaters. Most places have a vegetarian omelet, but Veggie here means vegetarians and vegans will have more than a couple of choices. A few places really hang their hat on this category. Examples: Vita, Paradox, Prasad.

DEFINING THE LOCATIONS

In addition to category, I sorted Portland's breakfast places by location, with the understanding that all location names are negotiable to some extent. In some cases I didn't use the "real" name of the neighborhood; rather, I used the name of the area's main street, because neither I nor anyone else really knows where these neighborhoods begin and end.

Downtown: South of W Burnside St. and bounded by I-405.

E Burnside: So close to E Burnside St. that it doesn't seem like it's in NE or SE.

N/Inner: North Portland, from N Killingsworth St. to the south.

N/Outer: North Portland north of N Killingsworth St.

NE/Alberta: On or near NE Alberta St. between MLK and NE 33rd Ave.

NE/Broadway: On or around NE Broadway and NE Weidler St. between MLK and the Hollywood District.

NE/Fremont: On or around NE Fremont St. between MLK and NE 82nd Ave.

NE/Hollywood: Around the Hollywood District, roughly NE Sandy Blvd. from 30th Ave. to 50th Ave.

NE/MLK: On or around NE MLK Blvd. south of NE Killingsworth.

NE/Outer: Northeast Portland beyond about NE 60th Ave.

NW: In Northwest Portland, outside the Pearl District.

Pearl District: North of W Burnside St. and bounded by I-405.

SE/Belmont: On or near SE Belmont St. between SE 12th Ave. and SE 50th Ave.

SE/Division: On or near SE Division St. between SE 12th Ave. and SE 82nd Ave.

SE/Hawthorne: On or near SE Hawthorne St. between SE 12th and SE 50th Ave.

SE/Inner: Between the river, SE 12th Ave., and SE Powell Blvd.

SE/Outer: Southeast, just a little farther out, but not in Sellwood.

SE/Sellwood: South of SE Powell Blvd. and/or in the Sellwood neighborhood.

SW/Inner: Southwest Portland, beyond I-405 but fairly close to downtown.

SW/Outer: Farther west from downtown than SW/Inner.

New Places for This Edition

Wow, when I look at it this way, it looks like I've actually been working.

Here's a list of places newly written up in this 2014 edition. Some of them are actually new, but many are just places I finally made it to.

So, for you folks who say you've eaten at every place in the second edition, well…get to eatin'!

NEW PLACES FOR THIS EDITION

23 HOYT

Weekend/Classy

Good food, great area…where is everybody?

529 NW 23rd Ave. (NW)

503-445-7400

23hoyt.com

Weekends 10 a.m. to 2 p.m.

$15–$20 (all major cards)

23 Hoyt is a funny place to me. It's in a cool neighborhood, NW 23rd Avenue, and a prime location in the middle of the action. It looks nice, has some pleasant outdoor seating, and is filled with light. It was founded by famous restaurateur Bruce Carey. It serves weekend brunch. And yet, in all my time as the Breakfast Guy, not one person has ever mentioned it to me. Over on PortlandFood.org, nobody has even bothered to post about it in more than three years. It's like the place doesn't exist.

Well, I've been there twice now, and I think it's great. No lines, nice atmosphere, excellent food, pleasant staff, outdoor seating with killer people-watching. How many Portland brunch places can you say that about?

So am I chump or something? Or are the "experts" missing out on something? Or are the real chumps waiting in massive lines just down the street at Stepping Stone and Besaw's (no offense)?

Another nice touch: As soon as you sit down, you can order a Bloody Mary or mimosa, and meanwhile they drop a couple of citrus buttermilk scones on you.

The weekend brunch menu (served from 10 to 2) is basically some classic stuff—Benedict, hash, biscuits and gravy—without too much fanciness. There's a corned beef hash and a veggie hash with butternut squash, kale, peppers, onions, goat cheese, and fennel crème.

My friends have gotten the Benedict and the biscuits and gravy, both done very well, without major tweaks. The B&G, which I don't usually get excited about, was a real highlight for me. They make it with spicy fennel sausage, and there's something sweet in the gravy, too, like sherry. It was outstanding, and the biscuits stayed firm throughout the meal. I think that means they were originally like hockey pucks, but in this case I don't care, because they don't turn to mush like a lot of biscuits do under all that gravy.

And finally, because I have an insatiable sweet tooth, I had to share some warm donut holes with cinnamon sugar and salted caramel. I was expecting something appetizer-sized, but this thing defeated two of us.

All in all, a really great brunch. And I still don't know what to make of it. I eat there and look around and think, "Where is everybody?" Maybe the Portland brunch scene is so overwhelming that people just stick to their favorites. Maybe I'm a chump and am falling for less-than-stellar food and a nice room and staff. Maybe it's the prices, which are a little higher than average.

The more I think about it, though, the less I care. I like 23 Hoyt, and that's what matters. I'll keep it in mind for an easy, convenient weekend brunch in Northwest Portland.

WAIT: None that I've seen, but you can make reservations online. **LARGE GROUPS:** Make a reservation. **COFFEE:** Caffe Vita. **OTHER DRINKS:** Full bar. **FEEL-GOODS:** They say it's "farm-to-table." **HEALTH OPTIONS:** Limited for vegetarians. **WIFI:** No.

ACCANTO

New/Classy/Weekend	
The Legend's casual sibling.	
2838 SE Belmont St. (SE/Belmont)	
503-235-4900	
accantopdx.com	
Brunch weekends 10 a.m. to 2 p.m.	
$13–$15 (all major cards, no checks)	

On my freelance writer's budget, a restaurant like Genoa is saved for once a year—maybe. If the folks are in town, or some magazine is paying, or I'm desperately trying to impress somebody, I can see it. Otherwise I leave it to rich folks and serious restaurant people.

Well, there are a lot more of me than them. And the owners of Genoa know this. So in late 2009 the new owners, having renovated the legendary restaurant, did the same to the storage area next door and opened Accanto, which their website says it all about fresh, seasonal Italian food that's "simple yet sophisticated, with the warmth and welcome of a true neighborhood corner café.

For once, a website has undersold a place. I'm writing this a few months after the Breakfast Crew descended upon Accanto—10 of us, with notice, at 11 on a Sunday—and some of them are still asking when we're going back. Or they're just going back on their own.

I don't know about "a slice of Italian café life," but I do know that it shares a kitchen and some staff with Genoa (*accanto* is Italian for "next to"), as well as the same philosophy—and some amazing food. The service was top notch, the atmosphere both classy and casual, and the brunch entrées all priced at $8–$10. It's like the serious restaurant world opened a door "next to" it for the rest of us to come through.

Once through that door, you can sit in a spacious, naturally lit room with wood floors, an open kitchen, and a seating area filled with Italian cookbooks. The menu has 10 main dishes, nine sides (like fennel bacon and a sage biscuit), and nine cocktails—most of these are a classy, Italian twist on an old favorite.

Consider the salmon scramble: hardly unique in Portland, but Accanto's version came with fennel, red onion, and crème fraîche for only $9. There was a frittata with mushrooms, arugula, mascarpone, and truffles ($9); poached eggs over polenta and pancetta hash with leeks, fennel, and piquillo peppers ($10); and panettone French toast with amaretto syrup, blueberry compote, and whipped cream ($9). No one in the Crew can describe that French toast—because I ran off and hid with it.

If you don't know what panettone is, here's a little education. It's a sweet bread, traditionally made with candied oranges, citron, lemon zest, and raisins. It's made to rise over 20 or more hours, which makes it so fluffy, you have to hold it on the table, and in Italy it's a big deal around Christmastime. I mention all of this for two reasons: one is to try to tell you how good Accanto's French toast is—although I can't—and the other is to point out that Accanto isn't just a great brunch without a huge line. It's a place to sample Italian culture for a bit, have a nice meal, and even learn something.

WAIT: A little; reservations available. **LARGE GROUPS:** Parties up to six. **COFFEE:** Heart. **OTHER DRINKS:** Cocktails, espresso, very good Bloody Mary. **FEEL-GOODS:** Eggs are fresh from Sweet Briar Farms; bacon, sausage, pancetta, quick breads, and panettone are all house made. **HEALTH OPTIONS:** Vegetarian friendly. **WIFI:** Yes.

ALAMEDA CAFE

New/Classy
The French invade New Mexico.
4641 NE Fremont Ave. (NE/Fremont)
503-284-5314
thealamedacafe.com
Daily, 8 a.m. to 3 p.m.
$13–$15 (Visa, MasterCard, no checks)

When I see white tablecloths, paintings of flowers on the walls, the staff wearing black, and bottles of wine in a display on the counter, I might think, "Great, welcome to Pompous Valley." Had I looked at the Alameda's menu and seen an omelet with blue cheese, eggs Benedict with chili-infused hollandaise, and French toast named for Santa Fe, I might have left.

But at the Alameda, on top of the white tablecloth is paper for kids to draw on; they're even given crayons. All the omelets, scrambles, and even the eggs Benedict are $10 or less—and big! When I saw all this, I thought, "Hey, being kid friendly and serving big portions for reasonable prices isn't pompous!"

The Alameda suits its neighborhood perfectly. Is the area defined by grand homes along Alameda Ridge? Or is it the streets north of Fremont without sidewalks? Yes and yes. Is it Stanich's old-school burgers? Or is it Starbucks and the Alameda Brewing Co.? Yes and yes, again.

Such is this café's food, which is part stylish (the Southwest Benedict also comes with sweet and spicy cornbread) and part, well, kind of down-home. You can, for example, build your own omelet with any three ingredients for $9.25, and it's served with potatoes and toast.

The Alameda has new-agey stuff like the Klickitat Omelet with bleu cheese, apples, and bacon. Then there is a Belgian waffle that's only $5.25; oatmeal with cranberries, shaved almonds, season fruit, and brown sugar for $4.95; and a granola-yogurt parfait with seasonal fruit for $5.25.

And the French toast. Giving in to their elegant, stylish side, the Alameda chefs couldn't just do French toast; they had to fancy it up. And yet they didn't do anything *too* fancy. They make it with thick baguette bread, dipped just enough to hold a crust of cinnamon-and-sugar crushed corn flakes, and then fried. As my friend Beth said, it looks like the pieces of cod in fish and chips. It's called Santa Fe Railroad French Toast because, apparently, the recipe originated on the old Santa Fe Railway.

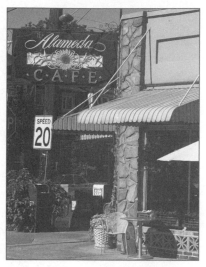

The first time I had it, I wasn't sure what to make of it. I like my French toast soaked, and this was dry in the middle. The second time? Well, now I'm thinking that the cinnamon is a nice touch, the crunch of the crust plays well with the soft bread, the syrup takes care of the moisture, and it reminds me simultaneously of Navajo fry bread and breakfast cereal with Saturday morning cartoons. Clearly, more research is required.

WAIT: Can be bad on Sunday, mostly outside with some cover. **LARGE GROUPS:** Not more than eight on weekends. **COFFEE:** K&F. **OTHER DRINKS:** Mimosas, homemade Bloody Marys, teas, juices, full bar. **FEEL-GOODS:** Some veggie options, tofu, a variety of gluten-free items. **HEALTH OPTIONS:** Soy and 2% milk. **WIFI:** Yes.

AQUARIVA

Weekend/Classy
Are we still in town?
0470 SW Hamilton Ct. (SW/Inner)
503-802-5850
riversedgehotel.com/eat_drink.php
Brunch Sunday 8:00 a.m. to 2:30 p.m.
$14–$18 (all major cards, no checks)

Brunch at Aquariva feels like eating in somebody's back yard—if that "somebody" had a gleaming, multi-windowed home next to the Willamette River, and was a gourmet chef.

It's in kind of a secret neighborhood that looks like just a bunch of offices as you whip down Macadam toward Lake Oswego. But it's in there, next to the fancy River's Edge Hotel and Spa, and one nice bonus is that for parking you have to make use of the hotel's valet service, which is provided at no charge. So you feel kind of special on arrival.

Then you walk through the spacious bar area into the dining room, and if the weather's good—make sure the weather's good when you go—you then pass through another door and out onto a little patio, with about six tables, surrounded by brush and trees, less than 50 feet from the banks of the river.

Sure, the Willamette Greenway runs between you and the water, so the occasional jogger or bicyclist will pass by, but hey, that just makes you feel cooler, right? Look at you, on the nice patio, having your nice meal, while people go jogging or boating by.

Aquariva is in a quiet, semi-secret little stretch of Southwest Portland. Even its street address, which starts with a zero, suggests a forgotten

corner. If you don't live in John's Landing or South Waterfront, you may not even know it exists—same for the stretch of paved trail along the riverbank that connects downtown to the Sellwood Bridge and beyond. In there, you'll pass boat docks, condos with sprawling, goose-filled lawns, Willamette Park, the Butterfly Park (who knew?), a creek with a salmon run, and some awesome trees.

Brunch at Aquariva isn't cheap, nor is it outrageously expensive for the cuisine and experience. Mains average about $12. They start you off with a build-your-own Bloody Mary and mimosa bar featuring 26 ingredients and 10 types of vodka. From there, you choose from six "light" dishes like oatmeal, granola, a lox plate, or a Continental. They have buttermilk and buckwheat pancakes, as well as a French toast encrusted with hazelnuts and oats and served with vanilla-cherry compote. Dang!

There are 10 main options, a mix of breakfast (smoked pork loin Benedict, chicken-fried steak with fennel sausage gravy) and lunch (burger, cobb salad). I have taken friends there a few times, always walking from my place in South Waterfront, and they are amazed each time at the setting, the restaurant, and the food.

It's a fine thing to sit out there munching on Benedicts and omelets, chatting with the charming young servers, gazing out upon the river and feeling like you're cool and in on a little secret. You're welcome.

WAIT: None. **LARGE GROUPS:** Definitely; make a reservation. **COFFEE:** Caffe Vita. **OTHER DRINKS:** Espresso, tea, full bar, build-your-own Bloody Marys, and mimosas. **FEEL-GOODS:** "A farm-to-table menu." **HEALTH OPTIONS:** Not much for vegetarians; omelets can be made with egg whites. **WIFI:** Yes.

ARLETA LIBRARY BAKERY AND CAFE

New/Mom & Pop
From secret spot to pillar of the scene.
5513 SE 72nd Ave. (SE/Outer)
503-774-4470
arletalibrary.com
Weekdays 8 a.m. to 2:30 p.m., weekends 8:30 a.m. to 2:30 p.m.
$11–$15 (Visa, MasterCard)

When Arleta first opened, I had this sense that I was one of the few people who knew about it. I kept having to explain to people, for example, that it's not in a library. It's also just about the least pretentious place you'll ever walk into; in fact, much of the decor is recycled doors, and the walls remain unadorned. So it didn't exactly scream its arrival on the scene.

Those days are gone. The Arleta is now a massively popular place, with the usual Portland-style weekend lines, and it made the TV show *Diners, Drive-Ins, and Dives*. They even flattered me by quoting this book on their menu. The name still confuses people a little, though. It's named for a library that used to be at SE 63rd and Foster, which the owner says was a gathering place back in the streetcar days.

The word *bakery* very much applies to this place. When I was there, they had a moist date scone, morning glory muffins, almond anise biscotti, triple gingersnaps, coconut macaroons with bittersweet chocolate, and sour cream coffee cake. There's always something new. My favorite is the coffee cake, which uses various fruits, mostly those in season. One day it was pineapple, another time blueberries, and without exception the crust was perfectly crunchy and the inside moist but light. Just what you want, along with the French-press Stumptown, while waiting for your order.

If the cake doesn't make you feel good, then you can bask in the mission of the place, which, according to the website, includes the ambitious hope that the restaurant "will continue the trend toward revitalization in the area." Arleta is also committed to "sustaining its neighborhood and foodshed by purchasing as much organic food from local farmers and producers as possible and by paying its employees an equitable, living wage."

Such innovation would be admirable even if the chefs weren't fantastic. Everything I've eaten has been not only delicious but also cooked just right, and Nick, the owner, seems to have brought some Italian tastes with him from Philadelphia. The Tuscan Scramble has roasted red peppers and spicy sausage and Romano cheese. The Florentine has spicy greens, basil, ricotta, Parmesan, and breadcrumbs. On the expanded weekend brunch  menu, you can get a Sicilian Hash, which they call their signature: beef braised overnight then sautéed with peppers, onions, and potatoes and topped with Parmesan scrambled eggs. For the sweet tooth, beware the Pane Dolce ("sweet bread"), a Pearl Bakery brioche with whipped honey butter, organic maple syrup, and seasonal fresh fruit.

They can get a little Southern, too. The sweet potato biscuits and rosemary sausage gravy come with a thin slice of slow-roasted pork loin that our server said had been in a brine "for a few days." It's waaay good.

I could go on, but by now you have either been there or decided to go. In fact, I already feel sentimental about Arleta's small, charming old days, back in foggy 2007 when only a devoted few of us knew about it and the rest were wondering why we ate in a library.

WAIT: Quite long on weekends; summertime patio helps. **LARGE GROUPS:** Yes, but a heads-up is good (and no larger than 14). **COFFEE:** French-press Stumptown. **OTHER DRINKS:** Fresh juice, sparkling apple cider, organic OJ. **FEEL-GOODS:** Most ingredients are local and organic. **HEALTH OPTIONS:** Good for veggies. **WIFI:** Possibly from a coffee shop next door.

ATAULA

Weekend/Classy		
What is Catalan for "Are you kidding me?"		
1818 NW 23rd Pl. (NW)		
503-894-8904		
ataulapdx.com		
Sunday 10 a.m. to 2 p.m.		
$12–$15 (all major cards)		

There are three ways a Portland brunch or breakfast place can make an impression on me and my Breakfast Crew, and two of them are bad. One is if the food just sucks, but that almost never happens. (If it does, the restaurant probably doesn't make the book). Another is if the food makes me wonder why people wait in line for it. Those places go on my Cadillac List of places that are fine but not worth waiting for.

Ataula remains memorable for that third, good reason: it rocks.

Some of my more experienced (read: jaded) Crew members came along for this one, and there was more than one occasion when somebody said, or the look on their face expressed, a joyous, amazed "are you *kidding* me?"

Ataula does things in a Spanish style. Ever since Toro Bravo came along, followed by its uber famous Portland brunch cousins, Tasty n Sons and Tasty n Alder (see page 234), the small-plate thing has been sweeping the town. Thus, when I heard of a new Spanish place serving small-plate brunch, I kind of thought, "Here come the copycats."

Well, maybe they're riding a wave Toro Bravo created, but Ataula (it's ah-TOW-la) is a classy, comfy, super tasty treat—and a killer Northwest Portland brunch without lines? Are you *kidding* me?

We started, and would end, with sweetness. The Xuxos de Crema was described as a "house pastry fritter" with cream and looked like a sugary donut. But it was like the opening jab in a series that would eventually knock us all out. It was perfectly fried and a little over-the-top sweet (and that's not a complaint). Ataula's name, by the way, means "to the table," (as in "let's eat"), and the sight and taste of these things was like a Pavlovian brunch bell to me and the Crew.

The two nice things about small-plates brunch are that you share everything and they just bring it out when it's ready. So just as I was polishing off a yummy coffee with sweetened milk, out came the savory.

Round one was an omelet with farm eggs, Mahón cheese, seasonal mushrooms, and bacon. Right on the heels of that simple, subtle masterpiece came a little party in a platter: Huevos al Plato, with farm soft eggs, blood sausage, stewed vegetables, and Catalan beans. There was so much going on here, I got a little dizzy. Again, you get two or three bites of this stuff, so it's like a lovely bird flying past, a song disappearing on the breeze, a pretty face on a crowded street.

I can't even keep up. Now there's this amazing open-faced sandwich, covered in luscious greens, and underneath is perfect bread, serrano ham, tomato jam, every bite of this meal a glorious moment.... And now the delightful chef was at our table, telling of his father's 37-year career running a restaurant in Barcelona, bragging about the sausage that Greg Higgins makes for him. *Wait, have we had that yet?*

No, we had not had the special sausage, nor the Spanish Fried Egg, which is cooked in olive oil until almost poached and basted with the oil so the egg whites get extra firm while the yolk stays soft. This is put next to oil-soaked white beans and the special sausage—the butifarra that so stoked the chef's pride, and which completely finished me off.

We sat back, let our minds wander off to the late nights of Southern Europe, and we swapped tales of 11 p.m. dinners, of walks with gelato, of the joy of the Spanish over their national soccer team.

Then more plates hit the table, and we all looked around...to see Jon of the Crew half-covering a devilish smile. "I got us some churros," he said—one for each of us—with a rich, fine chocolate dipping sauce.

Ataula is one of the best brunches I've had in researching my book, and it goes right to the top of my list when people ask what's my favorite Portland brunch.

WAIT: None—for now? **LARGE GROUPS:** Up to 20; Call for reservations. **COFFEE:** Local Roasting Co. **OTHER DRINKS:** Bloody Marys, café con leche, house-made Sangria. **FEEL-GOODS:** Local ingredients whenever possible. **HEALTH OPTIONS:** "Open to creative tapas for vegetarians." **WIFI:** No.

AUTENTICA

New/Classy/Weekend
Mexican sophistication, Portland relaxation.
5507 NE 30th Ave. (NE/Alberta)
503-287-7555
autenticaportland.com
Brunch weekends 10 a.m. to 2 p.m.
$15–$20 (all major cards, maximum of two per table, no checks)

Among the many signs that a neighborhood is changing, one that will really catch your eye is a man doing tai chi in the middle of the street. That's what we found when we arrived at the corner of NE 30th and Killingsworth in search of Autentica as a wellness fair was in full swing, complete with booths from local yoga classes and meditation programs. "Yep," I thought, "this end of Killingsworth ain't what it used to be!"

From what I had been reading online, a Mexican brunch ain't what I thought it was, either. In other words, it's not a pile of breakfast tacos and eggs. Autentica is a serious restaurant that happens to serve dishes from the owner's home state of Guerrero, Mexico.

The owner, Oswaldo Bibiano, has cooked in restaurants like Basilico, Southpark, and Pazzo. He uses local meats and produce and features vegetarian and vegan options as well as freshly made tortillas—a treat, if you don't know that already.

Eager to check this out, the Breakfast Crew headed out for what the real estate world now calls the Upscale Killingsworth Strip. At 10:30 on a lovely Saturday morning, we perused the fair, shot a curious glance at the line outside Cup & Saucer, and walked into the half-filled Autentica.

Long before Alice uttered the day's first astonished "damn!" upon biting into her *sope*, we knew we had found something pleasantly out of the ordinary. I had spotted huevos rancheros on the menu but told the server I wanted something I can't get anywhere else. Her response was, "Everything here is something you can't get anywhere else."

Some of the items, I was familiar with—like enchiladas. I had no idea people ate enchiladas for breakfast, but after trying these (stuffed with chicken and a red mole sauce, topped with iceberg lettuce, avocado, radishes, and Oaxacan cream), I would have eaten them at any time of day. As for the *sope*, which elicited Alice's "damn," it was a little like an open-faced soft taco with refried beans, cheese, onions, salsa, and your choice of meat. We were amazed at the number of flavors in that little thing!

It sounds like the Mexican food you know, right? Well, how about this: a cactus salad with crispy pork skin, onions, tomatoes, avocado, and fresh cheese. Or a crispy tortilla shell filled with octopus and prawns, topped with spicy cabbage salad. Or a *torta* (sandwich) that features pickled jalapeños. Or *huevos ahogados*, which is eggs poached in a traditional chicken broth with cilantro, lime, onions, and serrano peppers. I'm telling you, Autentica is a culinary tour of the Mexican countryside!

Alice, Rick, and I ordered four dishes among us, shared them all, and then kicked back and had a long, rambling discussion without ever feeling pressured to leave. We admired the down-to-earth nature of the menu and the place, with its ceramic dishes and its photos of families on earth-tone walls.

You'll pay a few more dollars at Autentica than, say, Cup & Saucer, but the food is so much better and the scene so much more chilled out that when you leave, you'll see all the folks waiting across the street and be glad that you, too, found out about Autentica.

WAIT: Maybe a little. **LARGE GROUPS:** Yes, groups of 10 are okay, with notice. Also a private dining room seats 15-30. **COFFEE:** Caffè Umbria. **OTHER DRINKS:** Cocktails, juice, homemade sangria, Bloody Marys. **FEEL-GOODS:** Only free-range organic eggs and local ingredients are used. **HEALTH OPTIONS:** Many vegetarian options, and some dishes can be made vegan. **WIFI:** No.

BAR CARLO

New/Hip/Veggie	
Decent breakfast, or frontier outpost?	
6433 SE Foster Rd. (SE/Outer)	
503-771-1664	
barcarlo.com	
Monday through Wednesday 8:30 a.m. to 3 p.m.,	
Thursday through Sunday 8:30 a.m. to 10 p.m., closed Tuesdays.	
$12–$15 (all major cards, no checks)	

When Bar Carlo opened in 2007, lots of folks took the opportunity to make socioeconomic statements about its neighborhood. Local media ran articles that read like reports from the land of savages, telling us there are actual reasons to go "out there." "My gosh," they collectively exclaimed, "healthy, tasty food on Foster!"

Think I'm exaggerating?

The *Mercury*'s blog: "Foster: not just for felons…. SE Foster is starting to get some attention (and this time it's the good kind)."

The *Mercury*'s (mostly positive) review: "I probably wouldn't make the trip out to SE 64th and Foster for lunch alone…."

A *Willamette Week* review of new restaurants in the area referred to it as a "fast-food vortex" and a "dusty, urban frontier." The only other preexisting businesses mentioned were a strip club, a tobacco shack, a "variety store selling windup toys," and a gun shop.

That *Willamette Week* story set off quite a discussion in its online comments area, with readers lobbing grenades like "gentrification," "meth houses," and "white trash." Others ridiculed the area's new name, FoPo (for Foster-Powell). Purely entertaining—and none of it had anything to do with the food at Bar Carlo.

Now open for seven years, Bar Carlo has kind of settled into a Cup & Saucer space. That is, some folks love it, some folks hate it, and some folks don't get what either kind of hype is about. It does move rather slowly: they took about five years to finish the room next to the dining area, which offers booths and a slightly more comfy vibe. The main room itself still feels a bit raw—or maybe I just expected more decoration. (Of course, it's an outpost on a "dusty frontier.")

My girlfriend and I went there twice and found no lines; friendly staff; strong, tasty coffee; and food that made us shrug. Like I said, in any other neighborhood this would be a fairly run-of-the-mill place, with loyal followers and others who find it disappointing. And Bar Carlo does have both.

A recent menu revamp included a build-your-own section, which I must admit, confounded my bacon-addled brain. You pay $9 for a three-egg (or tofu) omelet or scramble, then you pick from one-, two-, and three-star columns of ingredients, and your first five stars are included in the $9, but after that a star is 75 cents each.... I think I got that right. Anyway, you can get what you want there, which I guess is what matters. And it probably won't be the best of that thing you ever had. But you might love it. I'm confused.

All in all, it sounds like a pretty decent breakfast place, right? That's what Bar Carlo is to these eyes: a pretty standard Portland breakfast place that a lot of folks like. It just happens to also be in the crosshairs of some weird sociological energy.

WAIT: A little on Sundays. **LARGE GROUPS:** No. **COFFEE:** Nossa Familia. **OTHER DRINKS:** Tea, DragonFly Chai, juice, soda, and cocktails. **FEEL-GOODS:** Ingredients are local and organic whenever possible. **HEALTH OPTIONS:** Plenty for vegetarians and vegans. **WIFI:** No.

BEAST

New/Classy/Weekend
They don't care. They just cook.
5425 NE 30th Ave. (NE/Alberta)
503-841-6968
beastpdx.com
Brunch seating Sunday at 10 a.m. *or* noon
$35 plus beverages (all major cards, no checks)
Optional $20 wine or beer pairing

Beast just doesn't care.

For one thing, they don't care what you want to eat. It's four courses, and you'll find out what you're getting when you get there. It's on the little menu, right above *substitutions politely declined*.

They also celebrate meat, and serve lots of it. There's a famous picture of the chef hugging a pig in a field. If that's a problem for you, well, they don't care. There are plenty of other places in town.

They're expensive—as in $35 per person. See above.

Their chairs are uncomfortable and are apparently well-known carryovers from another restaurant. They crank rock music. They make you sit with folks you don't know. See above.

But they also "don't care" in the way my friend John T. means it. You don't know John T., which is a shame, but when he gets all worked up about something he likes, be it John Irving's writing or the University of Arkansas football team or Arlo Guthrie's version of "Gates of Eden," he will pronounce that his current hero "doesn't care!" As in, dude just hammers out the good stuff like he knows how, the Big Magic Way, and *does…not…care* what folks think.

That's how they cook over at Beast. They don't care.

Here's the magic they threw at the Crew and me one time. We sat down, got a French press, and they laid out a brioche and baguette bread pudding with maple-bourbon sauce, candied hazelnuts, and glazed bacon. Right there, on that plate, was a breakfast not to be messed with. It was course number one. Of four.

Next up, the hash: duck confit, prosciutto, sweet potatoes, brussels sprouts, rapini, and market potatoes with a poached farm egg and hollandaise. Don't know what confit or rapini are? Me neither. You won't care.

They had us on our heels now, could have thrown anything at us. "I eat like this in my dreams," I thought. They hit us again with a selection from Cheese Bar. I don't remember what they were, because I think in all the excitement, I ate my notes. But just think four or five cheeses that you've never heard of, come from all over, are several different kinds of amazing, and come with some greens and a sherry vinaigrette.

Did I mention that there's a wine pairing available for every course? That's right—imagine eating this way *and drinking*.

For closers, what do you think about a chocolate truffle cake and a cream puff with soft vanilla whipped cream? I'm still thinking about it. Consider it a nice, sweet kiss after a…um, no, can't say that here. The staff at Beast sure is hot, though. Did I mention that? Adds a certain something.

I guess the owner/chef was involved in some weird restaurant drama that I probably should know about. Changed the restaurant scene, blew the foodies' minds, fell from the throne, relationship ended, rose from the ashes…honestly, I don't care. Beast almost killed me, and I thank them for it. Go there if you dare.

Either way, they don't care.

WAIT: Reservations strongly advised. **LARGE GROUPS:** Reservations required. **COFFEE:** Extracto in a French press. **OTHER DRINKS:** Mimosas, wine or beer pairings available with each course ($20), juice. **FEEL-GOODS:** None that they tout. **HEALTH OPTIONS:** Vegetarians beware! (Though they can make you a veggie hash with notice.) **WIFI:** Yes.

TOP HASHCAPADE (SEE PAGE 301)

BEATERVILLE CAFE

Hip/Mom & Pop/Veggie

They put the fun in funky.

2201 N Killingsworth St. (N/Inner)

503-735-4652

beatervillecafeandbar.com

Weekdays 6 a.m. to 2 p.m., weekends 7 a.m. to 2 p.m.

$9–$13 (Visa, MasterCard, Discover, no checks)

Folks often ask how I got the idea for a book about breakfast in Portland. Well, in my 14+ years as a travel writer for the *Memphis Flyer*, I often described a place by describing a meal I ate there, because a place's essence shines through its restaurants. Generally, because of a combination of personal preference and budget, the meal I wrote about was breakfast.

One day a few years back, I was sitting at the Beaterville Cafe with my friend Craig Schuhmann, who writes fishing books. Just as we arrived, the front room of the cafe had come to a standstill because a regular had come in with photos from a vacation in France. I also noticed a stream of UPS drivers heading for the back room. The server told me the drivers were a regular Bible-study group, and I told Craig, "See, friends coming in from a trip and people meeting every week to get religion: *that's* the kind of thing you write about when you write about breakfast." Then Craig asked if I'd ever written about breakfast in Portland, and I said, "Man, I could write a whole book about places to eat breakfast in Portland!" We looked at each other, and that moment, this book was born.

So the short answer to how this book was born is, "I got the idea sitting in Beaterville," and I couldn't think of a more appropriate place for that inspiration to have struck. It's hard for me to think of the Beaterville and not have the phrase "perfect Portland breakfast place" come to mind. Maybe not the best or most innovative, but the most Portland, like a drizzly day is perfect Portland weather or like Bud Clark was our perfect mayor. Beaterville is a little strange, really friendly, colorful in both the paint way and the people way, and in a part of town that is seeing both grassroots changes and intensive urban planning.

It has a good story as well. A *beater*, you may know, is an old, beat-up car that is street-legal but barely runs. And, of course, our fair city has a club—people who are into this kind of thing—and, of course, they occasionally parade their beaters, which is a perfect Portland thing to do. Beaterville's owner is one of these folks, and he still keeps some of his beaters out back, as well as who-knows-what assortment of automotive parts on  the walls. And an odd collection of art. And a backward clock.

Oh, and the food is solid and consistent. The car theme is carried into the menu, which includes up to eight yummy, filling scramblers (get it, like Ramblers?) such as the Onassis (tomatoes, spinach, red onions, garlic, Greek olives, and feta cheese). There are also up to eight omelets and hashes, several combos, and plenty of vegetarian options. (Tofu and egg substitutes are available in all the scrambles and omelets at no extra charge.)

None of this stuff is likely to knock your socks off, but it's all solid and consistent, and there's no more relaxed, fun place to hang out than Beaterville.

WAIT: Long on weekends, even after another room was added a few years back, with space inside and some cover outside. **LARGE GROUPS:** Best on weekdays. **COFFEE:** Caffé D'Arte. **OTHER DRINKS:** Numi teas, espresso, full bar. **FEEL-GOODS:** Humane cage-free eggs. **HEALTH OPTIONS:** Egg substitutes, tofu, veggie sausage, home-made gluten-free biscuits. **WIFI:** Yes.

BERTIE LOU'S CAFE

Mom & Pop
1940s diner with a dash of goofiness.
8051 SE 17th Ave. (SE/Sellwood)
503-239-1177
Weekdays 7 a.m. to 2 p.m., weekends 8 a.m. to 2:30 p.m.
$8–$12 (all major cards, local checks)

There's a sign on the wall in Bertie Lou's that captures the essence of the place: "Unattended children will be given a shot of espresso and a free puppy." It conveys both the reasonable (control your kids) and the whimsical. Think about it: is there anything cuter than a wound-up kid with a puppy? That would be *fun*, right?

Another item on the wall is a picture of Bertie and Lou standing at the same counter in the 1940s. Though they are long gone, their presence brings in an added depth: if there's an old-time Portland breakfast place in nearly original condition and still in its original neighborhood, it's Bertie Lou's. The only major change is that the second room, which was a barber shop also owned by Bertie and Lou, now has 18 seats at tables to go along with the six at the counter.

Well, that and the fact that the 1940s menu probably didn't say, "Parties of 24 or more require a reservation and 80% gratuity." Probably also didn't say you could get a half order of biscuits and gravy that's "no biscuits…or no gravy." Or that you can get a signed copy of the menu for $10…plus $50 for framing, $25 for packaging, and $50 for delivery.

Get the picture? There's definitely a sense of humor about Bertie Lou's as well as a very friendly vibe. One of their mottos is "Portland's best mediocre breakfast." Sit at the counter and join in the conversation with the regulars

and the staff, because at Bertie Lou's, about 25 percent of the diners at any given time can reach out and touch the cook.

There's nothing fancy about the food—seven omelets and scrambles, four Benedicts, a couple of breakfast sandwiches, waffles, a burrito—but it's all solid. Egg Beaters and soy bacon are available for non-meat eaters, as is a veggie scramble "made with one, some, or all of the following, depending on what we have at the time you order: mushrooms, eggplant, zucchini, spinach, tomatoes, peppers, onions, and provolone."

Two items do stand out, if only for their difference: the potatoes are deep-fried reds, golden brown on the outside and soft on the inside, just about perfect to my Southern palette. In one dish, they're grilled with onions and peppers and laid over a bed of sautéed spinach. The other standout is the French toast, which they make with two croissants sliced lengthwise and serve with fruit and thick maple syrup. If that isn't enough sugar for you (and if it isn't, I'd like to meet you), usually there are cinnamon rolls and bear claws.

So sit back, chat with the folks at the counter, have some carbs and locally roasted coffee, then look at that old picture on the wall and ask yourself how much has really changed. Oh, and control your kids, or you might take home more than a full belly.

WAIT: Long on weekends, mostly outside. **LARGE GROUPS:** Five and under are fine. More would be a hassle. **COFFEE:** Happy Cup. **OTHER DRINKS:** Tazo teas, fresh OJ and grapefruit juice. **FEEL-GOODS:** Bear claws feel good, right? **HEALTH OPTIONS:** Egg Beaters, soy bacon, and Morningstar sausage patties, some veggie options. **WIFI:** No, but if you're sitting outside, you can steal from the bar across the street.

BESAW'S

New/Old School/Classy

Where new cuisine meets Old Portland.

2301 NW Savier St. (NW)

503-228-2619

besaws.com

Breakfast weekdays 7 a.m. to 3 p.m., weekends 8 a.m. to 3 p.m.

$13–$18 (all major cards, no checks)

My personal history of breakfast in Portland began with Besaw's. I was staying with my friend Chip, who then lived on the edge of Forest Park, and each morning we'd stumble down to Besaw's to warm up. I'd get the Farmer's Hash, apple-cranberry juice, and coffee, and Chip and I would sit for hours, read the paper, and marvel at our new home. Anyplace where a guy could get good food and friendly service, chill out with the paper, then go walking in a 4,000-acre forest was a place to call home.

And why should you care? Well, it's impossible to discuss breakfast and Portland history without getting Besaw's into the mix. It's been there since 1903, when two French-Canadian loggers got seed money from Henry Weinhard to start a tavern. In fact, back in the corner on the right, there's a photo that shows Besaw's with a steeple on top, before a 1922 fire took out the second floor.

So when you sit at or near the 19th-century oak bar to enjoy your classic Portland breakfast dishes like Wild Salmon Scramble, you're literally surrounded by Portland history. You may even see Cousin Maurice's Eggs on the menu, a Brie-scallion-tomato dish that used to be a staple at Zell's; the two restaurants have swapped ownership and staff over the years.

The weekend wait can be historic as well, but the staff serves coffee outside, and it's quite a social scene out there. Inside you'll find the perfectly Portland combination of class and chill.

44

The staff is in black and makes a fine Bloody Mary, and many are actors, hired for their charm and wit. The clientele is as likely to be mountain bikers in from Forest Park as high-end shoppers ready to cruise Northwest 23rd Avenue. You can sit inside under the ceiling fans or out back on the covered patio, and you'll find the menu extensive and the dishes full of fresh, local ingredients.

The salmon scramble is spiced with dill and smoothed by cream cheese. The potatoes are big chunks of reds tossed with garlic and rosemary. The Croque Madame has buttered Pullman brioche, shaved ham, gruyere cheese sauce, two over-medium eggs, and chives. The Farmer's Hash, a longtime favorite, is three eggs scrambled with potatoes, roasted garlic cloves, bacon, onions, peppers, and cheddar cheese.

The priciest entrée, the breakfast burger, is $13, and all the scrambles average around $12, so it's not a budget-busting place. And for $8 or less, you can get organic oatmeal, organic homemade granola, buttermilk pancakes, or a big, tasty Belgian waffle.

And—sitting under the twirling fans, listening to the creaking wood floor—you can try to decide (as my friends Linda and Rich and I once did) if Northwest Portland reminds you more of a relaxed San Francisco or a hilly version of Boston's Back Bay. Then you can hop the streetcar to go downtown, stroll the scene on Northwest 23rd, or head up to Forest Park for a woodsy walk. In other words, you can relax, eat well, and feel right at home.

WAIT: Way long on weekends after about 9 a.m. **LARGE GROUPS:** A mild hassle on weekends; reservations available for parties of six or more. **COFFEE:** Water Avenue. **OTHER DRINKS:** Espresso, Steven Smith teas, fresh juice, DragonFly Chai, mimosas, and Bloody Marys. **FEEL-GOODS:** The menu says, "Fresh, local and organic ingredients whenever possible." **HEALTH OPTIONS:** Egg substitute for $1.50, plenty of gluten-free options. **WIFI:** Yes, but you have to ask for the passcode.

BIJOU CAFÉ

New/Classy/Veggie

You can be healthy/progressive and *be a "real" restaurant!*

132 SW 3rd Ave. (Downtown)

503-222-3187

bijoucafepdx.com

Weekdays 7 a.m. to 2 p.m., weekends 8 a.m. to 2 p.m., closed Tuesdays

$14–$17 (Visa, MasterCard, local checks)

Consider the Fresh NW Oyster Hash, one of my favorite plates in Portland. Four or five cornmeal-dredged grilled oysters sit on thin strips of onion and potatoes with an over-easy egg, parsley, and a dash of lemon. Sorting through all this for variations on the perfect bite might be the highlight of your day. It's serious food. It's also $15, with no toast or other sides.

The Bijou's old brick walls and exposed wood beams say *history*; the modern art on the walls say *style*; the coat racks on each booth say *utility*; the blue-and-white checkered tablecloths, old-timey sugar pourers, and muffins in a basket say *down-home*. You'll see business-people going over charts, friends planning a wedding, tourists poring over maps, conventioneers reuniting, and regulars chatting with the staff.

The Bijou is darn near the prototypical Portland breakfast place. It's not necessarily the best, and it's certainly not the cheapest, but it's perhaps the one place you'd take your parents or other visitors who want a nice, safe dose of Portland's organic, progressive, friendly, homey culture without the tattoos, hairy armpits, and all-out vegan fare. Your server might be wearing rainbow stockings, though.

Another telling tidbit: They serve Carlton Farm bacon, Bravo sharp cheddar cheese, Tracy's Small Batch granola, Ayers Creek Hominy grits, and Cascade Natural Beef, and they don't offer a word of explanation regarding what these ingredients are. It's like what was once a radical idea—using artisan and (presumably) local ingredients raised in a healthy way—now doesn't even need an explanation.

It's also true that a lot of folks in town think this is all very uppity and just an excuse to charge $10 for bacon and eggs or $11.50 for a cheese-and-mushroom omelet (ah, but they're *local* mushrooms!).

It's not the kind of place for slackers stumbling in hungover and surfing the web for two hours. It's like a grown-up breakfast restaurant—but a relaxed, Portland breakfast restaurant. (And thanks to a 2012 renovation, it's much roomier, too.) One of several hashes is made with cauliflower and black kale, harissa for spice, sheep-milk feta, and olives. Daily special muffins (I had banana hazelnut) are made fresh. Brioche, French, or  whole-wheat toast is available, as are cornmeal, buckwheat, or buttermilk pancakes, all with real maple syrup.

The Bijou feels like the oldest breakfast place in the new Portland.

WAIT: Long on weekends; sometimes a wait during the week. Small indoor waiting area. **LARGE GROUPS:** Could be a seriously long wait. No reservations. **COFFEE:** Organic Café Femenino. **OTHER DRINKS:** Illy espresso, Holy Kakow hot chocolate, Tao of Tea, juices, Bloody Marys, mimosas, full bar. **FEEL-GOODS:** Heavy emphasis on organic and local ingredients. **HEALTH OPTIONS:** Tofu, granola. **WIFI:** Yes.

BRASSERIE MONTMARTRE

Classy/Weekend
Mon cher ami, allons prendre un brunch!
626 SW Park Ave. (Downtown)
503-236-3036
brasseriepdx.com
Sunday 10 a.m. to 2:30 p.m.
$15–$20 (all major cards, no checks)

I often run screaming from fancy brunches. Or I load up my Sarcasm Cannon and prepare to let fly. White tablecloths can set me off a little, but anything French takes it to another level, and just the slightest pretension from the place sends me to the foulest backwaters of my dark soul. But hey, I'm kind of an ass sometimes.

So when word came that Brasserie Montmartre is now doing Sunday brunch, my first thought was, "Great, that's two words I can't even pronounce!" So I loaded the Cannon and headed down there with my best-looking female friend. I was single at the time, and a dude can't be hangin' in a swank place downtown with other dudes, or himself.

Well, it's a beautiful place, tucked away on a little side street that really does feel kind of European; that is, it's narrow, packed with shops and a hotel, and I almost got run over by a car. We settled at the bar for a quick cappuccino, and I felt .04 percent more Euro.

We were gathered up by a disarmingly lovely hostess and walked over to a slightly raised booth under a chalkboard advertising oysters. If you lead with good looks, sleek decor, and oysters, I spare the sarcasm.

Then out came the menu, and the first four things made me cringe again: French Onion Soup (can't stand it), two salads, and a Lobster Croissant for $12. Ah, but right after that, they got me. You can be stylish and located in a cool place downtown and have cute young staff (of both genders, by the way)—all that, and I can still dislike you—but if you hit me with five kinds of French fries, you can even call them Les Frites and I'll want to hug you.

That's right, five kinds of frites! Pomme Frites. Pork Belly Frites. Duck Fat Frites. Truffle Frites. Foie Gras/Szechuan Pepper Frites. I was beside myself. The only comparable moment in my Portland breakfast career was when I saw the Kenny and Zuke's soda lineup. We ordered *les truffle frites*, and I felt .03 percent more sophisticated.

Out they came in good order, and they were precious. And yummy and cooked just right. I was feeling a little swirly, what with all the taste and fancy and good looks going on.

Whenever I'm in a new breakfast place I have to check out the Benedict—kind of like getting the Caesar salad in an Italian place, or a macchiato in a coffee shop—and Montmartre has one with sautéed spinach (Florentine) and one with Smithfield ham. Actually, when I was there, Dungeness crab was in season, and I got a Benedict with that. I loved every bite of it. My friend had the ham and cheese omelet, loved it, and couldn't even finish it.

Other dishes of note include Quiche du Jour (the Cannon almost backfired on that one!), which was arugula and shrimp when I was there; Pork Confit Hash with delicata squash, roasted cipollini onions, and two fried duck eggs; huckleberry pancakes with vanilla chantilly cream and candied almonds; and a braised pork shank with poached eggs, chanterelle mushrooms, and hollandaise.

This isn't one of the top five brunches in town, but it's a nice one, and I've never even heard of a line there. And the atmosphere is terrific, like a real French place without too much attitude and with evening jazz. Looking around downtown, I guess it's a little short of the Heathman for classiness, but it's also a dollar or two cheaper per dish. It's fancier than Mother's without the line. It's more chill than the Bijou, also without the line, and with more options.

Nice scenery, good food, five kinds of fries, and a touch of Euro class is a good combination. See if you can't arrange for some nice-looking company like I did—for the record, I have since taken my even lovelier girlfriend—and you might work up to 1.1 percent more Euro sophisticate.

WAIT: Not usually. **LARGE GROUPS:** Yes, with notice. **COFFEE:** Happy Cup. **OTHER DRINKS:** Espresso, juices, sodas, sparkling wine, cocktails, Perrier (of course), bottomless mimosas. **FEEL-GOODS:** Local eggs. **HEALTH OPTIONS:** Nothing in particular. **WIFI:** Yes.

BREAD AND INK CAFE

New/Classy/Kid Friendly
A classy old lady down on Hawthorne.
3610 SE Hawthorne Blvd. (SE/Hawthorne)
503-239-4756
breadandinkcafe.com
Daily 8 a.m. to 3 p.m.
$14–$18 (all major cards, checks)

Down in New Orleans there are restaurants called "old line." They aren't cutting edge, and a lot of folks consider them stuffy, but they are immensely popular and traditional. The Grand Dame is 100-plus-year-old Galatoire's, with its tuxedoed staff twirling under massive chandeliers and the debauchery of Bourbon Street right outside the door.

Bread and Ink Cafe may be the Galatoire's of the Portland breakfast scene. It opened "way back" in 1983 and was sort of a pioneer on then run-down Hawthorne; it was also one of the first places in town to commit to buying from local farmers.

To this day, it's definitely aiming for the area between classy and casual. It has fresh flowers to greet you and high-backed green chairs with armrests. Its white-tablecloth reputation has labeled it as a high-end, expensive place—but the drawing paper on the tables marks it as kid friendly. And when you walk out of Bread and Ink, you have a decent chance of hearing a drum circle or seeing somebody in a Guatemalan skirt.

I should tell you that in my research, no other place got quite the negative online reviews for service like Bread and Ink. The reviews spanned several years and may or may not have been the result of Southeast Portland slackerness running into the high expectations that come with a $12 eggs Benedict. Among the more serious food-oriented sites and blogs, it's often damned with the "ain't what it used to be" designation. On the other hand, it's packed every weekend.

Now you can even get a little something on the street. Inspired by an owner's son's trip to Holland, they opened the Waffle Window (8 a.m. to 5 p.m. seven days a week; until 9 p.m. in summer) with a wide range of sweet waffle flavors like chocolate dipped, apple pie, and banana Nutella. All of these run from $2 to $6. They now have a Waffle Window location at 2624 NE Alberta, as well.

At Bread and Ink, the menu changes regularly. Some of the things I've had or seen include the basic Skillet Scramble (red onions, herbed potatoes, Italian sausage, spinach, and cheddar cheese) and the more sophisticated Smoked Trout Scramble with onions, pepper bacon, spinach, and Jack cheese topped with horseradish sour cream. I've also seen an omelet unique to Portland, as far as I know: the Apple Omelet, which includes Granny Smiths with caramelized onions, pepper bacon, and Gruyère cheese. Their French Toast is made with Frisian (Dutch) sweet bread with cinnamon, topped with seasonal fruit. Note that the menu changes pretty frequently, which is a good thing; check the website for the latest.

I ate there once on a weekday with my girlfriend at the time, and when I looked around, I realized (this was at 11 a.m. on a Friday) that I was the only male! Seven tables were occupied, two of them with kids, and they were girls, too. I had gone through the looking glass, transcended the pseudo-hippie Hawthorne, and arrived in the land of the leisurely. Me and all the ladies, having a late breakfast!

Still caught up in the moment and feeling a bit old line, I took my girlfriend's hand and said, "I wonder what all the employed folk are doing today?"

WAIT: Can be long on weekends (20-30 min. average). **LARGE GROUPS:** Sure. **COFFEE:** Kobos. **OTHER DRINKS:** Espresso, tea, fresh juice. full bar. **FEEL-GOODS:** Local ingredients whenever possible. **HEALTH OPTIONS:** Substitute fruit for potatoes for $2. **WIFI:** Yes.

BRIDGES CAFE

New/Hip/Veggie
It was cool before MLK was cool.
2716 NE MLK Jr. Blvd. (NE/MLK)
503-288-4169
bridgescafeandcatering.net
Weekdays 7 a.m. to 2 p.m., weekends 8 a.m. to 3 p.m.
$11–$15 (all major cards)

Everything happening these days on Martin Luther King Jr. Boulevard—all the new construction, redevelopment, and old homes getting fixed up—was only a twinkle in some city planner's eye when Bridges Cafe first opened in 1994. In fact, when Bridges opened, it was one of only two restaurants in almost two miles along MLK.

What happened next was a classic example of the effect a little neighborhood restaurant can have. A crowd of regulars formed, and the new owner teamed up with the owner of another business to start events called Saturday Stroll and the Dog Days of Summer to get people walking around and noticing the neighborhood's businesses.

Word spread around the city: *there's this cool place to eat breakfast up on MLK!* From the beginning Bridges was known for a laid-back atmosphere, good Benedicts, local organic ingredients, and the best mimosas around. And believe me, in the mid- to late-1990s, this was exciting news in pretty much any Portland neighborhood, let alone MLK.

All these years later, Bridges hasn't changed that much. It still has the same tile tables, the same big windows, some of the same staff, and the same down-to-earth menu, Portland style: four Benedicts (Carlton Farms Canadian bacon, smoked wild salmon, Florentine, and a seasonal); around four omelet and scramble options; a wide range of basics like oatmeal, granola, and biscuits and gravy; and seven specialties that range from waffles and challah French toast to catfish hash, a breakfast burrito, and Eggs Fiesta, a Mexi-mix served on cornbread.

Their remarkable consistency means that Bridges isn't often thought of as one of the "it" breakfast places in Portland, especially since the rest of the neighborhood has blossomed and countless other breakfast places have spread like moss throughout the city. Since I have fond memories of Bridges (I'm fairly sure I saw my first hipster there), I go back about once a year to check it out. A typical visit goes like this: I walk in at about 10:30 a.m. on a weekday, just like the old days, and see a guy hunched over his computer, two contractors talking shop, an older couple looking around as if they'd never been there, and four young women talking about their favorite teacher.

The specials, each about $9 or $10, are old standards: a bacon-onion-mushroom-cheddar scramble and another scramble with garlic, spinach, roasted red peppers, and Jack cheese. I always get my old favorite, the Catfish Hash, and the rest is a trip down memory lane. It's still a big pile of potatoes with grilled onions and peppers and chunks of fried catfish in a stiff batter spotted with sesame seeds, topped with two perfectly poached eggs and creole hollandaise, which is a spicy version, still one of my favorite sauces in town. It's still served with big slices of yummy toast that somehow play perfectly with the savory festival on the plate and the house-made marionberry jam on the table. And all this for $11.95!

Neighborhood joint, indeed. An old friend in a rapidly changing neighborhood, I say.

WAIT: Pretty long on weekends after about 10 a.m., with limited space inside and cover outside. **LARGE GROUPS:** Yes (with notice), but not the best place for it. **COFFEE:** K&F. **OTHER DRINKS:** Soda, apple juice, espresso, DragonFly Chai, cocktails, mimosas, bottled beer. **FEEL-GOODS:** Many ingredients are local and organic. **HEALTH OPTIONS:** Good options for vegetarians. **WIFI:** No.

BRODER

New
More than just the best Swedish breakfast in town.
2508 SE Clinton St. (SE/Division)
503-736-3333
broderpdx.com
Breakfast daily 9 a.m. to 3 p.m.
$13–$16 (Visa, MasterCard, Discover, no checks)

Note: Just as this book was being wrapped up, Broder Nord opened at 2240 N Interstate Ave., apparently with the same menu and hours.

I am guilty of being hyped-out about Broder. When it opened in 2007, so many people wrote about it that it was a little overwhelming. Every review pretty much said Broder is a cute, popular place that serves authentic Swedish cuisine—the reviewer knows because of various Swedish connections or experiences—and this food, when you eat it, will make you want to ride a reindeer or something.

Some folks think it's great food at a good price; others think it's a novelty restaurant with bland food. The *Oregonian*, in a generally positive review, wondered why the food couldn't be more interesting, even if a little less authentic. The *Mercury* said, "Breakfast at Broder is a dainty affair, with modest portions and an emphasis on adorability. But the preciousness wears off if you realize you've ordered the most expensive breakfast item and you're still hungry."

I tended, at first, to fall into the "novelty" camp, and I wondered why people would wait for so, so long to eat there. Broder aims for a cross between old-timey (dark wood and light fixtures that everyone

compares to antlers) and the sleek-modern-Euro feel (with white tiles, stainless steel, and lots of powder blue that reminded me of flying on KLM). Handwritten specials on a mirror offer a form of a.m. booze called

Damenel Dansk (whatever that is) and desserts like Swedish cream, Danish buttercream, applesauce cake, and bread pudding.

The menu is surprisingly close to what you're used to seeing, just with little twists and different names. *Aebleskivers* are Danish pancakes, tasty little fried balls of dough served with lingonberry jam, lemon curd, and syrup on the side. Options for baked scrambles (served with walnut toast and a choice of roasted tomatoes, green salad, or potato pancake) include arugula, chèvre, and shaved Romanesca cauliflower; baked Northwest salmon with preserved lemon, pickled shallots and fresh dill; and pork belly, Brie, and Fuji apples. And yes, everything is served on a board, which is spelled *bord*. Cute, huh? The signature dish, in fact, is the Swedish Breakfast Bord, a sampler plate of rye crisp, walnut toast, salami, smoked trout, grapefruit, yogurt and honey, lingonberry jam, and hard cheese, for $12.

For some reason, my first impressions of the food were not that great. Then I attended a New Year's Day brunch with a fun group called Portland Food Adventures. And sure, we were getting some special treatment, but after they'd hit us with the breakfast bord, aebelskivers, smoked trout hash, Swedish meatballs, and then Swedish cream with blueberry compote, lemon curd, and a chocolate cookie, I was forced to look up and exclaim, "*Mitt fel!*" I think that's Swedish for *mea culpa*.

Broder has earned every bit of its popularity, but I still stick to weekdays!

WAIT: Very long on weekends, but coffee is available. Most waiting is outside, but they do open up the inside seating area when it's cold. **LARGE GROUPS:** Yes, but no reservations. **COFFEE:** Stumptown. **OTHER DRINKS:** Orange and grapefruit juice; wine and beer, cocktails. **FEEL-GOODS:** Menu says, "We always use cage-free eggs and organic produce and meats whenever possible." **HEALTH OPTIONS:** Almost any dish can be made vegetarian. **WIFI:** Yes.

TOP HASHCAPADE (SEE PAGE 301)

BRUNCH BOX

Hip
Now scattering gut bombs from a "restaurant" too!
620 SW 9th Ave. (Downtown)
503-287-4377
brunchboxpdx.com
Daily 8 a.m. to 10 p.m.
$6–$10 (all major cards, no checks)

When I heard that Brunch Box was adding a restaurant to their cart operation, I admit, I was worried. You know, some of these carts get a little carried away, think they're something they aren't, or just over-stretch and lose their way. In the case of Brunch Box, the cart that gave us the Redonkadonk—a hamburger with egg, bacon, ham, Spam, and American cheese between two grilled cheese sandwiches—I was actually worried they might try to get respectable or something.

Then I walked into the tiny little place (a good sign) and was blasted by Led Zeppelin's "In My Time of Dying" (a better sign). At the register was a customer reeking of weed leaning against the counter, saying, "Dude, are all these *sandwiches*?"

Fear not for Brunch Box, for they know who they are.

Yes, they still have the Redonkadonk, as well as the Monstrosity, which is double beef, double cheddar, four strips of bacon, ketchup, mayo, and "No veggies!"…on two grilled cheese sandwiches. Oh, and 13 other burgers. But for breakfast, it's actually the same menu as at the cart: 10 sandwiches with various combinations of egg, cheeses, meats, Spam, onions, Texas toast, bun, English muffin, bagel, biscuit, or wheat bread.

You can also build your own sandwich using a little menu pad on the counter. (This, by the way, was completely beyond the stoned guy.)

What they have added at the restaurant are more items along the same lines: fried chicken, French fries, and milk shakes. Again, fear not for the Brunch Box. When you start seeing mixed veggies or something, it'll be time to move on.

One time I got a Double Down, with two eggs, bacon and ham, and American and Swiss. The guy asked what kind of bread; I said Texas

Toast, and as he wrote it down he nodded slightly and said, "Atta boy." I felt a little warm and fuzzy for a second there.

Another time I got the Black and Bleu: sausage, bacon, bleu cheese, grilled onions, Cajun sauce, and (atta boy) Texas Toast. (By the way, you can get any sandwich with French toast for the buns; that would be the Breakfast of Champions.) They have daily specials, too, like Happy Hour All Day on Thursday and free fries (if you buy a sandwich and drink) on Fridays. For breakfast specials, buying a breakfast sandwich gets you free hash browns and coffee on Monday and free hash browns plus a $2.50 mimosa on Sunday.

If the Portland food scene was a giant band, Brunch Box would be the big ol' tuba, just poundin' out the beat and layin' down the bottom, leaving the higher, more sophisticated stuff to somebody else. Eating there is like swallowing a bomb. In a good way. You know how sometimes you want subtlety and nice combinations, maybe something green and fresh…and sometimes you want to plug your gut and lie around? Brunch Box is for the latter times.

WAIT: Never. **LARGE GROUPS:** No. **COFFEE:** Portland Roasting. **OTHER DRINKS:** Beer, OJ, shakes, sodas, iced tea. **FEEL-GOODS:** The nap is nice. **HEALTH OPTIONS:** Yeah, right! **WIFI:** Yes.

BYWAYS CAFE

Hip/Old School
Can you resist the kitsch? What about the French toast?
1212 NW Glisan St. (Pearl)
503-221-0011
bywayscafe.com
Breakfast weekdays 7 to 11 a.m., weekends 7:30 a.m. to 2 p.m.
(breakfast only on weekends, no lunches)
$10–$13 (Visa, MasterCard, no checks)

Just for kicks, I took a couple of serious restaurant people to Byways Cafe to get their impression. I think it might have been like taking a classical musician to a Grateful Dead concert.

Byways isn't as wacky as a Dead show, and Dan and Amy are not snooty by any means. But seeing these two fairly serious people sit in a springy booth that makes the table a little too high, under a collection of national park pennants, and with their coffee in a House of Mystery Oregon Vortex mug…well, I had to chuckle.

When Amy said the amaretto-infused French toast with honey-pecan butter probably wasn't on real challah, and Dan grudgingly admitted that his omelet was at least well cooked, it was a little like a non-Deadhead pointing out that Bob Weir forgot the words to "Truckin'." I wanted to say, "Yeah, but it was still fun, right?"

Maybe I'm just a sucker for kitsch, particularly of the travel variety. (I once made out with my girlfriend while watching a PBS documentary about the Lincoln Highway.) When I see a place decorated with souvenirs from the 1910s to the '70s—plates from various tourist sites, luggage, a globe, postcards, View-Masters—on the tables, the cases along the walls filled with trinkets, and Roger Miller on the stereo, it could even smother previously frozen semichallah with butter and syrup and still make me happy.

The place even has a history of kitsch. It used to be Shakers, a similar breakfast place with, instead of all the travel knickknacks, the biggest, freakiest collection of salt and pepper shakers you'll ever see. I still wonder what happened to those shakers.

It's funny: My notes from three research trips to Byways include phrases like "chic greasy spoon: just a marketing theme?" and "down-home feel, food not exceptional." And yet I kind of like the place; hell, I kept going back to "research" it! It's like listening to a tape of a Dead show I had a good time at and finding out they repeated verses and missed solos and did all kinds of other stoner stuff. Does it even matter? Maybe I'm just a rube.

So now I think back on the meals I've had at Byways. One time I had eggs, sausage, and mushy-yummy blue corn pancakes, topped with honey pecan butter and organic maple syrup. But were those 'cakes supposed to be mushy? Another time, while waiting for a friend who was late, I had a blueberry crumble muffin that my notes say was "more crumble than blueberry, but good. Dry and sweet." Of course I ate the whole thing.

Now I'm confused. The rest of the menu is just classic stuff—hashes, scrambles, taters, and so on—and I have always enjoyed chatting up the staff. I guess I'm just a little more slacker than foodie, just like I'm a lot more Deadhead than symphony orchestra. And Byways seems to fit all that: it's a casual place in the middle of the foodie-infused Pearl, and I'm glad it's there, even if I can't tell if it's any good.

WAIT: Long on weekends, almost entirely outside and uncovered. **LARGE GROUPS:** Would be a hassle on weekends. **COFFEE:** Stumptown. **OTHER DRINKS:** Stash teas; hand-packed milkshakes. **FEEL-GOODS:** House-made baked goods. **HEALTH OPTIONS:** Egg whites and tofu available for $1. **WIFI:** No.

CADILLAC CAFE

Old School/Classy

The one place everybody knows about.

1801 NE Broadway St. (NE/Broadway)

503-287-4750

cadillaccafepdx.com

Weekdays 6 a.m. to 2:30 p.m., weekends 7 a.m. to 3 p.m.

$12–$18 (all major cards, no checks)

Whenever I visit my hometown of Memphis, certain traditions must be observed—one of which is to stuff myself with barbecued pork. And when Memphians think of *tradition* and *barbecue* together, one place always springs to mind: Charlie Vergos's Rendezvous. When visiting the Bluff City, you pretty much *have* to eat there, after which you have a drink at the Peabody Hotel and then go boogie to the blues and R&B down on Beale Street.

But the lines at the Rendezvous are insane, sometimes up to two hours. Old-timers rue the massive expansion that happened in the 1990s, and not many locals actually think it's the best barbecue in town. It's just the place to go. In fact, part of the reason everybody goes there is that, well, everybody goes there.

Well, the Cadillac Cafe is the Rendezvous of Portland's breakfast scene. The lines are insane, it isn't often considered the best in town, and some folks say it used to be cooler in the old location…but seemingly everybody has been there.

Folks do flip over the size of the portions and the variety of choices: eight specialties like Filet Mignon Steak and Eggs, Cajun Catfish, and a breakfast burrito, in addition to seven omelets and eight items listed as "Simple Fare," including basic egg plates, granola, oatmeal, pancakes, and French toast.

About that French toast: it's the Cadillac's calling card, and I add my voice to its chorus of praise. It's done two ways: three pieces soaked in custard egg batter for $7.50 (or $9 with seasonal fruit and roasted hazelnuts) or Hazelnut French Custard Toast, which is covered in hazelnuts and powdered sugar and served with one egg and either bacon or chicken apple sausage for $9. You can also get a slice of either kind as part of the Bunkhouse Vittles, a terrific combo plate with sausage, potatoes, and two eggs ($9.25). A waiter told me the French toast bread was developed specifically for the Cadillac.

The main gripes against the Cadillac boil down to either "Why would I wait 90 minutes for breakfast?" or "It's more of a suburban chain feel than a 'real' Portland breakfast place." On the former, I have to agree. If you're standing in line for an hour and a half, it's because you've already decided you love it, you're determined to check it out, you just don't know any better, or you're entertaining some out-of-town guest who just *has* to experience the tradition.

As far as the "real Portland" argument, well, that just depends on your style. The Cadillac definitely has an upscale, pink-walls, cosmopolitan, flowers-on-the-tables vibe, made a little theme-y by the presence of a pink Cadillac. It is not, in other words, a hippied-out place like the Utopia or the Cricket or a serious foodie palace like Simpatica.

And yet the Cadillac is pure Portland, in an older, richer, Irvington kind of way. But why should I bother to describe it, anyway? There's a 90 percent chance you've already been there and made up your own mind. And if you haven't, well, I suppose you should, at least once.

WAIT: Legendary on weekends: up to 90 minutes in good weather. **LARGE GROUPS:** With notice. **COFFEE:** Kobos. **OTHER DRINKS:** Espresso, breakfast martinis, hot liquor drinks, Oregon Chai, fresh-squeezed juice and lemonade, Tazo teas, sparkling cider. **FEEL-GOODS:** None that're touted. **HEALTH OPTIONS:** Substitute fresh fruit or tomatoes for potatoes or toast ($1); staff will make two-egg or whites-only omelets. **WIFI:** Yes.

CAFE DU BERRY

Classy

French café, with French prices and French staff.

6439 SW Macadam Ave. (SW/Inner)

503-244-5551

cafeduberry.ypguides.net

Breakfast weekdays 7 a.m. to 3 p.m., weekends 8 a.m. to 3 p.m.

$10–$13 (all major cards, no checks)

After the first edition of this book came out, folks often asked if I wrote anything negative about a place in my book. To this, I always said, "Kind of." About a couple places I said the food is not that great but I don't care (RIP, Tosis). But more often I think of what I wrote about Cafe du Berry.

It's not that I trashed the place. I even said the food was good—in fact, I said their custard-recipe French toast was borderline orgasmic. It's just that my Snootiness Alarm went off—the prices seemed ridiculous, our server was rude, and I said at the time that only the French toast would bring me back.

Here's a sample:

My omelet, which wasn't on the menu, was $14, which the server didn't mention. Sure, I could have asked, but a $14 omelet? The server didn't mention the sauce, either, which was tasty but doesn't generally appear on omelets. In fact, whenever he came to the table, we were left somewhat dazed by his rapid-fire, straight-to-the-point, not-even-looking-at-us delivery. He greeted us, described three specials, poured water, and was gone in about 5.2 seconds. So, is that efficient or rude?

Jean rightly pointed out that the French toast with potatoes and fruit was one piece of the toast, one smallish helping of potatoes, one strawberry, and half of a banana. That ain't much for $7.50.

I confess I did get rather snarky (you should have seen the first draft!). In short, my whole thing with the cafe felt a little off, like nobody was getting along, and I didn't know why.

So I decided to go back. And I have to say, I now wonder what I was so worked up about.

Our server was fine, the food was fine (the hollandaise in particular), and this time the place came off a little more "creaky grandma's house" than "snooty French place." Even the prices have stayed the same and don't seem too high anymore—though the portions are a bit small. Hell, even the French toast wasn't as good as I recall. It was really good, but I didn't want to run into the kitchen and make out with whoever created it, like I did the first time.

So here's my new take: Cafe du Berry is a popular, French-style bistro that serves pretty good food in a casual, old-timey feel, has a unique and tasty French toast, and otherwise isn't really my kind of place. And in reading other bloggers and reviewers, I've found that folks seem to feel about the same way.

Do with that as you will. And try the French toast sometime.

It's a French custard dessert recipe, made with Hawaiian egg bread thoroughly soaked, then grilled to just crisp on the outside, with a touch of lemon in the finish, dusted with powdered sugar, and served warm, syrup be damned. I could add details like the firmness of the bread and how it played perfectly with the bouncy delight of the custard, but I'm on my way to have some right now.

WAIT: Some wait on weekends, mostly inside. **LARGE GROUPS:** Upstairs, with some notice. **COFFEE:** Kobos. **OTHER DRINKS:** Tea, cocktails, sparkling wine, fresh juice. **FEEL-GOODS:** None that I noticed; it's French food! **HEALTH OPTIONS:** I think if you eat the custard-based French toast, or the béarnaise sauce, or the hollandaise sauce 10 times, you get a punch card for a free angioplasty. **WIFI:** No.

CAFE NELL

Classy/Weekend	
Casual...in a fancy kind of way.	
1987 NW Kearney St. (NW)	
503-295-6487	
cafenell.com	
Weekends 9 a.m. to 2 p.m.	
$16–$20 (Visa, MasterCard, American Express, no checks)	

In restaurant world, the word *casual* has to be taken in context. So Stanford's might seem casual to some folks and fancy to others. What seems casual on Hawthorne might seem filthy to somebody in the Southwest Hills.

I say all this because you should know that Cafe Nell is a particular kind of casual restaurant. You can hang out as long as you want (at least at breakfast, which is the only time I've been), it's in a quiet little nook of Northwest, and it feels like a little neighborhood place in Paris or something.

But it's a fancy and sophisticated casual. And it ain't cheap. Benedicts, for example, range from ham for $15 to braised pork tenderloin for $20. Their basic burger (available at brunch) is $15. Ah, but it's Cascade Natural ground beef, with balsamic caramelized onions, a fried egg, and aioli on a Pearl Bakery brioche bun.

So Nell is casual in a high-end Northwest Portland kind of way: sleek, with black and white and tile dominating, accented by a red fireplace, and the mere presence of wine cooler buckets holding bottles of Pellegrino telling you, "You're not at the Cricket Cafe." But it is certainly relaxed, and the combination of tall windows, high ceilings, and several large mirrors makes it an open and attractive place.

Cafe Nell has really blown out its brunch under new ownership. There are now more than 10 starters and salads, 12 or more mains, six artisanal cheeses, oysters, and a full range of cocktails. Though I should say the menu changes frequently, and this is what they had when I was there.

One thing that has survived since Nell's founding in 2008 is the Mary Nell, a Bloody Mary that could probably pass as a meal in itself.

Along with the vodka (you can also get pepper-infused vodka) it comes with house-roasted pepper-tomato mix, skewers of shrimp, chorizo, cheddar cheese, and pickled vegetables. It actually looks like somebody stuck a breakfast on your cocktail. Oh, and you can add bacon for $2. I mean, why not?

If I were suggesting a breakfast place for out-of-town visitors whom I wanted to impress, and they just wanted a tasty little something in a casual setting, Cafe Nell would be perfect.

WAIT: Not usually, but they take reservations. **LARGE GROUPS:** Up to 20, with notice. **COFFEE:** Caffè Umbria. **OTHER DRINKS:** Espresso, full bar. **FEEL-GOODS:** Emphasis on local, organic, and sustainable ingredients. **HEALTH OPTIONS:** Limited vegetarian and vegan options; a number of gluten-free options. **WIFI:** Yes.

TOP HASHCAPADE (SEE PAGE 301)

CAMEO CAFE EAST

Mom and Pop/Old School
Grandma's Kitschy Korean Roadhouse!
8111 NE Sandy Blvd. (NE/Outer)
503-284-0401
cameocafe.com
Daily 6:30 a.m. to 3 p.m.
$10–$16 (all major cards, no checks)

Argue all you want about the best or worst breakfast places in Portland, but the Cameo is definitely one of the strangest.

I used to drive by and think it was a roadhouse or greasy-spoon joint, with a cheap motel behind it and highways all around. But inside, the décor practically screams *Grandma*, with flowered wallpaper, tea sets on shelves, and clay figurines of chefs over the stove. The *Mercury* said it "looks a little like an insurance office," and my friend Jane said it looked like an ice cream parlor. Keep looking and you'll spot a bulletin board covered with signed photos of Miss America contestants who apparently ate there. There's also an accordion, a flashing carousel, a parasol, and more clay figurines of hillbillies, Cupid, and a naked lady.

When you sit down and check for the specials, there's another shock. Nothing can prepare you for the words *Kimchee Omelet*. When I told Jane that kimchee is a very spicy fermented cabbage dish popular in Korea, she asked, "And they make an omelet with it?" Well, apparently. And it took me years of telling my friends, "You eat it, I'll buy it!" before my friend Mike finally took me up on it. He says he loves kimchee, and reported it was "good, but not the best kimchee I've ever had."

When I first saw that omelet, I wondered, "What kind of place is this?" Well, it's a, um, kitschy Korean roadhouse. I guess.

After you peel through the layers of oddness, you'll see that Cameo is in most ways a pretty straightforward breakfast joint—with big portions and high prices. It shares the famous "acres" of pancakes from the old and famous Cameo West on NW 23rd, but Cameo East's Full Acre is listed at market price (I forgot to ask why, but it's $10.95). The 'cakes come with apples, bananas, strawberries, raspberries, or peaches.

But there is a Korean thread running through the menu. There are tofu pancakes (made with mung beans and rice) with vegetables and cheese. And there is Sue Gee's fusion Pancake (that's how it's written on the menu) with rice and vegetables in a "special prepared batter" with cheese. And then there's what I had, the Pindaettok, which is pronounced pin-day-tuck and is, according to the menu, "a Korean word meaning pancake."

I was on my way out of town for a hike, which might be the only time that a soy-based pancake with vegetables, beans, spices, and ground rice in a "flavored batter," cooked thin and crispy and with something called Duck Sauce on the side sounds about right for breakfast. It also comes with two eggs, bacon, and two pieces of their yummy, multigrain, house-made stong bread. (Again, that's how it appears on the menu. I don't know what it means.)

Cameo also has the usual assortment of waffles (plus a coconut option), French toast, and about a dozen combinations of egg, meat, and carb. But the Pindaettok defined the place for me. I had never heard of it, wasn't quite sure what it was, and was not at all used to spicy vegetables at breakfast.

But I also liked it, and there was more of it than I could eat. And walking out of a breakfast place, all filled up and ready to hike after admiring a bunch of beauty pageant ladies, was the first non-strange thing that happened to me that day.

WAIT: Sometimes on weekends. **LARGE GROUPS:** Up to 10, with notice. **COFFEE:** Farmer Brothers. **OTHER DRINKS:** Tea, juice, hot chocolate, regular sodas (including RC), and local Shirley Temple Soda Pop. **FEEL-GOODS:** The house bread is preservative free and baked fresh locally. **HEALTH OPTIONS:** Pretty good range for vegetarians; many gluten-free options. **WIFI:** No.

CITY STATE DINER

Hip/Old School

The name kind of says it all.

128 NE 28th Ave. (E Burnside)

(503) 517-0347

citystatediner.com

Weekdays 8 a.m. to 3 p.m., weekends 8 a.m. to 4 p.m.

$13–$16 (Visa, MasterCard, Discover, no checks)

Okay, just settled in for a late breakfast at City State, figured I'd write it up as I go.

It's on NE 28th, just up from Burnside, in that row of places with La Buca, Beulahland, and so on. I guess it was a wine place before, couldn't say for sure. A lot going on in this strip.

The menu is pretty much all classics, with a couple of things that jump out: a peppercorn pork loin with redeye gravy, loukanika Greek sausage scramble, and a pancake o' the day, which today is coconut. (Why on Earth would somebody ruin a perfectly good pancake with coconut?)

I ordered the country-fried steak because (A) I'm hungry as hell, (B) I figured I should check out a "diner" on their gravy and fried stuff, and (C) I live on Heart Attack Road. All the plates come with either house potatoes or seared grits. I got the latter. Curious.

Not much in terms of decor: black booths and table tops, grey and white walls, a few photos around, big close-up shots of rustic kitchen utensils. It's maybe half-full, and seems louder than it should be for this number of people. About six booths, three or four tables, and a counter. Kind of a hipster vibe; the waiter was cut straight from the mold (skinny, tight black jeans, flannel shirt, Adidas shoes, working on his sideburns) and the waitress is sporting a little color striping in her hair. I think 1974 Arlo Guthrie just sat down at the table next to me.

Food came fast! About the time it took me to type the previous paragraphs. Smells nice, looks nice. "Seared grits" look just like polenta, cut into wedges. Chunks of sausage in the gravy. Two scrambled eggs and two pieces of toast, all for $10.50. Solid portion for that price.

Tried the grits; taste like grits. Not being a smart-ass—not more than usual anyway, just not sure what the searing did, other than pack

68

them into a cake-like form. Tried the eggs; a perfect scramble. Tried the steak and gravy. Didn't get much taste there, better try again. Hmm, same deal. Clear the palate with some toast, drink a little water, try it again. Nothing. Nicely fried, meat is tender, gravy is a good consistency, just not a lot of pop in there. Tried the eggs again to check my palate; they have more taste than the gravy. What, am I losing it?

A girl with blue-and-yellow hair just sat down with a guy with one of those 1930s paperboy hats and sideburns you could farm in. And it's seriously filling up; it's now 12:20 p. m. on a Monday, and we are in Slacker City. Wait, that makes me a slacker...

Let's check the online reviews, try to get a little perspective. The Yelpers are typically all over the map, but mostly positive. One person called it "chi chi," and I'd like to see her version of casual. The *Mercury* said it would be successful despite slow service. One breakfast blog dug it, without being too convincing. And the *Tribune* said it was "comfortingly, self-consciously generic." They also said it "takes a concept and doesn't run with it."

Me? I could do with some more running. Strikes me as a casual neighborhood place that wouldn't be worth a drive. It does serve breakfast all day, and there are cocktails and everything, and WiFi. And you can do worse than getting filled up for $10. But I can probably walk out the door of this place, turn in a circle, and see five better restaurants. If I lived nearby and, like today, was starving, low on cash, and wanting to do some writing for a while, I'd probably be back. Otherwise, I think I'm good.

I've now heard the waitress, in discussing coconut pancakes, say three times, "People love it or hate it." I would be surprised if people felt either way about City State.

WAIT: A little on weekends. **LARGE GROUPS:** During the week; groups of six or more will be split. **COFFEE:** Cellar Door. **OTHER DRINKS:** Espresso, tea, juice, soda, cocktails, beer. **FEEL-GOODS:** None they brag about. **HEALTH OPTIONS:** Good veggie options, and you can substitute tofu for eggs for $1. **WIFI:** Yes.

CLYDE COMMON

Weekend/Hip/New
A place to be checked out, apparently.
1014 SW Stark St. (Downtown)
503-228-3333
clydecommon.com
Weekends 10 a.m. to 3 p.m.
$13–$17 (all major cards, no checks)

I don't mean to get all psychoanalytical, but in some situations I feel like a silly, crude imposter, or worse. Among the situations that bring this up are hanging out with Serious Food People, eating at highly regarded Portland restaurants, and attending soccer games in England. We'll set the last aside for a future book project.

When I heard that Clyde Common was doing brunch, I actually felt a little reserved about it. Nothing to do with them, of course, but all the Serious Food People in town regard it highly, and I wasn't sure that my inane scribblings would contribute much to the discussion. At some point, though, I was speaking with my friend Jen Stevenson, who goes out to eat about 13 times a day, maintains two blogs, and wrote and published a book called *Portland's 100 Best Places to Stuff Your Faces*…which sold more copies than my book did! And she, who had of course been there for drinks and dinner, mentioned brunch at Clyde Common.

I thought, "What the hell, let's combine all my fears at once and go eat at Clyde Common." It's in the Ace Hotel downtown, and both have the reputation of hosting the "in" crowd and being a place to see and be seen. First I cruised the website and found praise from *Esquire* and *Food & Drink* magazines. Even the motto, "Domestic and Foreign Cooking," was somehow so smug I found it intimidating. Like, *who am I to ask what they cook?* I was nervous and almost told Jen, "Screw it, let's go down the street to Kenny and Zuke's and get some pastrami and soda." That stuff, I understand.

Alas, I braved on, and soon we were sitting in a spacious, classy-but-comfortable room, with huge windows (to see and be seen through, I guess), big wooden community tables, and this kind of simple, elegant feel to the whole place. I felt a little better, but soon developed a new problem: I couldn't take my eyes off our gorgeous waitress. Now I felt like a silly, crude pervert.

Well, the food made all these non-worries go away. The menu changes here more than in many places, because, after all, this place is Serious. In March we had buttermilk waffles with bacon marmalade (!) and pear preserve, and I think Jen said something about the balance of savory and sweet. All I know is, after one bite I was doubly distracted. Next came a caramelized onion and potato quiche, which I enjoyed so much I started to think maybe I belonged here.

What killed me was the seared lamb pancetta with bulgur (which I thought I didn't like), broccoli rabe (which I had to Google), and cipollini (ditto). Turns out, the lamb and pancetta were rolled into a loaf and laid on top of this nutty, green bed with tiny grilled onions on the side. Wow, is she pretty was it good! As I write this, I am looking at a picture of it and feeling all warm and fuzzy. (No, I didn't take a picture of the waitress; I'm not that bad.)

When Jen published her second edition (which you should go buy at bestplacestostuffyourfaces.com), I read what she had to say about Clyde Common. After raving about the food and its "popular-kid hipness," she closed with a suggestion to sit at the bar so you can admire the bar manager's "renowned tushie."

I feel vindicated all around, and I can't wait to head back to Clyde Common for the food, feel, and scenery.

WAIT: Can be long on weekends. **LARGE GROUPS:** Limited reservations for groups of six or more. **COFFEE:** Stumptown. **OTHER DRINKS:** Cocktails, including make-your-own mimosas, Steven Smith Tea, house-made sodas, espresso next door at Stumptown. **FEEL-GOODS:** None they tout. **HEALTH OPTIONS:** Not much. **WIFI:** No.

TOP HASHCAPADE (SEE PAGE 301)

COUNTRY CAT DINNER HOUSE & BAR

New
A new happening in a newly happening area.
7937 SE Stark St. (SE/Outer)
503-408-1414
thecountrycat.net
Brunch daily from 9 a.m. to 2 p.m.
$14–$18 (all major cards, no checks)

Used to be you could just about drive right past the Country Cat and never notice it. The same was true for the Montavilla neighborhood. Those days are getting further in the past all the time.

The Country Cat's generic exterior hides an exquisite interior made of wood, with shades of blue and brown, spacious booths, hanging lights, and an open kitchen. It's modern yet comfy. Only the lines will tell you how good the food is.

Like the exterior, the brunch menu at first seems rather down-home: pancakes, a Benedict, a basic breakfast, a couple omelets, and lunch items like chicken wings, a meatloaf sandwich, and fried chicken (more on that later). But the details tell you that you're dealing with something different: the pancakes come with roasted apples, salted caramel butter, and maple syrup. One omelet has butter-braised leeks, three cheeses, and wild mushrooms. The Benedict is on a sweet cream biscuit with smoked steelhead or house-cured ham and preserved lemon hollandaise. The Cast Iron Skillet Fried Chicken comes with mixed greens and toasted pecan spoon bread, all of it dressed in maple syrup.

See where I'm going here? The Country Cat aspires to be both

a cozy neighborhood place *and* a new-Portland-style cutting-edge restaurant. And more folks than the locals have noticed. The owner/chef, Adam Sappington, has gotten nominations from the James Beard Foundation, and the Country Cat has been written of glowingly in *Time, Bon Appétit,* and *Gourmet,* and featured on Food Network.

At the Country Cat, a pig is butchered once a week; bacon, ham, and other meats are made on-site. Almost all other ingredients are local. After it opened in 2007, the picky folks over at portlandfood. org went nuts over the place. Some were from the neighborhood and were excited about the Cat in conjunction with the Academy Theater, a wine bar, and a new farmers' market on Sundays. Others were just fired up about such serious cooking with fresh, local produce and an ever-revolving menu based on the season.

And then there is the fried chicken. Just about everybody mentions the fried chicken, for two reasons. One is the decent chance that it will be some of the finest fried chicken you've ever eaten, unless you're a purist and believe that fried chicken should still have the bones and skin. The Cat's is a brined, skinless piece of thigh meat with seasoned breading; at brunch (for $15) two pieces come with a mixed green salad and a slab of toasted pecan spoon bread, which is at the same time moist and cakey, firm and soft, and sweet and crispy. It and the chicken are drizzled with real maple syrup.

The $15 price tag is why some folks get a little sideways about the Country Cat. The theme here is, "What's a place, much less in this neighborhood, doing charging $15 for fried chicken?" Some folks even lobbed the nuclear bomb of these conversations: *gentrification.*

I don't wade into such chatter. If a guy can get $15 for fried chicken, I say more power to him. All I can tell you is that the chicken is darn good, as was everything else we had at the Cat, and who cares what neighborhood it's in? My friend Alice spent the whole meal saying, "Wow, this is good," and "I need to come back here for dinner." I'll just agree with Alice.

WAIT: Quite long on weekends. **LARGE GROUPS:** Yes. **COFFEE:** Stumptown. **OTHER DRINKS:** Espresso, Steven Smith teas, Bloody Marys, mimosas, fresh juice. **FEEL-GOODS:** Plenty of local ingredients, and much of the meat is prepared on-site. **HEALTH OPTIONS:** Some veggie options. **WIFI:** No.

CRICKET CAFÉ

Hip/Veggie
Dude, dig the size of this menu!
3159 SE Belmont St. (SE/Belmont)
503-235-9348
cricketcafepdx.com
Breakfast daily 7:30 a.m. to 3 p.m.
$11–$15 (all major cards, no checks)

The Cricket is nearly the perfect Southeast breakfast place: good ideas, good food, slow pace (for better or worse), good folks, and a little rough around the edges. Colorful artwork featuring baked goods and outdoor scenes adorn the simple white walls. Bamboo blinds block the summer sun and Belmont Street traffic noise. The ceiling and concrete floor used to be crisscrossed with cracks, but they cleaned that up a few years back

In fact, I went back for this edition of the book to see what had changed over the years. The extent of my notes from that day was "Indian music, smaller than I remember, redid the ceiling." I guess the pace of change is slow at the Cricket, and why wouldn't it be? It has settled in as one of the most popular, enduring, and endearing off all the Portland breakfast places.

The Cricket roasts its own coffee and buys from local growers and farmers, which suggests a commitment to health and community. It also serves a large list of "liquid breakfast" cocktails. The baked goods are made from scratch, and the Cricket is known for absurdly good cinnamon rolls, which are only available some weekends. The apple bread is served warm, soft in the middle, and crunchy outside—rather like the whole place, now that I think about it.

And the menu! It's an awesome level of variety: about 20 omelets, scrambles, hashes, skillets, plates, and specialties, *plus* you can build your own omelet, scramble, or potato dish. And there are two other wonderful touches: $3.99 specials before 9 a.m. and $2.99-3.99 to-go orders. And you won't leave hungry. You can get the Big Farm Breakfast with potatoes, pancakes, *and* toast, if you want. The bacon is thick and crispy. The pancakes are thin but very flavorful and crisp around the edges, served with pure maple syrup. They have home fries (simple, lightly peppered, with the smaller pieces crunchy) as well as crispy shoestring hash browns. The granola is excellent—of course.

Still, what I am going to remember about the place are two things. One is the relaxed vibe that exists, whether it's crowded or calm. The other is an interaction we had with the ~~hipster punk~~ young man pouring water for us. There was some music playing, and we were discussing whether it would be called rap

or hip-hop. (We're very white.) Pitcher Boy mumbled loud enough for us to hear, in a voice dripping with disdain, "Just call it *music.*"

Then he walked off, and we all looked at each other for a moment, caught between shock and humor. Then we remembered where we were, shrugged it off, and dived back into our food.

WAIT: Long on weekends after about 10:00 a.m.; coffee available; some chairs and cover outside, very little room inside. **LARGE GROUPS:** Groups of six or more should expect a longer wait. **COFFEE:** Millar's Wood Roasted Organic Coffee house blend. **OTHER DRINKS:** Variety of teas (Numi, Tao of Tea, Tazo), DragonFly Chai, full bar. **FEEL-GOODS:** Local fruits, veggies, cheeses, butter, and meats. **HEALTH OPTIONS:** Egg whites or tofu in any dish for $1.75; vegetarian gravy; vegan and vegetarian options. **WIFI:** Yes.

CUP & SAUCER CAFE

Hip/Veggie

Like an old friend: dependable and nonthreatening.

3566 SE Hawthorne Blvd. (SE/Hawthorne)

503-236-6001

Daily 7 a.m. to 9 p.m.

3000 NE Killingsworth St. (NE/Alberta)

503-287-4427

Weekdays 8 a.m. to 4 p.m., weekends 8 a.m. to 3 p.m.

8237 N Denver Ave. (N)

503-247-6011

Daily 8 a.m. to 3 p.m.

cupandsaucercafe.com

$10–$13 (Visa, MasterCard, no checks)

You wake up medium-late, like 10 in the morning. You want some breakfast, but you don't want to spend 15 bucks. You want something more than a coffee shop, something less than a fancy brunch. You don't want to go too far. You figure the lines are already huge at the local giants. You talk it over with your friends, you waver for a minute, and then somebody says, "Screw it, let's just go to the Cup & Saucer."

Now, you might think I just demeaned the Cup & Saucer. Not so. In fact, here's another way of saying the same thing: The Cup & Saucer is *The Princess Bride* of Portland breakfast places. Get some friends together to pick a movie sometime, let them hash it out for a while, and then say, "What about *The Princess Bride*?" Somebody will say, "Oh, I love that movie!" And everybody will agree it's all right. It's got something for everyone.

That seems to be how Portland feels about the Cup & Saucer. It's friendly and casual, and it's in three very happening neighborhoods. It's hippie, hipster, kid-friendly, and dependable. They serve breakfast at all hours, and the menu is bursting with options. Chances are, nothing you eat there will be the best you ever had, but chances are even better that whatever you want, they'll have it.

The 18 egg or tofu plates include just about every ingredient you can think of, and you can add the works (cheddar, salsa, and sour cream) to your side of potatoes for $2.75. Split plates for these 18 options come with a scone and a side of potatoes for $2.75, and you can substitute fruit for your potatoes for $1.75. Oh, and there are five house specialties (a regular and Florentine Benedict, biscuits and vegetarian gravy, huevos rancheros, and the Super Saucer, which is two eggs, a meat choice, and a pancake), challah French toast, granola, oatmeal, and four pancakes: buttermilk; ginger buckwheat; vegan, gluten-free cornmeal; and a daily special. There are more than a dozen side dishes, including brown rice, sautéed veggies, muffins, toast, and tortillas.

See what I mean? Just try to go into the Cup & Saucer and find nothing you want. Can't eat sugar or wheat? Dig into the Basil Pesto Scramble with spinach and sun-dried tomatoes. And, for the record, before I even read this review to one non-wheat-eating friend, she said, "That place is like a generic breakfast place, but it's pretty good!"

Other than the variety and dependability, the Cup & Saucer is known for scones and their spin on breakfast potatoes. The scones… well, they're called the Cup & Saucer Classic Buttery Vanilla Delight. Need to know more? A basket of three is $2, so don't skip them. The potatoes are a combination of russets and sweet potatoes, with cloves of roasted garlic thrown in. They come with most dishes and are $3.50 as a stand-alone.

Now I'm hungry and need a break and some food, so what the heck, I'll just walk over to the Cup & Saucer.

WAIT: Medium on weekends, with some space inside and cover outside. **LARGE GROUPS:** Good choice (up to 10). **COFFEE:** Happy Cup. **OTHER DRINKS:** Espresso, DragonFly chai, Italian sodas, cocktails at some locations. **FEEL-GOODS:** Some organic ingredients. **HEALTH OPTIONS:** Egg substitute or tofu; gluten-free pancakes; vegan and vegetarian options abound. **WIFI:** Yes, in all.

DELTA CAFE BAR

Weekend/Veggie/Hip	
Sit ya'self down and let's eat!	
4607 SE Woodstock Blvd. (SE/Outer)	
503-771-3101	
deltacafepdx.com	
Weekends 9 a.m. to 2 p.m.	
$12–$14 (all major cards, checks)	

So, there's this way we like to do things down South. It's part food, part booze, part folks, part music, part attitude. It's a little hungover, and it's a little drunk. It's slumped back in the chair too. It ain't light, but it's serious—like when a blues band hits its groove: nobody's smiling, exactly, but it's just right. It's gettin' down.

The Delta Cafe just about gets me to this place every time I go in. I say "just about" because I'm getting a little old for the hipster vibe, and no place does the hipster vibe like the Delta. Still, it's got some old-school funk in there, and I don't mean filth. I mean soul. Somebody's got a Southern groove goin' on there, more my kind of South than, say, the Screen Door.

The Screen Door, God bless it, is all foodie and stuff. Excellent place. But the Delta is a Smoked-Brisket-Hash kind of Southern. Eggs scrambled with andouille sausage, crawfish, onions, bell peppers, celery, and garlic. Po' Boys! Beignets!

Okay, so there's a barbecued tofu Po' Boy in addition to the barbecued pork and fried oysters—and a lot of other tofu available—but hey, this is Southeast Portland, not the French Quarter. I can get with that. Nothing wrong, either, with a Brioche French Toast served with berry compote, organic maple syrup, and whipped cream.

I went there with a big Breakfast Crew one time—foodies, friends, and assorted loonies—and I'm not sure it was the best meal we ever had, but it was one of the longest and one of the loudest. That's in part because they're not afraid to crank up the tunes at the Delta, nor are they afraid of Johnny Cash, or some occasional hard rock. But it's also because there's booze going around and some folks are either hungover or still working on something from the night before. And there're some wacky decorations that I can't even describe, but I can tell you that the whole place is kind of a trip. And none of the chairs match. And you might get sweet tea in a mason jar. And their lunch- and dinnertime Creole Gumbo with shrimp, chicken, and sausage is just about my favorite plate in town.

So it's right at a cool intersection between the groovy Southeast Portland thing and that down-home, get yourself-a-cocktail Southern thing. Sit yourself down and fill yourself up. Take a little tour of the PDX Southern food thing.

WAIT: Maybe a little. **LARGE GROUPS:** With notice. **COFFEE:** Happy Cup. **OTHER DRINKS:** Beer, cocktails, Bloody Mary bar, juice. **FEEL-GOODS:** None in particular. **HEALTH OPTIONS:** Good veggie variations. **WIFI:** Yes.

DETOUR CAFE

New/Veggie
A literally hidden gem.
3035 SE Division St. (SE/Division)
503-234-7499
detourcafe.com
Daily 8 a.m. to 4 p.m.
$9–$13 (Visa, MasterCard, Discover, no checks)

One of these days I'll be sitting around in who-knows-what kind of breakfast place, telling folks I was in Portland when the organic/local-grown/sustainable revolution happened—a time when so many good places opened all over town that a yummy, cool place like the Detour Cafe could exist right under my nose and I wouldn't even know about it.

I mean that literally: starting in 2001, this little place hid behind all the vegetation on its porch for six years before I knew of its existence. I guess the folks in the neighborhood didn't want the rest of us to know about it.

Detour represents everything the "new" Portland is all about. Its website says, "We use free range eggs, organic flour, and when possible, organic and/or locally farmed produce and meats. We also feature freshly baked pastries of all kinds, house-made vegan soups, and Stumptown coffee." It then goes on to offer a feel-good hodgepodge of links: Gathering Together Farm, the Oregon Humane Society, Planned Parenthood, art studios, bands, you name it. Actually, I think the place is defined by one item on its menu, the Division Street Farmer's Breakfast: organic potatoes, blanched kale with toasted seeds, house-made bread, choice of meat/faux meat, and an egg. Have you ever heard of another place that would call that a "farmer's breakfast"?

Detour is cute and friendly, with yellow and green dominating the décor. Plastic chairs and tables give it a semigoofy feel, and on the shady porch the overhanging plants cut down on the noise from Division Street. They serve house-baked goods, including one of the finest cheddar biscuits in town, spiced with scallions and sweetened with corn.

What really sets Detour apart, though, can be stated in four words: build your own frittata. As soon as I saw my smoked-salmon-and-goat-cheese three-egg frittata sitting on my plate with roasted potatoes and whole-wheat toast (all for just $9.25), I thought, "Why doesn't everybody do this?" My frittata was the perfect combination of egg, cheese, and meat, with just a little crust from the baking and plenty of fresh, creamy, cheesy goodness.

The basic option is any two of 24 frittata ingredients, so a vegetarian can do well. Extra ingredients are only $0.75, and you get organic roasted onions for free. You can get any three of the same ingredients from the same list with potatoes for only $8.50, so even the vegans can get their groove on (there's a daily vegan and gluten-free soup, as well). And for only $4 you can get toasted focaccia with cream cheese, Roma tomato, and fresh basil.

The portions aren't overwhelming, but everything looks nice and colorful. My friend Chela's French toast was made with cardamom bread, which sort of grounded the sweetness from the custard dip; the topping of cherry compote, toasted almonds, and organic maple syrup brought it home wonderfully. One slice of this for $5 (two slices is $8) was just what she wanted.

My friend Tom, ever on the search for the perfect bacon-and-egg sandwich, was mighty impressed by his B.E.L.T., with pepper bacon, two eggs sunny side up, mixed greens, and tomato, on house-made mayo on focaccia ($8.50). Other sandwich options included the Original, with baked eggs, cream cheese, Roma tomatoes, fresh basil, and pepper bacon ($8.50); the All Fired Up, with spiced cream cheese and red peppers ($7.75); and the Don ($9.75), with portobello mushrooms, onions, and feta mixed into the eggs and topped with Italian sausage, avocado, tomato, and basil.

Everything was fresh, tasty, and down-home in that "new Portland" way. That seemed to perfectly wrap up Detour, that home of the Southeast Portland farmer set.

WAIT: Long on weekends, with self-serve coffee and some cover outside. **LARGE GROUPS:** Yes, with notice. **COFFEE:** Self-serve Stumptown. **OTHER DRINKS:** Chai, Foxfire teas, Brew Dr. Kombucha on tap, soda, juice, and full bar. **FEEL-GOODS:** Organic, local ingredients and cage-free eggs. **HEALTH OPTIONS:** Plenty here for vegetarians and vegans. **WIFI:** Yes.

DIN DIN

Weekend/New/Hip
It's so small and adorable!
920 NE Glisan St. (NE/Inner)
971-544-1350
dindinportland.com
Sunday 10 a.m. to 3 p.m.
$12–$15 (all major cards, checks)

One's first impression of Din Din might be that's a little, well, odd. For one thing, it's located in a forgotten corner of Northeast that seems somehow hard to find even though it's just a few blocks off Burnside. Then there's the website, with a drawing of a loin-clothed hunter stalking beets and a running ham. The family-style dinners are called *din dins*, the light daytime menu is called *fee fee*, and the Sunday brunch *matinee*. And the picture on their About Us web page…I don't know where to start.

But when you get there, you'll probably walk in and say what a few of us in the Crew said: It's small and adorable. We were there just after the holidays, and the lights were still up, along with paper cut-out ceiling decorations and evergreen centerpieces. Also on the table: slabs of black slate, taking us back toward "odd" just a little bit. There are just five big tables and a tiny kitchen left wide open for you to admire the magic. The staff is all young and delightful, and the whole vibe is a cool combination of down-home and whimsical. Even the sinks in the bathroom? That's right: Tiny.

When you see the plates, you might also think more "small" than anything else. The brunch menu, which changes weekly, is not quite "small plates," but

it comes close. At any rate, our collective advice was to think community style and go for it. And it's French: I've seen a lamb crépinette (sausage sautéed in butter) with walnut-lemon hollandaise and a crème fraîche pound cake.

Again, small but adorable: You might order a $7 salad, for example, thinking you're getting a great deal, and want more food. But it will be a greens dressed with white balsamic and bleu cheese custard with a soft-boiled egg. Or you might get a plate called simply Ham and Whole Grain Mustard for $3.50, and you'll get two pieces of ham with some mustard—which doesn't sound like much, of course, but my, was it adorable, as well as tender and tasty. Same thing for a plate with the day's cheese (in our case, Langres, from Champagne) and pear slices. Again, nothing much to it, except it was perfect.

For me, Din Din isn't the kind of place where you go and stuff yourself, but it could be the kind of place where you and your somebody spend a leisurely brunch touring the tastes of French cooking. With mostly community seating, you'll probably meet some new folks, too.

It's *definitely* the kind of place where you and a half dozen friends can have a community feast, get to eat all sorts of different things, and marvel at how small and cute everything is.

WAIT: None. **LARGE GROUPS:** Yes, but make reservations. **COFFEE:** Sterling Coffee Roasters. **OTHER DRINKS:** Espresso, T Project tea, wine, cocktails, beer **FEEL-GOODS:** "We enjoy conscientiously sourcing local ingredients." **HEALTH OPTIONS:** Good for vegetarians, not vegans. **WIFI:** Yes.

DOUG FIR LOUNGE

Hip/Old School

Live music and good food, at the same place.

830 E Burnside St. (E Burnside)

503-231-9663

dougfirlounge.com

Breakfast daily 7 a.m. to 2:30 p.m.

$10–$14 (all major cards, no checks)

Perhaps you've heard that the Doug Fir Lounge, that "music place" on East Burnside, serves breakfast. And perhaps when you heard it, you thought, "Bar, club, breakfast…no, thanks." Well, the Doug Fir is trying to be more than a music place, and its food is definitely beyond bar chow.

First and foremost, the Doug Fir is a music place featuring bands that this 40-something has absolutely never heard of. Maximo Park's bus was parked outside when I ate there, and had the entire band been sitting at a table next to me singing its number one song, I wouldn't have known them.

Like any music place, the Doug is trying to be young and hip—trying too hard, if you ask its detractors, who also bemoan its stylishly casual approach to service. Supporters generally chime back with, "Chill out, it's a rock-and-roll place." Even among rock-and-roll places, though, it's going for a particular niche. The shows start on time downstairs in the smoke-free room and are finished around midnight—both attempts to draw a wider range of audiences. Its owners told *Willamette Week* that their goal was to make the club itself a destination, "like Disneyland."

You might think you've walked into LoggerLand when you come into the ground-floor restaurant. Or maybe RetroLoungeLand. The walls and ceiling are a fancy-looking version of a log cabin, bulbous chrome fixtures drop amber light on Formica tables and round booths, and the colors are various shades of brown, from the two-tone padded chairs to the etchings on the ubiquitous mirrors. In the lounge area you'll find couches, padded ottomans, a glass moose head, and a fireplace. It's Retro Maximo.

Be sure to check out the bathroom, too. The women's room, in particular, inspired my friend Kelly Melillo to write an entire book about Portland bathrooms, called *The Best Places to Pee: A Guide to the Funky & Fabulous Bathrooms of Portland.* She says walking into the bathroom at Doug Fir is like "walking into the inner core of a disco ball," with everything covered in mirrors and both light and drunk patrons bouncing all over the place.

The menu is as down-to-Earth as the décor is over-the-top. There's a Logger Breakfast of eggs, hash browns, and various options for meats and breads. There are whole-wheat pancakes with apple butter, as well as French toast made with croissants and a touch of orange zest, served with bourbon-currant compote. There are two Benedicts (smoked salmon or house-cured pork loin) and my favorite, the Cascade Scramble with wild mushrooms, fresh herbs, shallots, and Gruyère.

As for the feel of the place, I found the defining moment to be when the heavily tattooed (and entirely pleasant) bartender shut off the start of Lynyrd Skynyrd's "Free Bird," put on some '70s funk instead, started trying to charm a two-year-old boy to get him to eat, and served a (reputedly strong and expensive) Bloody Mary to a scruffy-looking, twitching dude in a flannel shirt sitting at the bar with a very attractive young woman. Somehow, everything about the Doug Fir was right there: the family eating a hearty breakfast, the pre-9 a.m. booze, the guy who may well have been with the band, the staff dancing on the line between rockin' and professional, and the whole place eating surprisingly well and moving to a funky '70s groove.

WAIT: Maybe a little on weekends. **LARGE GROUPS:** More than six might be tough, but they do host events. **COFFEE:** Sisters Coffee Company. **OTHER DRINKS:** Cocktails, Shangri La organic teas, Red Bull. **FEEL-GOODS:** Many of the ingredients are local. **HEALTH OPTIONS:** Good options for vegetarians (but not vegans); grass-fed beef. **WIFI:** Yes.

EAST BURN

Hip/Weekend
A neighborhood semigourmet hangout.
1800 E Burnside St. (E Burnside)
503-236-2876
theeastburn.com
Weekends 10 a.m. to 3 p.m.
$13–16 (all major cards, no checks)

There is a *lot* going on at East Burn.

I had no idea how much was going on there before the Crew and I went there for brunch, and even after we'd gone—after we'd been completely impressed by many things there, including the food—I had to go to the website to see all the other stuff I'd missed.

I'll get to all of that, but first let's set the scene a little. I stay away from the whole "bars that do breakfast" category, because I have enough trouble keeping up with actual restaurants that do breakfast. So I almost didn't go to East Burn. Ah, but East Burn is a public house. And they don't seem to use that term lightly.

Consider: You walk in on a weekend morning, and a long row of beer taps atop the wall says *bar*. But a 1930s cartoon on a giant projection screen says *kids*. Or maybe *hipsters*. But the hanging basket chairs definitely say *kids*. Or maybe *drunk hipsters*. Ditto for the skateboard seats in the corner. Wood-paneled walls say *'70s,* as do green wine-bottle light fixtures, and yet the crayons and paper bring us back to *kids*. "What the hell is this place?" I wondered to myself.

Well, let's diverge for a moment and bring you up to speed. East Burn is a full-on bar, with a happy hour and everything, and is open till 2:30 a.m. Tuesday is Craft Beer Appreciation Night, with pints from 19 rotating taps going for $2.50. Downstairs is the Tap Room, with arcade games and a DJ booth, and they also have an Annex, where you can have meetings. They show local artists' work for no commission and have live music most nights (usually with no cover). Their motto is Eat-Drink-Play.

And then there's the semicovered patio, which is just a den of hipness, with porch swing seats, bamboo growing next to a fountain with a blue fish spitting water out of a wall of iron art, a dartboard, overhead heaters, and fire-pit tables. It's really kind of awesome.

Ah, yes: the food. Like I said, there's a lot going on. We sat down (eight people, no notice, no problem) and perused the menu, me still expecting something like standard bar fare. I can't say what that is, really, but it isn't a Caprese Benedict with polenta cakes, fresh basil, poached eggs, and fontina cream sauce. It certainly isn't a Lobster and Crawfish Benedict, nor Danish pancakes with cinnamon bun batter, golden raisins, and house preserves. And a Warm Quinoa Salad…I mean, *what is this place?*

The chef is from Philadelphia and apparently worked at some high-falutin places back there, and they've got everything from the above to a pork medallion sandwich with bourbon-apple chutney and caramelized onion to biscuits and gravy and a grilled cheese sandwich "recognized as being one of the best in the country by *Food & Wine* magazine," according to their website.

I had no idea *Food & Wine* magazine even recognized the existence of grilled cheese sandwiches, and it was just one more piece of information that kind of overwhelmed me on my first visit to East Burn. Oh, the food was outstanding, by the way. I got two meals out of my $12 lobster-crab Benedict, and everybody else was happy with what they ate.

Still, I felt like I needed some more "essence" of the place, so I went back alone one Saturday afternoon. It was a similar feel, and I got the country-fried steak with elk gravy (I won't live to see 50)…and then the cartoon gave way to a Timbers game, and the place slowly filled with all ages, and some of the staff came out of the kitchen to check on the game, and then I got it: It's a neighborhood semigourmet hangout place.

WAIT: None—and anyway, they take reservations. **LARGE GROUPS:** Yes. **COFFEE:** Happy Cup. **OTHER DRINKS:** Stash teas, fresh-squeezed juices, full bar. **FEEL-GOODS:** Mostly local ingredients. **HEALTH OPTIONS:** They say can make almost anything vegetarian. **WIFI:** Yes.

EaT: An Oyster Bar

Weekend
New Portleans!
3808 N Williams Ave. (N/Inner)
503-281-1222
eatoysterbar.com
Sunday 10 a.m. to 2 p.m.
$14–$17 (all major cards, no checks)

Loud, friendly, loose, and boozy—that's what a New Orleans brunch ought to be. So when I put out the EaT invite to the Crew and only three people said yes, I was worried. Had we, and Portland, lost the NOLA magic when Roux closed and Acadia quit doing brunch?

I could feel the vibe forming when I realized those who had accepted were all women whose names started with J: Juliet, Jean, and Jeanette. That has to mean something. Then we got to walk past the immense line at Tasty n Sons and sit right down in the big, spacious EaT. There was a jazz trio playing, just loud enough that you had to raise your voice a little, but you could still hear. Yep, startin' to feel it.

Our server came dancing over to say howdy and take drink orders, and we dug into the menu. It's about one-third food and two-thirds booze. Even their signature oysters, at brunch time, are bathed in lemon and alcohol: vodka with spicy red sauce; chili-infused bourbon; chili-infused tequila; and beer with Tabasco. When ocean brine meets citrus, spice, and liquor, something good is bound to happen.

In fact, most of the vast media praise for EaT (the name is a compilation of the owners' names) has to do with the oysters, which come in throughout the week from local waters. Most of the complaints have to do with slow service. At brunch, the Crew's opinion was that oysters were beside the point, and slow service—even though we didn't have that problem—would have fit just fine. Remember: loud, friendly, loose, and boozy.

We were all about the eggs and protein, New Orleans style. Juliet got the Eggs Sardou, which is poached eggs on top of artichoke hearts filled with creamed spinach, all covered in hollandaise sauce. I went for the Shrimp and Grits with a spicy, buttery Cajun sauce, and even had fun teasing the ladies with the heads of the shrimp; the server, still spinning, told me to play nice with the girls. Jean had the Hangtown Fry, which is actually a San Francisco dish, but who cares? It's a scramble with bacon and oysters, and at EaT the latter are fried in cornmeal and sitting on top. Jeanette, meanwhile, wanted a Po' Boy, which on our visit was done open-faced with soft-shell crab. If you don't know, the magic of a soft-shell crab is that you eat the whole thing, shell and all. Sadly, she couldn't bring herself to chomp down on the big bug on her sandwich, perhaps because she was lacking in the boozy part of the brunch equation.

Now, you want some Portland flavor? Apparently, some of the band, Reggie Houston's Box of Chocolates, work at New Seasons! Can't get any more PDX than that. Sitting there watching all my friends meet each other, watching the NOLA-transplant server boogie around (and insist she's a shy mom during the week), listening to the jazz blow, with my belly full of shrimp and grits, I felt myself start driftin' down South for a spell.

WAIT: Not much. **LARGE GROUPS:** With notice; reservations for six or more. **COFFEE:** Rotates. **OTHER DRINKS:** Sweet tea, sodas, juices, house-made ginger beer, full bar. **FEEL-GOODS:** Local oysters. **HEALTH OPTIONS:** Not much for vegetarians; less for vegans. **WIFI:** Yes.

EQUINOX

Weekend/New	
More like a paradox: good place, short wait.	
830 N Shaver Ave. (N/Inner)	
503-460-3333	
equinoxrestaurantpdx.com	
Brunch Wednesday through Sunday 9 a.m. to 2 p.m.	
$12–$14 (all major cards, no checks)	

Folks often ask me, "Why isn't so-and-so place in the book?"

Well, when I wrote the first edition of this book, I knew there was a place called Equinox, but somehow I had it in my head it was a coffee shop. Or it was so hippie-granola that I didn't want to go there. And therefore, Equinox just slipped through the cracks. Bottom line: I'm kind of an idiot sometimes. In my defense, two people I met there recently both told me they had driven by it many times and didn't realize there was a restaurant back behind that patio.

So now I have a question: Why the hell is everybody waiting in line at Gravy when Equinox is less than a block away?

For one thing, Equinox has a fine patio, removed from the chaos of Mississippi Street and set off by brick walls and an iron gate. It also doesn't seem to have much of a wait—and anyway, they take reservations. While the portions don't come close to Gravy's, there's only one dish on the brunch menu (steak and eggs) above $12, so the value is there. And it has the Breakfast Nook. Or Cave. Or Lair. The Crew and I called it all of these. It's a little…closet…off the main dining room, where you can just barely pack seven people, and you can even close the curtains. This led to quite a few strikingly crude jokes.

Despite our silly behavior, Equinox is a young, family-friendly place with some pretty classic breakfast fare, often served with a little twist—and by a particularly cute and friendly staff. (My lady friends agreed with this take.)

I particularly like the Breakfast Pillow, a puff pastry stuffed with roasted bell peppers, Parmesan, mushrooms and caramelized onions, topped with two poached eggs and chipotle cheese sauce. There's just a bit of a kick to it, and the sauce is like a cross between cheese dip and hollandaise. There's also steak and eggs, smoked salmon hash and Benedict, crème brûlée French toast with seasonal fruit, and one of my favorite breakfast names in town, the Back to Bed. That would be two fried eggs and peppered bacon over a baked puff pastry with chili pepper aioli and potatoes.

If I was really looking to "tank down," as we used to say in the fishing business, and go back to bed, I'd probably hit the Equinox Bowl: roasted potatoes with pork sausage, peppered bacon, spinach, roasted red peppers, caramelized onions, and cheddar, topped with poblano cheese sauce, salsa and sour cream. That's only $8, or $10.50 with two eggs added to it.

I would share more details, but really, these Breakfast Crew gatherings are too damn much fun for "research." I'd recommend you try to lock yourself in a Breakfast Lair with my friends Shari and Jerry and the rest of the Crew and see what you remember of the food. I'd also recommend you not do what I did originally, which is miss out on eating at Equinox.

WAIT: A little on weekends, but they take reservations. **LARGE GROUPS:** Notice helps. **COFFEE:** Stumptown. **OTHER DRINKS:** Espresso, fresh juice, Bloody Marys, mimosas, other cocktails. **FEEL-GOODS:** Local ingredients. **HEALTH OPTIONS:** Good veggie options. **WIFI:** Yes.

FAT ALBERT'S BREAKFAST CAFE

Old School

No nonsense, from them or you.

6668 SE Milwaukie Ave. (SE/Sellwood)

503-872-9822

Weekdays 7 a.m. to 2 p.m., weekends 7 a.m. to 3 p.m.

$8–$12 (cash and checks only)

Nobody is going to kiss your ass at Fat Albert's. The staff will seat you, feed you, and move you out, professionally and efficiently. And you'll get only a single page of options to choose from; that's one way to keep both the kitchen and you moving right along. So sit down, eat, and then go do whatever it is you're supposed to be doing.

Another couple of things, as a sign will inform you as soon as you walk in: cash and checks only, and incomplete parties will *not* be seated.

So, as you might sense, there can be an edge to the place, and sometimes there seems to be an "in" crowd that's treated better. Marginally. I think the signature dish is the egg-and-ham breakfast sandwich; my friend Jeff once told me, while wiping off the excess moisture with a napkin, that it "went over the butter line." I loved it, but I'll probably die of a heart attack when I'm 50.

You could also be thinking, "Finally, a breakfast place that doesn't try to be what it isn't, doesn't encourage people to surf on their laptops all day, doesn't try to break new ground in cuisine." Well, that's Fat Albert's, too.

Eggs, meat, potatoes, bread, and something sweet. That's the menu. Six omelets, pancakes, the sandwich, bottomless oatmeal, and biscuits and gravy. The omelets are straight to the point: one has good ol' ham

and cheese; the Yuppie has sun-dried tomatoes, artichoke hearts, and feta; Kim's Fave has avocado, cheddar, and bacon; the Salad Eater, with its spinach, tomatoes, onions, and mushrooms, is a nod to the veggie crowd.

I'm not much of a biscuits and gravy guy, but I can tell you that most reviews I've read don't consider them the café's strong point. The pancakes, however, are quite popular: big, fluffy, and a little crisp around the edges (of course). The maple syrup is nice and light; that's because, as the menu says, Fat Albert's uses "*real* maple syrup" and "*real* butter." Okay, then.

In fact, the menu also explains that it's the restaurant's policy to ask you to leave after you're done eating. You'll appreciate this when you're waiting in line for a table, but one online review recounted having fresh silverware placed in front of the reviewer along with the check! Every time I've been there, the food has arrived so quickly I was astonished.

Jeff and I had a quick work-lunch there, and as we were leaving, I wasn't sure who was paying. We stood at the register, each with a $20 bill at the ready, and after we hesitated for about one breath, the server dinged open the register and said, "I know! Why don't you pay separately!" Then she rolled her eyes, took our money without another word, and went back to serving food and coffee.

We were briefly stunned, then remembered where we were, admitted she had a point, and hauled our full bellies back to our day.

WAIT: Fairly long on weekends. LARGE GROUPS: Possible, but be prepared for a wait. COFFEE: Rose City Roasters' Fat Albert Blend. OTHER DRINKS: Tea and juice. FEEL-GOODS: None in particular. HEALTH OPTIONS: None in particular. WIFI: No.

FAT CITY CAFE

Mom & Pop/Old School

In a small town, a long, long time ago…

7820 SW Capitol Highway (SW/Outer)

503-245-5457

Daily 6:30 a.m. to 3 p.m.

$8–$11 (all major cards, no checks)

Here's how you do a breakfast with the fellas. You meet too damn early on a weekday, 'cause one of the fellas has to work. (On weekends, fellas have to sleep.) You show up on time so you can give a load of crap to the guy who shows up late. You say something about not being awake until you've had your coffee. You order the same thing you always do. Any mention of an attempt at weight loss is completely understood but thoroughly ridiculed.

Most importantly, you don't go someplace that has candles on the tables, or *bistro* in the name, or Asiago cheese. You go to a place like Fat City Cafe.

Ponder the name for a moment: Fat City. Every time I've been there, the special on the chalkboard was some kind of sausage: Italian, Cajun, spicy, smoked. The spicy sausage is precisely that, and a guy can earn points for eating it without complaint. The menu includes omelets, scrambles, and sizzles, and the only difference is consistency and egg-to-potato ratio. The bacon is crisp, the coffee never stops coming, and the servers work hard, do a great job, and take no slack.

I eat there with Bob, Phil, Al, and Mick, and one time I told the server that we don't hang out with guys who have two syllables in their names. I always get the Fat City Sizzle—a pile of hash browns, ham,

green peppers, onions, and cheddar with two eggs on top that's so big it looks like it may have been dished out with a shovel.

The website, when they had one, for years touted their "Best of Portland" designation in 2008 (for a hungover brunch) and the fact that their owner was once in a punk band. The décor of the place is kind of a road theme, with old signs and license plates stuck up on the wall, plus seasonal decorations and Fat City T-shirts. The bathroom is pure American goofy: a super narrow door between the counter (which is always filled with fellas) and the kitchen (don't look!), and once you're in you'll pretty much have your knees under the sink if you need to sit on the toilet.

If the restaurant looks like it's old and in a small town, it is. Multnomah Village dates back to the 1910s, when a community sprang up around an Oregon Electric Railroad station. Today, the Village itself is much more of a natural lady habitat, with shops and bookstores and whatnot; it's often called quaint.

On your way back to your table, you might notice an *Oregonian* article on the wall: the account of the 1987 Fat City Firing, perhaps the ultimate breakfast-with-the-fellas gone wrong. In this very booth, the mayor of Portland, Bud Clark, fired his police chief, Jim Davis.

I mean, where *else* would two fellas who needed to talk some stuff out go for breakfast? It wasn't the Alameda Ass-Kicking, was it? Or the Bread and Ink Bashing? Tin Shed Tanking?

Nope. It was the Fat City Firing. Mmmmmm.

WAIT: Long on weekends, mostly outside. **LARGE GROUPS:** Not at the same table. **COFFEE:** Organic Cafeto Coffee. **OTHER DRINKS:** Tea, milkshakes, hot chocolate, sodas. **FEEL-GOODS:** You don't have to eat the whole thing. **HEALTH OPTIONS:** Ditto. **WIFI:** Check back in 30 years.

FULLER'S COFFEE SHOP

Old School/Mom & Pop

Some call it old-fashioned.

136 NW 9th Ave. (Pearl)

503-222-5608

Weekdays 6 a.m. to 3 p.m., Saturday 7 a.m. to 2 p.m., Sunday 8 a.m. to 2 p.m.

$9–$11 (cash and checks only, but there's an ATM on-site)

A common misconception about Fuller's Coffee Shop is that it's in a place called the Pearl District. The folks at pearldistrict.com say Fuller's is "a reminder of when the Pearl District was into lifting heavy loads off the docks." But the Pearl District never did an ounce of heavy lifting; the name was created as a marketing tool in the 1990s when a warehouse-brewery district was being turned into a land of condos, art galleries, and boutique shopping.

Although Fuller's is geographically in the Pearl, it's really in the 1940s. And although there's nothing wrong with yoga and doggie day care, it sure is nice to have an old-style coffee shop around.

Perhaps I sound snide. I will miss the old warehouse district when it's totally gone, but I don't think of Fuller's as a reminder of times gone by. I think of it as a place where people eat breakfast, read the paper, sit close to one another, and have conversations. Somehow that has become quaint, which seems a shame. I'm just glad I can still do it.

Fuller's has all your old favorites: pigs-in-a-blanket, strawberry waffles (in season), great hash browns, crispy bacon, chicken-fried steak smothered in gravy, huevos rancheros, and that homemade bread sliced by a machine you can spot from the counter. Actually, you can spot the whole kitchen from the counter.

The prices, many of them written by hand on the menu, top out around $9. Newspapers are generally strewn on the counter, and the photos on the walls are of the same place in 1955, back when it was at Union (now MLK) and Pine. It moved to 9th and Davis in 1960.

Michael Stern, of *roadfood.com* and *Eat Your Way Across the USA*, had Fuller's in his first book. Then he came back 10 years later and found that it hadn't changed at all! He even found a man at the counter who ate there 30 years ago and said it hasn't changed since then, either—other than the prices.

It's funny that people expect a place like Fuller's to change. Why should it? It's pretty simple, really: cook basic, good food; charge reasonable prices; treat people nicely; otherwise, stay out of the way and let folks be.

My friend Craig used to work with the homeless population downtown, and he loves Fuller's. I think it's because he sees the Pearl as a land of posers and Fuller's as a place where nobody's full of it and a guy living on the street can be welcomed. I don't see the Pearl so harshly, but to see Fuller's getting some notoriety for being old-timey is somewhat humorous.

After shaking hands with Craig on the sidewalk at 9th and Davis—with another condo tower rising behind the car repair place across the street and a stream of thirty-somethings walking their dogs by us—I can only rub my bacon-filled belly and hope the old way lives long into the future.

WAIT: Medium on weekends. **LARGE GROUPS:** If there's room at the counter; parties may be split. **COFFEE:** Boyd's. **OTHER DRINKS:** Stash teas, espresso. **FEEL-GOODS:** Getting to know folks at the counter. **HEALTH OPTIONS:** Egg whites available. **WIFI:** Hardly.

GATEWAY BREAKFAST HOUSE

Mom & Pop

Family, regulars, piles of food, and a touch of goofy.

11411 NE Halsey St. (NE/Outer)

503-256-6280

gatewaybreakfasthouse.com

Monday through Saturday 6:30 a.m. to 3 p.m., Sunday 7 a.m. to 3 p.m.

$9–$12 (Visa, MasterCard, Discover, no checks)

The defining moment of our trip to the Gateway Breakfast House was when Tom's pancakes arrived. Our table of friends let out a collective *wow* that was part awe, part humor, and part fear. Tom looked like he had walked into a pickup basketball game and found out he was guarding Wilt Chamberlain.

Diana said they were "pancakes you could sleep on," and when Tom cut somebody a portion, he said, "White meat or dark?" The server said that two or three times a year, one person eats the whole pancake order.

So, you get the idea. Very. Large. Portions. Seven of us each ordered something, we could have easily fed a dozen people, and the pre-tip bill was only $53. Gateway does breakfast the way James Michener writes books.

Gateway is cozy, crowded on weekends, and has a vibe that's part homey-family and entirely working-class. In fact, it's the one Portland place I know of that was visited by a sitting US President (during a campaign, of course). Barack Obama rolled in one day in 2012 (with about five minute's notice), had some split pea soup and a grilled cheese sandwich, and off he went. When I heard he had eaten in town, I was not the least bit surprised he chose Gateway.

The nice young women hustling food, the large wreath, and the painted skillets and washboards hanging on the wall all say *down-home*. Despite the long lines, the Gateway doesn't keep a seating list; it just sort of…works out.

You sit down to a cup of coffee in those truck-stop brown mugs and water in plastic cups. You read the menu and notice both hamburger steaks *and* hamburger patties (at which point you know you're not in for an exotic meal). The ribeye-and-three-egg platter is described as *seasoned*.

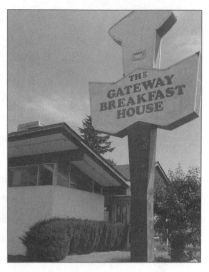

The building used to be a Chinese place and a doughnut shop (presumably not at the same time), so the architecture isn't much of a turn-on. The first description I heard, from my dedicated breakfast spotter, Linda, was that it was a "strange-looking place with a huge line." And there's still a tinge of strangeness to it; hanging from the ceiling are about two dozen large white orbs of different sizes, some of them lights, in a pattern that suggests a bizarro solar system or, as Leslie put it, "the molecular structure of fat." Her thought seemed reasonable when my pork-chop-and-eggs special arrived: two large pork chops, three eggs, a half plate of hash browns, and two pieces of toast.

The size of these portions, I mean…consider the Country Breakfast. You get a pancake or French toast or a waffle or toast or biscuits and gravy. *And* you get two eggs, hash browns, and bacon or links. *And* you get a choice of one pork chop or ham or sausage or pastrami or chicken-fried steak. For, like, eight bucks.

Though we could hardly walk out, we had a good time; good friends, big portions, and cheap prices will do that. The world o' pancakes (my term), for example, was only $3.75 (single big pancake) and the two big pancakes are $4.75. The staff was friendly and attentive, and they volunteered to let us pay separately at the register. (Even our check was about four pages.) We saw kids and old folks and families and loners and regulars and everyone, and now I know why they always have a line outside this place: they're nice folks, and they feed the hell out of you!

WAIT: Up to 30 minutes on weekends. **LARGE GROUPS:** Sure, but send somebody early on weekends. **COFFEE:** Farmer Brothers. **OTHER DRINKS:** The usual. **FEEL-GOODS:** Do the by-the-pound price comparison! **HEALTH OPTIONS:** Can't imagine. **WIFI:** No.

GENIES CAFE

New/Hip/Veggie	
Look at what these kids are up to!	
1101 SE Division St. (SE/Inner)	
503-445-9777	
geniesdivision.com	
Daily 8 a.m. to 3 p.m.	
$9–$14 (all major cards, no checks)	

Years ago, when Genies opened, the *Oregonian* raved about how Genies uses all local ingredients, serves fancy cocktails, has a chef (a chef!), and a menu with smoked tomatoes, cremini and oyster mushrooms, artichoke hearts, and an Italian sausage frittata with nettles and fiddleheads. Genies also got a lot of press for their cocktails, including the Emergen-C Elixir (orange vodka, Emergen-C, muddled lemon, and a splash of cranberry juice) and a Bloody Mary made with jalapeño-infused vodka.

Back then, such things were still rather new and exciting in Portland. Now they are just about taken for granted, and Genies has settled into a role as the anchor of a now-happening intersection at SE 11th and Division. The lines are still long, but long ago the cafe expanded and added an espresso bar where you can wait out the rain and breakfast list.

The space itself is large, open, and airy, but divided in a way that somehow still feels private; diners have the choice of sitting in the sun or in a shady corner. The decor is clean yet colorful, with slight art nouveau touches. The staff and the vast majority of patrons are quite young; I was there once for a crowded Monday lunch and, at 40, was among the four oldest people in the building.

The menu is massive: four omelets and scrambles, six Benedicts, six "specialty egg dishes," three kinds of pancakes (buttermilk, berry of the week, and white-chocolate-chip hazelnut), French toast made with house-baked brioche, more than a dozen sides, and rotating seasonal specials like a morel scramble with asparagus tips, or huckleberry pancakes. Goodness!

Here's a typical weekday visit: I take a table in the corner and immediately have a cup of strong coffee. I admire both the number and youthful energy of the staff and the other customers. After fighting through the menu, I force myself to rule out things like an omelet with locally grown button, cremini, and oyster mushrooms topped with shallots and chives. I settle on the Tasso Benedict featuring Cajun-style ham. For a $2 sweet treat, I toss in a single white-chocolate-chip-and-hazelnut pancake.

I see that on the table we are simultaneously old school (Heinz ketchup), local quirky (Secret Aardvark sauce), and artisan (house-made raspberry jam and orange marmalade). My big plate comes with two large portions of the Benedict and a heaping side of tender, flaky red potatoes seasoned with rosemary, thyme, and parsley. The ham had fat and just a little toughness and spice to it, the closest thing to Southern-style country ham I've found in Portland. Playing that against the thick, creamy hollandaise, clearing the palette with the occasional potato, I occasionally visit the massive pancake sitting nearby. It's just a little crunchy on the underside, giving it a nice snap to go with the chewy hazelnuts, fluffy cake, and fine sweetness of white chocolate.

By the end I realize, again, that I need to do two things immediately: quit taking great breakfast for granted and get back to Genies more often.

WAIT: Long on weekends, with uncovered benches outside but an espresso bar and full bar inside. **LARGE GROUPS:** Absolutely, but expect a longer wait. **COFFEE:** Oblique Coffee Roasters. **OTHER DRINKS:** Tao of Tea, espresso, beer, and a world of cocktails. **FEEL-GOODS:** Most ingredients are local and organic. **HEALTH OPTIONS:** Plenty of vegetarian options, and both tofu (free) and egg whites. **WIFI:** Yes.

GRAVY

New/Hip/Veggie
Once new-cool, now establishment-cool.
3957 N Mississippi Ave. (N/Inner)
503-287-8800
Weekdays 7:30 a.m. to 9 p.m. (breakfast all day), weekends 7:30 a.m. to 3 p.m.
$10–$14 (all major cards, no checks)

I'm not sure when Gravy stopped being a place that was new and exciting just because of what and where it is.

It isn't that the place changed so much. It's still got that sort of relaxed vibe about it, which some folks call funky and others call slow. The menu still offers a wide variety of down-home-style choices, often with locally raised, organic ingredients. It's still so miserably crowded on weekends that waiting outside for up to 45 minutes is an accepted part of the experience.

Gravy set up shop back in March 2004, when North Mississippi Street was just accelerating its fairly quick, and utterly inevitable, transformation from a neighborhood worried about abandoned homes and drug raids to one fighting over high-density housing and saving some diversity. You might say Gravy was to Mississippi sort of what Tin Shed was to Alberta. Suddenly, there was a place on Mississippi with local, organic ingredients, live piano music on weekends, modern art on the walls, a few tattoos on the staff, and food that is a kind of an homage to old-school diners.

In fact, the main gripe about Gravy is that the food is just that: basic breakfast food, not too exciting but in ridiculous portions. (Honestly, if you can knock back a full order of the challah French toast, I'd have you immediately tested for marijuana.) When I do go to Gravy, it's often to get a hash or pork chops and eggs as a kind of long-term investment: eat breakfast and walk out with dinner!

Still, there is a lot to be said for variety, and Gravy certainly delivers: numerous scrambles, hashes, omelets, meat-and-egg combinations, and griddle specialties. And if that isn't enough, there's a large build-your-own omelet section with vegetarian and vegan options. Also, the meals don't come with just potatoes; you can add bacon, sausage, ham, fruit, hash browns, or pancakes.

In a sense it's almost too much, and one can feel a little overwhelmed. Certainly, the weekend crowds are insane, but even during the week you may feel like the tables are pushed awfully close together. It's not a place to visit if you're looking for peace, quiet, and personal space. Or if you're impatient; complaints about slow and spotty service have been around since Gravy opened. My take has always been that the staff is just as overwhelmed as we diners sometimes are.

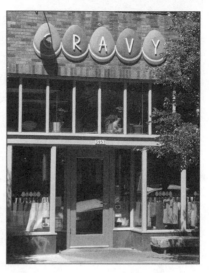

The décor might make you think the place is still evolving, with its bare ceilings, exposed pipes, mismatched light fixtures, a facade in front of the kitchen, and an old sideboard near the kitchen.

But why should Gravy change? Or start any kind of Internet presence at all? Even though you rarely hear it mentioned as one of the best places to eat breakfast in Portland, it's easily one of the most loved. I think it just quit being novel to people, sort of like Mississippi Street itself. Both are now more than discovered, and Gravy—as well as its lines—are now part of the neighborhood's lore.

WAIT: Legendary on weekends. Very small area for waiting inside, with self-serve coffee. **LARGE GROUPS:** Maybe during the week, with notice; parties may be split. **COFFEE:** Cellar Door house blend. **OTHER DRINKS:** Fresh orange juice, vegan Bloody Marys, full bar. **FEEL-GOODS:** Many ingredients are local and organic. **HEALTH OPTIONS:** Egg substitutes or tofu available, and build-your-own omelets offer plenty of options; vegan cheese and sausage. **WIFI:** Yes.

HANDS ON CAFÉ

New/Classy/Mom & Pop	
This is no student *cafeteria!*	
8245 SW Barnes Rd. (SW/Inner)	
503-297-1480	
Sunday 9:30 a.m. to 2 p.m.	
$13–$15 (cash and checks only)	

NOTE: Just as this book went to press, Hands on Café was taken over by Leather Storrs, formerly of Noble Rot. No doubt it will change, Storrs says he loves the place, so I doubt it will be *too* different.

So …

Here's what I once thought I knew about the Hands On Cafe: it's the student cafeteria at the Oregon College of Art & Craft, and it's really nice up there. I admit that it didn't overwhelm me, but at the time I was dating an artist, so I said, "Honey, let's go check out that place at the art school!" I had her at *art*.

We parked in a shaded lot and wandered down a path to a building in which we found an art gallery, a gift shop, and just the kind of "student cafeteria" you'd expect at an art school in the West Hills: a little fireplace, some art on the walls, jazz playing softly, flowers on the tables, and a room full of affluent-looking folks chatting amiably. It wasn't, in other words, the Mustang Cafe, which I used to haunt for chicken strips and pizza back at SMU.

The place must not be all that well-known, because we arrived at 10:15 on a Sunday morning and there was exactly one couple waiting for a table—who promptly informed us about the community table in the back corner near the wide-open kitchen. A moment later we were at that table, where we were instantly presented with a free plate of baked goodies, half a red grapefruit, and candied ginger. The other couple there told us the wait is never more than 15 minutes, and the server said that in the summer, when tables are set up under the trees, rhododendrons, and azaleas, "there's hardly ever a wait."

The staff, made up of students and the owner's family, was friendly, sweet, and efficient. While they got Jenny at *art*, they got me with grilled salmon cakes on corn, basil, and red peppers topped with poached eggs and hollandaise sauce. It was served with tomato, arugula, and avocado relish and roasted potatoes.

There are always four items on the menu—when you see the size of the kitchen, you'll know why—and one item is usually a pancake. When we visited, it was buttermilk 'cakes topped with winter-fruit compote, crème anglaise, sweetened whipped cream, and toasted almonds. It came with scrambled eggs and a choice of sausage or bacon for $10.50. So you'll spend about $14 to eat at Hands On Cafe, but considering what all you get, it's a bargain. I'm told there's always a meat dish as well (often lamb or pork), and the one I had was out of this world: sautéed tenderloin on a roasted red peppers and tomatoes topped with a pork demi-glace sauce and served with two poached eggs, creamy polenta, shaved Parmesan, and greens with pancetta and mushrooms.

I ate every bit of it, then shamelessly swooped in on the rest of Jenny's pancakes. We made a joke about telling the server this should be the Hands Off Cafe, because I would have hurt anybody who tried to get those pancakes from me.

WAIT: Maybe in winter, with a whole gift shop and gallery to explore. **LARGE GROUPS:** Sure. **COFFEE:** San Francisco Bay. **OTHER DRINKS:** Tea, juice, lemonade, iced coffee. **FEEL-GOODS:** None that they tout. (Supporting students, maybe?) **HEALTH OPTIONS:** Ditto. **WIFI:** Yes.

HARLOW

Hip/New/Veggie

Glowing with goodness.

3632 SE Hawthorne Blvd. (SE/Hawthorne)

971-255-0138

harlowpdx.com

Monday through Saturday 8 a.m. to 2 p.m., Sunday till 3 p.m.

$12–$14 (all major cards, no checks)

Every year, my sweetie and I retreat to Breitenbush Hot Springs to unplug from the modern world, get massages, soak naked in hot water, meditate, and eat piles of organic vegetarian food. In fact, we mark our anniversary there every December, and whenever we return we bring back peace, health, rest, and a determination to start cooking "Breitenbush food."

Of course, this resolve, as well as peace and health and the rest of it, slowly fades and is replaced by the usual stressors of daily modern life. It's pretty much official some late evening when I drive into a Burgerville or something, and I can feel my body kind of sigh and give in to reality.

The exact opposite of this happens when I walk into Harlow on SE Hawthorne. My inner Breitenbush Self, the one who doesn't drink coffee or eat meat or sugar, perks up and smiles, for Harlow—the food, the people, the setting—positively glows with goodness. To think that it inhabits a space that formerly hosted the Bridgeport Brew Pub makes it seem even more like a triumph of clean, healthy living. The inside is spacious and modern but with slightly funky touches like mismatched chairs and drinks served in various preserve jars.

In fact, before we even discuss the food, grab a menu (you'll be ordering at the counter) and look at the beverages. I mean, *look at the beverages!* The first thing I always wonder is, what process created this list? There are 18 "beverages," five "health elixirs," 20 smoothies (with 16 possible additions), and 17 fresh juices—with five possible additions there, as well! I confess that I imagine a gaggle of young, skinny, tattooed people sitting in the middle of a mountain of fruits and vegetables, a blender between their knees, smiles on their faces, and splattered plant flesh all over the walls.

Rest assured, the cooking at Harlow is much more serious than I am. And sometimes they don't even cook; some breakfasts are raw, like the granola, with gluten-free oats, toasted pecans, coconut, pepitas, sunflower seeds, and dried cranberries, with fresh fruit and your choice of milk. Pepitas are toasted pumpkin seeds. You can also add goji berries to this. I have no idea what goji berries are.

The whole menu, by the way, is gluten-free, and for more on GF dining, see Martha Wagner's contribution to this book on page 281 (Also check out their sister restaurant, Prasad, on page 200.) Another raw dish is the Lone Star: shredded collards and spinach tossed in jalapeno cashew "cream cheese" with dehydrated tomatoes, chili-lime walnuts, house-made guacamole, chipotle hot sauce, almond "Parmesan," cilantro, scallions and fresh lime. I do wonder if anyone in Texas has eaten something like that.

They do have pancakes (lemon-poppy-quinoa and oatmeal-banana-walnut) as well as some dishes made with eggs (or smokey tempeh) like Huevos Rancheros and a few scrambles. But when I go there, I like to get into the spirit of the place and get the tempeh instead of eggs. And sometimes, when they serve my smoothie—like a Spicy Stella with carrot-ginger juice, coconut milk, strawberries, banana, and cayenne—I just kind of stand there staring at it like a love-struck fool.

Perhaps one day Sweetie and I will go all-in and do the $150 four-day Juice Cleanse. Or we'll go back to Breitenbush. Or we'll just get a place in Southeast so we can walk to Harlow every day and feed our healthy selves.

WAIT: Some, on weekends. **LARGE GROUPS:** Some reservations available for parties of six or more. **COFFEE:** Cold-brewed organic Trailhead Roasters. **OTHER DRINKS:** My goodness! **FEEL-GOODS:** Local ingredients. **HEALTH OPTIONS:** Kitchen is 100 percent gluten-free and vegetarian; many vegan options. **WIFI:** Yes.

HAWTHORNE STREET CAFE

New/Hip/Veggie
We can all agree: it's a happy place!
3354 SE Hawthorne Blvd. (SE/Hawthorne)
503-235-8286
Daily 7:30 a.m. to 2:30 p.m.
$8–$12 (all major cards, local checks)

Among the many random moments that occur in an author's life—like, someone thinking you must be famous or that you must know some other writer—is the moment when someone reads your own words to you and you don't recognize them.

This happened to me toward the end of an enjoyable brunch with my Portland Breakfast Crew at Hawthorne Street Cafe. My buddy Al pulled out his phone and started reading about the place's "hippie-pagan vibe," and I looked around at the white tablecloths, hanging potted plants, pastel walls, and country-scene artwork and said, "Who the hell said it's got a hippie-pagan vibe?" As the words left my mouth and the table fell silent, a terrible realization dawned: I said that. Dammit.

So let's get something straight: There's nothing like a hippie or pagan vibe at the Hawthorne. It's a lovely, friendly place in a great location. I was probably thinking hippie because it's on Hawthorne and pagan because there used to be a Druid society or something upstairs. (Bad thing about being an author: Your "off" days stay in print for a long time.)

In fact, the interior and staff of the Hawthorne Cafe combine for one of the most pleasant experiences on the Portland breakfast scene. It's a big old house with several small rooms and patio seating, plus a lovely glassed-in porch with a charmingly sloping floor. Each room has only a few tables, so the result is that you feel rather private even when many tables are occupied. Our party of seven had a room to ourselves, and another party of six took up the only table in a back room. We never saw any evidence of a wait, and anyway, they take reservations.

The other thing the Crew got on me about was my brief summary in my iPhone app (RIP), from which Al was reading. It included the line, "There are a lot of options, none of them great." The Crew thought I was being harsh, but then I put it back on them: "Okay," I said. "Having now eaten your brunch, would you call the food 'great'?" And they all said, "Well, I'd say it was good…maybe even real good!" But "real good" isn't great.

I'll tell you what it's like: it's like the Grateful Dead of the local breakfast scene. Even folks who like it would never describe it as particularly efficient. I was a huge fan of the Dead, too, and whenever people get going about the band, it's always the same conversation. One group says, "Oh, I *loved* those guys!" Another group says, "God, they were hardly even proficient musicians!" And the majority of people just wonder, "What's the big deal about them, anyway?"

So, back to breakfast. Here's a typical batch of notes from a trip to the Hawthorne: "pear crepe super tasty, warm, and sweet…smoked-sturgeon Benedict interesting but not great…turkey wrap has a little spice to it, nice…sign near bathroom for a class called Wicca 101…staff friendly and cute, not too efficient…homemade marionberry coffee cake like a big ol' slab of goodness…"

See? Even somebody who's eaten breakfast in more than 100 places in town couldn't tell you if the Hawthorne is consistently good. For the record, I never made the argument that the Dead was a particularly good band, either—just that it was, and is, my all-time favorite. And a lot of folks feel that way about the Hawthorne Cafe, which explains why it's been open (and popular) for so long.

Looking for an amazing, life-changing performance every time? Skip the Hawthorne. And the Dead. Looking for a relaxed, friendly scene that does the basics pretty well, has fun, and doesn't take itself seriously? I recommend both.

WAIT: Medium on weekends. **LARGE GROUPS:** Yes. **COFFEE:** Kobos. **OTHER DRINKS:** Espresso, fresh OJ, organic apple juice, Stash teas, plus a house blend of fine quality tea. **FEEL-GOODS:** They love you; just ask them. **HEALTH OPTIONS:** Egg substitute available; many vegetarian and vegan options. **WIFI:** No.

HELSER'S

Hip/New
Open, spacious, simple, casually elegant.
1538 NE Alberta
503-281-1477
helsersonalberta.com
Daily 7 a.m. to 3 p.m.
$12–$17 with $5.95 portions available before 9 a.m. on weekdays
(Visa, MasterCard, no checks)

I went to Helser's once when I had been driving around Oregon for days, hosting a friend from Switzerland, staying in fancy hotels, and eating rich food. I was ready to settle back into my Portland routine, calm down, and eat something simple and tasty. Manuela was still looking for a place to eat breakfast in America where she could get only what she wanted—pancakes and fruit—and not leave a meal's worth of food behind. She said it made her feel guilty.

So we walked into Helser's, and I got the Yukon Gold Hash, lightly seasoned, with cremini mushrooms, scallions, roasted garlic, onions and poached eggs. Manuela asked about the pancakes, was told there were four to an order, asked if she could have only two, the server said absolutely, and she got a side of yogurt and fruit. Ate the whole thing. We spent $10 each. Perfect.

Another time I went to Helser's when I was heading out for a hike, and I wanted something filling but not too much so. I was there before 9 a.m. and got a ham, egg, and cheese crumpet sandwich with fresh fruit. I paid $5.95 for it and didn't eat a thing during the hike. Perfect.

Another time I just wanted to feed my sweet tooth, so I walked over and got the full portion of the brioche French toast, sliced thick and soaked in vanilla-cinnamon batter. I walked out with a little buzz. Perfect.

The feel at Helser's is very simple, in a good way. It's borderline Zen. Wood tables, comfortably spaced from one another. Wood chairs that are wide and comfortable. Tall ceilings. Plenty of windows and light. A few flowers on the table. Some bamboo. Beige walls. Servers wearing black. Simple light fixtures. Soft jazz playing.

The menu hits many classic breakfast themes: German pancakes, Scotch eggs, Russet potato pancakes, biscuits and gravy, smoked salmon hash, three Benedicts, and pigs in a blanket. (Any of these may rotate off the menu, by the way.)

I'm biased, because I used to live about five blocks away and had a crush on pretty much the entire wait staff. Consider that your disclaimer. All I know is that every time I go to Helser's, I'm in the mood for something in particular, and they always have it.

Here's perhaps the ultimate feedback: In 2010 I was approached by a guy named Rick Sebak, who was working on a PBS documentary called *Breakfast Special*. He had found this book online and wanted to know a couple places in Portland he should visit to see what our scene was all about. I said go up to Alberta Street and check out the Tin Shed and Helser's. (I apologize if I added to the wait at either place.)

He fell in love with the Scotch egg and Dutch Baby pancake, blogged about how passionate Portland is about breakfast, and when it came time for his crew to follow me down to tape my breakfast radio show, they decided instead to stay at Helser's.

Can't say I blame 'em. It's perfect.

WAIT: Up to 40 minutes on weekends. **LARGE GROUPS:** Yes, but this will extend your wait. **COFFEE:** Kobos, with French press available. **OTHER DRINKS:** Kobos loose-leaf teas, espresso, mimosas, breakfast cocktails. **FEEL-GOODS:** Local meats; pure maple syrup for $1.25 extra. **HEALTH OPTIONS:** Egg whites and meatless options at no charge; gluten-free bread. **WIFI:** No.

HENRY'S TAVERN

Weekend/Classy
Not your parents' Henry's!
10 NW 12th Ave. (Pearl)
503-227-5320
henrystavern.com/location-portland-OR.php
Sunday 10 a.m. to 2 p.m.
Buffet is $15 for adults, $9 for kids
$3 each for Bloody Mary bar and mimosa bar
(all major cards, no checks)

Sometimes I like to play the Old Portland Grump, even though I've only been here since 1996.

Eh, but since '96 is long enough to remember when Henry's was *Henry's*, and they made *beer*, and the whole place smelled like *beer-making*, and their trucks got in the way on Burnside, and there wasn't any such damn thing as the "Pearl District," just the Brewery Blocks…and then stupid Stroh's or somebody bought Henry's and moved them off to God knows where, and now there's some yuppie grocery store and this stupid giant "American bar and grill" with locations in Seattle and *Texas*, for God's sake, and they charge $13.95 for some damn thing called a Danish Bleu Cheese Burger with Tree Hugger Porter Mustard. And *arugula!*

And, fun as that is (for me, anyway), it pretty much fades when I walk into Henry's for the Sunday breakfast buffet and I'm greeted by nice young people who show me to a big, comfortable booth, then inform me that the buffet is $15 for all you can stand. Actually, they don't say that last part, but Paul vs. Breakfast Buffet is always a daunting game of strategy, endurance, glory, and gluttony. I always lose, of course, and generally regret even playing. But it's fun while it lasts.

The buffet at Henry's is impressive: an omelet station where you build it and they cook it and bring it out, and then a full lineup of honey pancakes, corned beef hash, chilaquiles, huevos rancheros, scrambled eggs, biscuits and gravy, peppered bacon, sausage, potatoes, cinnamon rolls, pastries, and fruit. All the meat is from Zenner's, a local company.

The buffet includes juice, coffee, tea and soft drinks, and there are also build-your-own Bloody Mary and mimosa stations for $3 each.

The space is epic—two stories high, with a big central staircase and upstairs seating and an open kitchen and what looks like seating for 200—but they designed it with plenty of little nooks here and there, so you can feel cozy in a corner booth or private in the balcony or conspicuous with your group of 12 or 20 at a long table by a window. This place is perfect for a big group, and in fact they have spaces like the Upstairs that seat up to 120 people. Now *that* would be a Breakfast Crew!

When I went with my group of eight, we made reservations and had no trouble at all. The place is big enough that I can't imagine it ever having a wait. And speaking of big, I think I made it through three entire plates of food. It's almost embarrassing (well, it should be) to munch a plate of biscuits and sausage gravy and bacon while you're waiting for someone to cook your omelet and honing in on your pastry and pancake selection.

But I have no pride in such matters, and when it comes down to it, I'm not too good at being a grouch, either. I'm all for progress, and if we lose a downtown brewery, we might as well replace it with good food and a place that serves about 100 kinds of beer. All in all, Henry's is where my gluttony overcomes my grumpiness.

WAIT: No, and they take reservations. **LARGE GROUPS:** Oh, yes. **COFFEE:** Boyd's. **OTHER DRINKS:** Juice and tea included with buffet; beer and cocktails available (all day happy hour). **FEEL-GOODS:** Local sausage. **HEALTH OPTIONS:** I *guess* you could stick with the fruit. **WIFI:** Yes.

HOLLYWOOD BURGER BAR

Mom & Pop/Old School
Just grabbin' a bite before I head into town.
4211 NE Sandy Blvd. (NE/Hollywood)
503-288-6422
Breakfast weekdays 7:30 to 11 a.m., Saturday 8 a.m. to 1 p.m.
$10–$14 (all major cards, no checks)

I sat on the little spin-around counter seat at the Hollywood Burger Bar—there's a counter and about three tables, total—and my knees hit the wall underneath. But since I was about to eat breakfast for around eight bucks, I didn't complain. What I thought was, "I bet this place has been here a long time." Folks used to be shorter, you see.

I asked the guy behind the counter, who was already pouring me a big mug of strong coffee, if this was true, and he said, "It's been the Burger Bar since 1954. The place was built in the '20s, been serving food since the '30s. Before that it was a dry cleaner. Before that it was a trolley stop."

A trolley stop! It all came together for me. The small seats. The tiny kitchen. The church bells I heard as I walked in. The pure simplicity of the menu. This used to be the hub of a little community.

Turns out two trolley lines ended here: the one that came out Sandy and the one that came up 39th. Back then, when Sandy was Highway 30 heading out toward the Columbia Gorge, what we now call the Hollywood District (named for the theater, which was built in the '20s) was a little village on the edge of the city, and folks would come in here to get a cup of coffee and a paper before hopping on the trolley to go into Portland.

Look around the neighborhood: Sam's Hollywood Billiards has been there since 1962, Pal's Shanty since 1937, St. Michael's church since 1910, Paulsen's Pharmacy since 1918 (and they have an old-style soda fountain, too!).

That morning at the Burger Bar's counter, there was a woman writing in a journal, a young guy waking up and stretching, an elderly couple being taken out by their daughter, and a man and woman talking religion and politics. Three bus lines run by the door, and I wondered how much had really changed.

But perhaps you're wondering about the food. Well, I can tell you this: for me, it's all about the bacon. I don't put a lot of energy into being a food critic, since I'm no good at it, and besides, I have never noticed any correspondence between my tastes and a place's popularity. But I do like bacon. And I like it just the way it is here: crispy, but not so much so that it snaps in my hand—lean, tasty, with some spice, but not chunks of black pepper. All this, and it should be shamelessly greasy.

Two other things I love about the place are both online. For one thing, back when they had a website (it seems to have vanished again) they were still touting that they won that they won the Hollywood Burger Battle…in 2008! Also, they have an ad on YouTube, linked from their site, which seems to be mainly a collection of people trying to speak with their mouths full of burger. It's truly awesome.

Old-fashioned pride and shameless kitsch, in an old trolley stop surrounded by longtime friends and neighbors. I love the Burger Bar.

WAIT: Maybe on weekends. **LARGE GROUPS:** No chance. **COFFEE:** Royal Cup. **OTHER DRINKS:** Juice, tea, and there're RC Cola signs all over the place; need I say more? **FEEL-GOODS:** You can see how clean the dishes are, because you're basically sitting on the dishwasher. **HEALTH OPTIONS:** Veggie burgers at lunchtime—and is RC healthy? **WIFI:** Hardly.

HOLMAN'S

Hip/Old School
F— it, I'm going to Holman's.
15 SE 28th Ave. (E Burnside)
503-231-1093
https://www.facebook.com/pages/Holmans-Bar-Grill/140011250809
Full breakfast menu: weekdays 8 a.m. to 11 a.m., weekends 8 a.m. to 3 p.m.
Limited breakfast items daily 8 a.m. to 2:30 a.m.
$12–$14 (Visa and MasterCard, no checks)

I wake up late, tired, and sore. In the old days, this would have been a hangover, and I'd have smoked something to start my day. Today it's from a steep 13-mile Saturday hike. My whole body hurts, I'm fuzzy, and the place where I'm dog-sitting is bereft of groceries. Semiconscious, I walk the dog to the park and contemplate my day.

Actually, I can't think beyond the way I feel, and I feel…hurting. And wait, I think that's hunger. Right, I slept 10 hours—probably hungry. Need coffee. Okay, breakfast.

Within a few minutes' walk, I can get to Kerns Kitchen, Pambiche, Screen Door, Navarre, East Burn…but shit, there'll be *people* there. Like, people who are awake and functional. Besides, I'm *hungry*. I don't want to shower or talk to people. I want a booth with springs sticking in my ass, a waiter who does nothing but fill my cup, and a gut bomb.

F--- it, I'm going to Holman's.

It isn't really very good, or good for you, or maybe even clean, I don't know. But stumbling down 28th past all the new-style places, I realize I'm just not up for it today. No local ingredients, no sustainable, no organic roasts. I know exactly what I want, and all I want: Today is the day I tackle the chicken-fried steak.

It's like my Great White Whale, the massive terror I've only heard of and not actually seen. You can't just, you know, go in and order it. It has to be a particular kind of day, a day when you don't care about your health, have absolutely no plans for the afternoon, and don't care who sees you doing what. And this is that day. Bring it on, Holman's.

I walk in and am hit with a rush of memories from my alcoholic days: the old neon sign, one tiny window in a brick wall, stickers everywhere on the wall, claustrophobic bathrooms…and ah, yes, my springy booth. Sure, I'll sit there.

Coffee—yes, please. Menu…uh, yeah, where is it, *right*. Chicken-fried steak. Two eggs over easy. That'll be all you hear from me today.

I glance around. About 11 a.m. on a Sunday, and folks are working the Bloody Mary bar pretty hard. Two young guys are staring at an NFL game on a big-screen TV, but not like a new HD plasma whatever. This is one of those with the three different colored lights, remember those? I wonder if those dudes couldn't have found a more festive place to watch the game.

I drift off, staring out the window at the young moms with strollers, the biker kids, the joggers. They all seem so…active. What's the rush, man?

The waitress reappears with a plate, and *are you kidding me?* People eat that thing??? It looks like an alien has landed on the plate she's carrying, and then puked runny eggs. It's like they coated a dog-chewed Frisbee with gravy. They should *require* you to be stoned before you tackle that damn thing.

She lays it in front of me, and all I can do is stare like a fool. It's awesome. I feel the need to document it, so I lay my fork on it—and it doesn't even stretch across it the short way! I am in serious trouble. This cannot end well.

And then I conjure the speech from *Lord of the Rings*, right before they wade into the sea of orcs: "Breakfast Guy, there may come a day when you cower at the sight of your meal, when you ask for a to-go box before you even start, when you ask if somebody wants to go… splitsies. *But this is not that day!*"

I take a bite. It is perfect. And so it begins.

WAIT: Sometimes, on weekends. **LARGE GROUPS:** With notice. **COFFEE:** Hot. **OTHER DRINKS:** Bloody Mary bar on Sundays. And it's a bar. **FEEL-GOODS:** Stop it. **HEALTH OPTIONS:** No, really, stop. **WIFI:** Yes.

INDUSTRIAL CAFE AND SALOON

Weekend/Old School
A quiet place with loud fans.
2572 NW Vaughn St. (NW)
503-227-7002
Breakfast served weekdays 8 to 11 a.m., weekends 8 a.m. to 3 p.m.
$12–$14 (Visa, MasterCard, American Express, no checks)

There seems to be a small number of people who absolutely adore this place, and a whole mess of folks who are starting to find out about it.

I used to be among the latter; I lived in Northwest Portland for years, and I only ate at Industrial when a friend thoroughly berated me for not having it in this book. Truth is, I didn't know it was there for a while, and then the name turned me off. Then I kept reading newspaper and magazine stories saying it had some of the best biscuits and gravy in town, and if you want my attention, saying "gravy" is generally a good start.

It sure doesn't look industrial from the outside, but it's right on the edge of the part of town called the Northwest Industrial District. Across the street you'll find Schmeer Sheet Metal Works and Reed Electric. Not far away are sprawling rail yards. And the outside of the cafe fits the name a little, with its tin walls and metal outdoor tables.

But the real "industrial" theme is on the inside. There's a big tangle of pipes and valves, an eagle painted on a saw, various pieces of metal all over the place, and even some of those metal hand puzzles sitting on the counter. The real fun is in the men's room, where the pipes for the urinal are exposed, so when you flush you can see the pressure drop and then build back up. They even added a red light and green light to show when water is flowing or not.

The food, even according to its biggest fans, is straight-ahead American diner chow—and lots of it. The best-known breakfast dishes seem to be the biscuits and gravy—the super firm biscuits are called "gears" and shaped like that—and the chipped beef on sourdough toast, which a glowing *Oregonian* review called "pristine, tender slices of organic beef doused in rich cream sauce, with paprika giving a dash of spice." Since the biscuits also come slathered in cream gravy, I think we can detect a pattern.

The rest of the menu is as down-home as their two signature dishes: steak and eggs; spicy Italian sausage scramble; hash, ham and cheese omelet; veggie omelet; breakfast burrito, etc. And other than the steak and eggs ($15), everything is $9.50 or less. On the sweets menu, there are a couple of things that seem a little out of the ordinary: the Industrial Toast is brioche French toast with candied walnuts and orange honey butter, and the Gingerbread Pancakes are topped with house-made lemon curd.

The Industrial fits a very welcome niche in the Northwest Portland food scene. It's got outdoor seating like Meriwether's, without the prices—and down-home food like the Stepping Stone, with less of a line. And if the food happens to turn you on, you can be on the short list of this place's ardent fans.

WAIT: A little on weekends. **LARGE GROUPS:** Decent options. **COFFEE:** Kobos. **OTHER DRINKS:** Juice, beer, wine, and cocktails. **FEEL-GOODS:** None they tout. **HEALTH OPTIONS:** A few things for vegetarians. **WIFI:** No.

IRVING STREET KITCHEN

Classy/Weekend	
Aren't we all stylish and fancy?	
701 NW 13th Ave. (Pearl)	
503-343-9440	
irvingstreetkitchen.com	
Weekends 10 a.m. to 2:30 p.m.	
$16–$21 (Visa, MasterCard, American Express, no checks)	

For some time now, I have been saying that the Big Lesson I've gotten from writing this book has been that there are good brunches all over Portland with little or no line. I think the crowds just naturally congregate at the Same Old Places—and I don't mean to trash those places. I just mean that some places always have really long lines. And yes, I also feel that some of them aren't worth it.

As of this edition, when people ask for a good place with no lines, and especially if they want something in the middle of town, I'll recommend Irving Street Kitchen.

It's a cool-looking place—spacious, with lots of wood, a big bar, open kitchen, and gas fireplace—and I guess the decor suits their descriptive phrase, "a soulful New American restaurant anchored in slow cooking and deep flavors." I don't really know what that means, but it sounds serious, doesn't it?

Irving Street Kitchen has a classy and casual feel, one that seems like it could do soft-lit romance at night, especially in curtained booths. It also works for a spacious, well-lit hangout brunch. In summer the long patio overlooking pedestrian-friendly 13th Avenue is pretty sweet, too. Sit up there with your cocktail, and you'll feel pretty darn special.

The menu has six starters; we got the Sugar and Spice Donuts for $7. (Hold that thought.) Others included Pain au Chocolat ($6), Pumpkin Chocolate Chunk Bread ($6), and a parfait of Greek yogurt, grapefruit marmalade, and house-made granola ($6).

I looked at those prices and remembered, suddenly, where we were: in a Pearl District restaurant, specifically one in which somebody spent a crapload of money making it nice. So they make it up by, for example, getting $7 for two donuts. Good donuts, sure, but at $3.50

a pop, they'd better be. In a related note, coffee or espresso is $3.50, lattes $5, tea $5, and cocktails $9-12. So it ain't cheap.

There are seven egg and griddle dishes, eight lunches, seven sides, and three or four desserts. And since I mentioned the cocktails, they also have a nice selection of booze-free cocktails (for the "Un-Spirited") like a Bed Head (ginger beer, honey, fresh lime juice, and a dash of bitters for $5).

As far as I know, everybody on the Crew dug everything they had. I got the Mary's Organic Fried Chicken and Pecan Waffles with a fried egg and buttermilk syrup for $15, and it was awesome. Somebody else got the smoked turkey stuffing hash with paprika hollandaise and cranberry compote ($12), and somebody else got a chocolate-banana bread pudding French toast with vanilla ice cream and bourbon sauce ($13). For what it's worth, I didn't get to try either, nor did I hear much from those people until they were done.

I thought this was a great brunch, and they handled our party of 10 with ease. They do strongly recommend reservations for groups of eight or more, and there are no substitutions on the brunch menu. We were there from 10 to 11:30 on a Sunday and the place never filled up. I had been worried about this after local reviewer Karen Brooks called it "one of the best brunches in the city" in *Portland Monthly* magazine.

As for the prices, I don't think they are unreasonable, given the quality and location. I just feel like I need to give folks a heads-up. The bottom line for me was half a donut, a few bites of muffin, the chicken and waffles, and espresso; with tip, that was $25.

So if you're downtown, don't mind spending a few extra bucks, and want a good brunch with no line, check out Irving Street Kitchen.

WAIT: None I know of, but they take reservations. **LARGE GROUPS:** Yes; reservations recommended. **COFFEE:** Stumptown. **OTHER DRINKS:** Steven Smith teas, juices, specialty sodas, regular and "un-spirited" cocktails. **FEEL-GOODS:** None they brag about. **HEALTH OPTIONS:** Vegetarians have some options, vegans not so much; kitchen can prepare veggie variations with notice. **WIFI:** Yes.

ISABEL

New
Sleek, healthy, and a little out of place?
330 NW 10th Ave. (Pearl)
503-222-4333
isabelscantina.com
Breakfast (and lunch) daily 8 a.m. to 3 p.m.
$14–$17 (all major cards, no checks)

The first person who told me about Isabel was my friend Wendy. She's very attractive, extremely fit and healthy, ambitious, upbeat, and all-around striking. The fact that Wendy told me about Isabel should tell you something about the place.

Isabel is a chain, with locations in Ashland and southern California as well as a farm in Sandy. And according to their website, "Chef and cookbook author Isabel Cruz [has a] trademark blend of Puerto Rican, Cuban, Mexican, Japanese, and Thai cooking." So that's ambitious.

The first time I walked into the place, I thought maybe they were still working on it. There's a lot of exposed concrete, virtually no art, big vents visible along the ceiling, and huge metal wheels along the walls. But those turned out to be for opening the massive, floor-to-ceiling windows, which makes it nice in the summer.

What's the food like? Well, consider the King Cakes, a stack of three pancakes with peanut butter, bananas, chocolate chips, raspberry puree, and powdered sugar. I like to get that, so I can fell like I'm getting some health (banana) and protein (peanut butter) with what I really want (pancakes). If I really want to get healthy, though, there are several "power" items, like the Original Power Breakfast, with scrambled egg whites, brown rice, steamed greens, and salsa cruda, or a Power Burrito: egg whites scrambled with grilled chicken, cheese, green onion, and tomatoes, wrapped in flour tortillas and served with black beans and salsa cruda.

Since I have become accustomed to heavier, probably less healthy breakfasts, I was initially underwhelmed, though the food was clearly cooked right and with fresh ingredients. I thought the artichoke scramble was too long on artichokes and otherwise short on seasoning, but the rosemary potatoes were good: mashed up, then grilled so there were little crispy bits throughout. But I am not used to fresh, healthy cooking.

Whatever you want, the 17 breakfast items and several sides will probably include it. There's coconut French toast with raspberry puree, blackberry pancakes with or without bananas, a hash, burrito, quesadilla, jalapeno scramble, oatmeal, fruit cup, etc.

There's another advantage, if you will, to Isabel: hardly anybody seems to go there. I've been twice and ridden the streetcar past it many times, and I've never seen it full.

When I first started writing this book, back in 2006, I said that Isabel and the Pearl had two things in common: they were both good ideas, and neither had caught on yet. Now I think both have changed; they both have a good-looking, young, healthy vibe about them, and they're both catching on pretty well.

WAIT: Expect a wait on weekends. LARGE GROUPS: With some notice; reservations available for parties of six or more. COFFEE: Stumptown. OTHER DRINKS: Juices, espresso, breakfast cocktails, iced tea, Mexican mocha and hot chocolate, Thai coffee. FEEL-GOODS: Organic ingredients (many from their own farm). HEALTH OPTIONS: Tofu and egg whites available. WIFI: Yes.

J&M CAFE

New/Classy/Veggie

A place where you can take your parents—and pay!

537 SE Ash St. (SE/Inner)

503-230-0463

jandmcafepdx.com

Weekdays 7:30 a.m. to 2 p.m. (full breakfast until 11:30, plus some limited breakfast offerings until close), weekends 8 a.m. to 2 p.m. (breakfast all day)

$8–$12 (all major cards, checks)

When my parents travel, they pick their restaurants from *Gourmet* and the *New York Times*. But my independent–publisher income is a bit more Beaterville than Morton's. Hence, I keep the List of Places I Want My Parents to Take Me to when They Visit.

There are two other lists. One is the Places My Parents Wouldn't Go to in a Million Years: Fuller's Coffee Shop, the Stepping Stone, and so on. And then there's the list J&M Café is on: Places I Would Take My Parents To. To get on this list, a restaurant has to be clean, comfortable, serve good and interesting food, not cost too much, exhibit some class, and yet include a touch of what makes Portland the great, goofy city it is.

Here's the case for the J&M: It's in an industrial neighborhood, within eyeshot of empty buildings, a rehab center, and busy, grimy Grand Avenue. But as soon as you walk in, you see high ceilings, wood floors, big windows, brick walls…and a restaurant design that could easily serve as a backdrop to the most stylish of foods. Nonthreatening modern art (just my parents' style) hangs on the wall, there's plenty of space between tables, and the clientele includes lots of families and young people.

And then there are the small-town Portland touches: self-serve coffee (Stumptown, of course) from an oddball collection of mugs hanging on a metal vine, water served in mason jars, an old-world wood-fronted refrigerator, the restroom keys on a burger and a lizard, butcher paper and crayons on the tables, a logo with a crowned flying pig.

J&M's food is a step above your basic breakfast place. One time my special was a scramble with Black Forest ham, shallots, zucchini, cherry tomatoes, fontina, and spinach pesto. The texture was perfect, and the pesto had just the right amount of zing. Another special had roasted eggplant, pine nuts, green onions, fontina, and fresh artichoke salsa. A regular item is a tofu, garlic, spinach, and feta scramble.

Even J&M's take on the basics has a classy twist. The J&M Plate has natural local bacon with basted eggs, fontina, cheddar, and Parmesan on a toasted English muffin. The Scrapple and Eggs is crispy grilled pork-cornmeal sausage glazed with maple syrup, served with two eggs, Como toast, and home fries. The Belgian Cornmeal Waffle is delightfully light and can come with pecans and ginger butter.

The wait staff shows up, treats you well, takes your order, comes back with food, and otherwise pretty much leaves you alone. I've seen some online reviews that consider such service unfriendly, but I think of it as, "You have your food, coffee, and water are self-serve, and if you need anything, we're right here."

Somehow, the basted egg captured the whole thing for me. The J&M could have just poached it or fried it, but instead they did something that was just a little different. Basting, by the way, means cooking an egg without flipping it; you cook the top by drizzling either water or fat on top, or just covering the pan until the top cooks just a little. Sipping my excellent local coffee and looking around at all my nice fellow citizens enjoying a relaxed, tasty meal in pleasant surroundings, I kind of felt proud of Portland.

WAIT: Not usually, but sometimes on weekends; there are a few padded benches to wait on inside, no shelter outside. **LARGE GROUPS:** Yes, up to 12. **COFFEE:** Extracto. **OTHER DRINKS:** Foxfire teas, the usual. **FEEL-GOODS:** Local, natural meats; wild-caught Pacific salmon; homemade granola. **HEALTH OPTIONS:** Some veggie options, and tofu can be substituted for eggs. **WIFI:** Yes.

JAM ON HAWTHORNE

New/Hip/Veggie
Clean, simple, basic, and sweet.
2239 SE Hawthorne Blvd. (SE/Hawthorne)
503-234-4790
jamonhawthorne.com
Daily 7:30 a.m. to 3 p.m.
$9–$13 (all major cards, no checks)

For the first edition of this book, I wrote a rather tortured comparison of Jam to Billy Joel, concluding that their lemon ricotta pancakes are, metaphorically, their "Piano Man." I'll spare you the rest. Truth is, I couldn't think of anything to say other than, "They're nice, and I love their pancakes."

The corner of Southeast Hawthorne and 23rd Avenue has been a breakfast destination for years; Cafe Lena was the previous inhabitant, and Jam fits in the same groove. It's long been a place that locals walk to, even if folks from other parts of town might not know exactly where it is. To them it may be "the little place across from Grand Central Bakery and that produce place (Kruger's Farm Market)." Jam's colors are bright, the staff is young and cheerful, and it's a relaxed, cozy place, with just six booths and eight tables.

Somewhere along the way, tough, word got out, and Jam became immensely popular. Then it expanded, taking over a larger restaurant space next door...and yet the weekend lines are long. Apparently, some people are waiting to sit in the older, smaller section, adding a whole new layer of mystery to the question, "Why do people wait so long for brunch in this town?" At least they converted some of the old space into an indoor waiting area, with couches and a coffee cart.

Jam leads with its signature namesake spreads, which are on the table before you order. Even disparaging reviews of the place say things like, "Don't go unless you just really like homemade jams." The *Portland Mercury* called them "spectacular," and the seasonal flavors I've seen include blueberry, strawberry-mango, and pear chai.

The other sweet signature dish is the lemon ricotta pancake, which the *Oregonian* showcased in a pancake special feature: "With a drizzle of warm blueberry sauce, these 'cakes sound more like a haute dessert than a flapjack breakfast. But the citrus hit is subtle, the mild ricotta lends body to the batter and the house-made topping is vibrant with fruit. A sweet way to start your day."

The rest of Jam's food seems to have gotten better over the years, or maybe my memory was fogged by the pancakes, which truly are among my favorites in town. I'll also add that the place is loud on weekends… but I'm getting to be a crank. The coffee is good, the service nice, the atmosphere relaxed, and the prices downright reasonable, so the Crew and I weren't upset. We walked away saying things like, "Well, it wasn't the greatest breakfast ever, but I liked it." Besides, I'm a sucker for sweets, although I wasn't quite up to the Grand Marnier French Toast or the wheat-free, vegan Oatmeal Chai Blueberry Pancake.

Jam also gets a stamp of approval from the veggie crowd. An Internet blog called Stumptown Vegans said Jam "know(s) what vegan is" and gave them credit for stocking Odwalla juices (plus a full bar with breakfast cocktails), local produce from Kruger's Farm Market and Uncle Paul's, and soy margarine (I wasn't aware it existed). Indeed, the veggie options do seem more interesting than most, including the much-appreciated build-your-own option. I also give credit for hash browns that are crispier and less greasy than many and how the Stumptown coffee is brewed: strong and smooth.

Jam has a lot of options and doesn't try to do too much. Being friendly and healthy, getting produce from the stand across the street, and having two or three items that really stand out are enough to make it a nice little big place for breakfast.

WAIT: Around 30 min. on weekends. **LARGE GROUPS:** Not a problem if it's not busy. **COFFEE:** Portland Roasting. **OTHER DRINKS:** Tazo and Stash teas, Odwalla juices, breakfast cocktails. **FEEL-GOODS:** Produce from Kruger's across the street. **HEALTH OPTIONS:** Good variety for vegans and vegetarians. **WIFI:** Yes.

JAMES JOHN CAFE

Weekend/Hip
More than a "coffee shop with breakfast."
8527 N Lombard St. (N/Outer)
503-285-4930
jamesjohncafe.com
Tuesday through Sunday 9 a.m. to 2 p.m.
$11–14 (Mastercard, Visa, personal checks)

Normally, when people tell me about a breakfast they loved at a coffee shop, I kind of cringe. This is for two reasons: one, they're usually telling me about a place they absolutely love, that they also want me to love, and I'm thinking that if I don't happen to love it, and don't put it in the book, then I'm an asshole. I got a lot of this for the Little Red Bike Café (RIP).

The second reason I cringe, which also explains the first, is that there are so many coffee shops in this town, many of which have an egg sandwich or two, that if I tried to visit all of them to check out their "breakfast" options, I'd weight 400 pounds, never finish the book, and die of a caffeine-induced heart attack.

So when people started telling me about brunch at the James John Café in St. Johns, I generally tried to change the subject, or wave them off with a "yeah, I'll go check it out." I thought it was a coffee shop, because that's what I saw when I drove by. Then I checked their menu, which I had to admit was more than pastries and egg sandwiches. "Fine," I thought, "let's go check it out."

When I walked in, I thought, "Hell, it's just a coffee shop; I'm about to disappoint some people." Then a few things happened very quickly: the floor creaked under my feet, I saw a stuffed animal head on the wall, I noticed an old-school chandelier hanging from the vaulted ceiling, I saw couches in a sunny window, and a cute barista caught my eye. I softly swore to myself, because it looked like I was about to be one of those people who just "happens to love" this coffee shop.

So I hoped they would at least have a real breakfast, and sure enough, there was a fairly thorough menu on a chalkboard. As I looked at it, the cutie behind the counter told me, without any context, that the food was "real sexy." That's when the hook went right down my throat.

A few friends met me, we all placed our orders at the counter, and we settled at a table in the back, surrounded by pictures of old Portland. I was watching the UP students, families, and random hipsters hanging out, thinking that I liked this place more and more. The water was served in old bourbon and Jack Daniel's bottles, the plates and cups were mismatched, we shared a  yummy cinnamon-apple muffin, and Cutie made me a fine cappuccino.

The food, obviously coming out of a very small kitchen, surprised me with how good it was (I had some lingering "just a coffee shop" reservations). Somebody had an eggs Benedict with just the right amount of sauce (a vanishing art in Portland) and English muffins that stayed crispy. I got pork chops that were tender and peppery. Somebody else had a bacon and egg salad, the bacon lean and chewy. The menu, by the way, changes daily and might not even be what they say it is online.

So, dang it, now I have to re-consider my whole "just a coffee shop" position. I really don't want to wander off into that whole realm of Portland, but I might have to keep the James John in mind—and, obviously, in the book. It still might not be a "big time" Portland breakfast place like its neighbor the John Street Cafe, but it is my kind of place. And saying that doesn't even make me cringe.

WAIT: Some, on weekends **LARGE GROUPS:** Yes, with notice. **COFFEE:** Water Avenue. **OTHER DRINKS:** Tea, juice, full bar. **FEEL-GOODS:** "We use as many natural, local, seasonal ingredients as possible." **HEALTH OPTIONS:** All sandwiches served with salad. **WIFI:** Yes.

JAMISON

Classy/Weekend

What a setting! Oh, the food is good, too.

900 NW 11th Ave. (Pearl)

503-972-3330

jamisonpdx.com

Weekends 10 a.m. to 2 p.m.

$12–$14 (Visa, MasterCard, American Express, no checks)

I see a restaurant experience as a formula, more or less. You take the location and atmosphere, add the people, and then the service and the food. Obviously, those aren't ranked in importance…or maybe they are? You'd put up with a lot, including high prices, for killer food, right? And many folks would tolerate mediocre food if the rest of it is right, or if they just have strong feelings for a place (see Shed, Tin.).

Jamison opened in 2012, taking a slot at the high end of Pearl brunch places. We already had the low end covered with Fuller's and Byways, plus the medium range with Daily Cafe. Now the high-end Portland brunch is coming through, as would be expected in the Pearl. We've got Irving Street Kitchen and now Jamison, the reincarnation of Fenouil in the Pearl—of which much fun was made in the first two editions of this book.

Jamison, which is much less pretentious than Fenouil was, delivers on a very basic premise: Let's sit outside on a beautiful, quiet patio and have a pleasant brunch, with cocktails and good food and a nice view of kids playing in the park. It's a fantastic combination, of course, and even when the weather turns and we have to go eat inside, the interior of Jamison is fantastic and fancy, as well. In fact, one might

call it epic, with sky-high ceilings, windows and light everywhere, and every part of it dripping with luxury.

I went with the Country Ham Benedict, because I have been on a quest to find real country ham in this town. They say they serve Johnson County Country Ham, a North Carolina outfit that knows what they're doing. Finding it in a place as glamorous as Jamison (much less with preserved-lemon hollandaise) was something of a culture shock, but I got over it in one bite.

But go back to the formula I mentioned above. Jamison has a built-in advantage in this regard: It is a beautiful place to eat, especially on that patio in nice weather. It's so nice it makes me think I should act better than normal, and bring my parents here next time they visit. The staff was awesome, even when our table hit our poor waiter with, yes, I am ashamed, eight bills for nine people. (I was *not* in charge of that!)

On opening, their reviews were so-so, but everyone agreed they needed time to work it out. Since then, reviewers have settled into two camps: love it and hate it—a distinction which I think is fueled by the ambience and ambition of the place. In other words, when you go to, say, a brew pub and your meal is okay, you don't go online and trash the place. You get an okay meal in a million-dollar room, and somehow you feel the need to vent.

I went about a month into their brunch service, and I found the food quite good, not awesome. But I don't care. My Benedict set me back $13, and I dropped another $4 on a cappuccino—not outrageous prices at all. The main plates average around $12 to $13, so for all you get in atmosphere and comfort—plus no wait on a sunny Sunday morning at 10:30—it's also pretty easy on the wallet and the schedule.

WAIT: Possibly on Sunday in good weather. **LARGE GROUPS:** Yes; make reservations. **COFFEE:** Cafffe Vita. **OTHER DRINKS:** Full bar, brunch cocktails espresso. **FEEL-GOODS:** None they tout. **HEALTH OPTIONS:** Decent options for vegetarians. **WIFI:** Yes.

JOHN STREET CAFÉ

Mom & Pop/Old School

Come out and eat in our backyard!

8338 N Lombard St. (N/Outer)

503-247-1066

Breakfast Wednesday through Friday 7 to 11 a.m.,

Saturday 7:30 a.m. to noon, Sunday 7:30 a.m. to 2:30 p.m.

$8–$12 (Visa, MasterCard, checks)

It can be (probably should be), pretty simple to run a successful restaurant. You get a nice space, pick a reasonable number of menu items you're good at cooking, act nice to people, and open up the doors. Folks can way overthink the thing, in concept and execution—but not the folks at John Street Café. There's hardly a sign outside, not much on the walls inside, a one-page menu with less than 10 items on it, no Internet presence whatsoever…and a huge crowd of loyal customers.

Oh, and among my two or three favorite pancakes in town. More on that in a bit.

It's the old, very popular Tabor Hill Cafe from Hawthorne, reborn in downtown St. Johns. The owners sold the old place and moved north in 1997, and it would seem the whole crowd just followed them up there. One thing they gained in the move: behind that bland-looking front is one of the warmest, most colorful outdoor seating areas in town.

Walking through the front room to the patio is like emerging into somebody's backyard. Before I knew it, the owner was pouring coffee while greeting two regulars among us by name, and we were looking at a simple menu with a major focus on omelets, none of them priced north of $11. The staff also calls hazelnuts *filberts*, like good Oregonians, and will give your kids Gumby dolls to play with.

Before we get to the food, here's a picture of the patio: A seating area with 10 or so picnic tables ringed by beds of fuchsia, bleeding heart, columbine, geranium, creeping phlox, Japanese maple, and bamboo. Dogs, welcome on the patio, sit curled up beside picnic tables filled with families. An enormous fig tree looms overhead, providing shade—and fruit in September.

The homey, simple feeling kept right on coming with the food. All the mains come with oven-roasted red potatoes and wheat toast. The day's special was huckleberry-blueberry coffeecake, which had just the right balance of fluffy, moist, and crunchy. The bacon was sweet without being too maple-y, cooked perfectly, and met the rousing approval of my 14-year-old "little brother" (through Big Brothers Big Sisters). The corned beef in a special hash had a little more zing to it than usual, and the leftovers were a meal in themselves. A spinach-and-bacon omelet had a hearty portion of greens as well as avocado, sour cream, and salsa. My friend Toni summarized her generous Shrimp Scramble: "Usually these things are egg-egg-egg-shrimp-egg-egg, but this one is more like egg-and-shrimp, egg-and-shrimp, egg-and-shrimp."

And then there's the pancake, a perfect example of what the café is up to: One black-currant-and-filbert pancake is $6.50, but it was the size of a dinner plate, thick, and perfectly cooked, with an almost-burned crust outside giving way to a light, fluffy inside made a little chunky by the nuts and sweet-chewy by the fruit. It was served with warm maple syrup, and we fought over it. If I had to choose between these and the sourdough flapjacks at the Original Pancake House (see page 178), I would just go up Lombard a ways and jump off the St. Johns Bridge.

John Street's signature dish—oatmeal—is another example of its homey friendliness. It comes with milk and brown sugar, plus your choice of two from this list: dried raisins, currants, apricots, or cranberries, and chopped filberts or walnuts. If eating a nice bowl of cereal at a picnic table in a sunny garden sounds like, well, your bowl of oatmeal, then head to John Street Cafe and see how good simple can be.

WAIT: Up to 20 min. on weekends after about 9:30, no cover outside. **LARGE GROUPS:** Yes, with notice. **COFFEE:** Kobos. **OTHER DRINKS:** Espresso, fresh orange juice, Kobos tea, hot chocolate, milk, beer, mimosas. **FEEL-GOODS:** None they brag about. **HEALTH OPTIONS:** Omelets can be made with egg whites only for $1; gluten-free bread and oatmeal. **WIFI:** No.

JOHN'S CAFE

Old School/Mom & Pop

A quiet corner, breakfast, and a friend.

301 NW Broadway St. (Pearl)

503-227-4611

Weekdays 6 a.m. to 2 p.m., Saturday 7 a.m. to noon

$10–$12 (cash only)

Sometimes I get kind of tired of Portland. I don't mean Portland the city, of course. It's my home, and I'm married to it. I mean "Portland," the hip town that magazines call "livable" and bike riders dream of and conservatives call a People's Republic. It's sustainable and local, and it uses words like *foodshed*. I want to punch people who say *foodshed*.

Sometimes I leave "Portland" and go down where my friend Wharf Rat John used to live.

Wharf Rat—we called him that because he was a clean and sober Deadhead, a member of the sober tribe within that traveling, partying supertribe, named for a song about a down-and-out guy who got a bad break and drinks down on the docks now. John walked that road for years—used to drink at a picnic table in Forest Park all day—then he sobered up. At first, when they put him in a treatment center and gave him his own bed, he couldn't sleep on it because it was too soft. He was used to hard, flat surfaces, the kind he'd slept on for most of 30 years.

One time we were walking by a church downtown, and he said that's where he met his wife. "I didn't know you ever went to church," I said. "No," he said. "I met her on the porch; they used to let us sleep out there."

Wharf Rat died a few years back, eight years sober, in the MacDonald Center, a few blocks away from John's. And I tell you this story not because everybody at John's Cafe is down and out, but because the streets of our city are absolutely packed with amazing stories, and not just the ones they write about in *Portland Monthly* or on foodie blogs.

Another friend of mine used to run the hotel upstairs, for Central City Concern. I know another guy who lives over on Burnside—indoors now—and is starting a yoga class for people in recovery. Down at Sisters of the Road, folks can get lunch for about two dollars or a volunteer shift. And at John's you can get breakfast for hardly any more than that. You can sit in the corner by yourself or grab some counter space and discuss the latest outrage on talk radio.

I used to sit with Wharf Rat in that little corner booth for two, between the register and the window, and we'd talk about getting sober and how crazy folks can be, and how good the Dead could be on the right night, and how much fun it all was. And is. Now he's gone, and I sit there with other friends and talk about the same stuff. We keep on truckin', and John's keeps serving breakfast.

And someday John's will close, too. The owners will retire, and probably nobody will want to keep it going. I've seen a lot of that around town: Tosis, Niki's, Johnny B's, Leo's Non-Smoking Coffee Shop, and so on. Or the building will get torn down and probably the lot will get turned into condos or something, and the whole neighborhood will get "fixed up." And I'll think about Wharf Rat and all the other folks down here and wonder where they've moved off to.

And then I suppose I'll find a new place to get out of "Portland" for a while for some simple breakfast and honest conversation. For now, though, I do love the way the world looks from a table at John's.

WAIT: Possibly on weekends. **LARGE GROUPS:** Up to six. **COFFEE:** Boyd's. **OTHER DRINKS:** Juices, teas, sodas, hot chocolate. **FEEL-GOODS:** Other people. **HEALTH OPTIONS:** Someplace else. **WIFI:** Turn that damn thing off.

JUNIOR'S CAFE

Hip/Veggie
Kitschy, cozy, comfy, cramped, and cool.
1742 SE 12th Ave. (SE/Hawthorne)
503-467-4971
Weekdays 8 a.m. to 2:30 p.m., weekends 8 a.m. to 3 p.m.
$7–$13 (Visa, MasterCard, Discover, no checks)

To look at Audra Carmine, you might not think she owns a restaurant. She seems so nice and sweet and young, not haggard and nutty like many restaurant folks are. Yet since 2005 she has owned Junior's Cafe on Southeast 12th Avenue, for years one of Portland's favorite little breakfast joints.

Although there have been some subtle changes to the menu and crowd, Junior's is still a friendly, popular place that will fill you up, not empty your wallet, and not rush you along at all.

Carmine worked for years at Dot's, the Clinton Street institution that spawned Junior's more than a decade ago. Still, she admits she had a lot to learn.

For example, there was the dedication of some customers. "People would call me over and be like, 'Why did you change the way you chop the zucchini?'" she says. "People have a huge emotional attachment to this restaurant."

And what were these radical changes? She tweaked some of the classic dishes like the Country Scramble (now with mushrooms, sausage, flat-leaf parsley, Jack cheese, and black pepper), the 12th Avenue (zucchini, corn, green onions, tomatoes, and Parmesan), and the Migas (green chiles, jalapeño, sausage, and tortilla chips topped with salsa, cilantro, and salty goat cheese). Several kinds of French toast replaced the waffles and pancakes, and she brought in fresh herbs for the first time. Crazy, huh?

The biggest change has been a greater emphasis on vegetarian and vegan options. Stumptownvegans.com gave the place high marks, especially the Superhero (sautéed tofu, tomatoes, garden sausage, green onions, and spinach).

"We don't use any partially hydrogenated oils or corn syrup," Carmine says. "We use real ingredients, and we make everything by hand. We try to use local providers and fresh eggs, and I handpick all the fruit, which is all organic."

I must admit, I was one of those old-time customers concerned about the changes at Junior's. I'm a dedicated meat eater, but I loved the heaping Vegan Potatoes, topped with mushrooms, corn, zucchini, and spicy tofu sauce for $7.50. I also got two meals out of it. And being a sucker for French toast, I liked that there were options: a regular 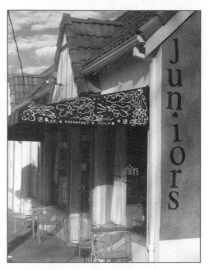 version, one topped with organic fruit, and another with yogurt, a whole chopped banana, and toasted almonds covered in honey. Of course there was also vegan version, soaked in bananas, applesauce, and soy milk.

There's still a relaxed, slightly goofy vibe to the place. About a dozen gilded mirrors adorn the walls, the booths are still a glittery gold, and the tiny bathroom is still a hallucinatory sea of graffiti.

For me, Junior's used to be a place I'd stumble to from an apartment down the street when I was hungover or still working on a buzz. I remember being impressed that staff applied butter to the toast with a paintbrush and often seemed to be as stoned as I was. Those days may be gone, in more ways than one, but Junior's is rolling right along with the times.

WAIT: Long on weekends, with very little room inside or cover outside. **LARGE GROUPS:** One booth could handle five or six; more could be a hassle. **COFFEE:** Happy Cup. **OTHER DRINKS:** Qu'an teas, juice, lemonade, full bar. **FEEL-GOODS:** Most ingredients are locally grown/made and organic. **HEALTH OPTIONS:** Plenty for vegetarians, vegans, and gluten-free folks. **WIFI:** No.

KELLS IRISH PUB

Weekend
A wee bit of Ireland in downtown Portland.
112 SW 2nd Ave. (Downtown)
503-227-4057
kellsirish.com/portland
Weekends 8 to 11:30 a.m.
$13–$16 (all major cards, no checks)

So, it's a weekend. You're downtown, looking for a brunch, and not up for the lines at Bijou or Mother's Bistro. You could hit a cart, a hotel, head over to the Pearl…or drop into Kells Irish Pub.

Did you even know Kells served brunch? I didn't, for longer than should have been the case. But there it is, with a big space, a central location (close to Saturday Market, for example) and a large menu that includes a rather unique corned beef hash—as would be expected from an Irish place.

Yes, Kells is a bar, and yes, it's a zoo on weekend nights. But by day it slips into the "public house" aspect of a pub's role, and so tables which host who-knows-what boozy shenanigans at night are, at brunch time, filled with diners grubbing down on Irish or American breakfasts.

And yes, the mysterious money-on-the-ceiling thing is laid bare in the light. I assume it has to do with magnets: you take a dollar, wrap it around a couple quarters, throw it up there, and it sticks. Try it; every St. Patrick's Day they sweep it clean and give the money to charity.

Slide into a booth, and it feels a little old-fashioned, with brick walls and your own lamp. There's even a (gas) fireplace, so it feels a little cozy, especially for a bar.

I also like various Irish, Celtic, and English touches, like the bathrooms being labeled Fír for gentlemen and Mná for ladies. There's a smoky cave of a Cigar Room downstairs (no cigs or pipes allowed) and live Irish music every night, plus an open "session" on Sunday. There is also a full schedule of both soccer and rugby, and around seven or eight on weekend mornings you'll find quite the scene as people watch live games from England. In fact, if you want to endear yourself to the (English) manager, a Manchester City fan, ask him where he was when Aguero won them the league. If he has time, ask him for the story.

The menu has eight options, and I figured I'd better get either the Irish Breakfast (two eggs cooked to your liking, banger sausages, rashers, grilled soda bread, potato bread, and roasted tomato for $10.50) or the corned beef hash. I went with the hash, since I have associated corned beef with Irish cuisine ever since I got cornered in an actual Irish pub years ago by a man determined to explain how, if you stuff yourself with corned beef and cabbage, you can then drink as much as you want. Still, though, I had to inquire as to the difference between a banger and a rasher. A banger is apparently just a sausage, with the name coming from their high water content, which may make them explode under heat. A rasher appears to be nothing more exotic than unsmoked bacon.

Now, I have had a lot of hashes, and Kells has one unlike any other in town that I know of. It's also one of my favorites. It's big and meaty, with fabulous chunks of tender, tasty beef, but what sets it apart are two things: it has no eggs, and the primary spice is stone-ground mustard. The result is a savory, sweet taste explosion that makes me wonder why we bother with eggs on hash, anyway. What do they add, really?

I am glad my friend Geralyn, who sells goods in local craft fairs, harassed me into going to Kells. I think it will make a fine weekend morning: stuff myself on corned beef hash, catch a game, and then perhaps wander over to the market and take a walk along the river. Since I don't drink anymore, this is about as Irish as I'm likely to get.

WAIT: Only on big game days (soccer, rugby). **LARGE GROUPS:** Yes. **COFFEE:** Caffé Umbria. **OTHER DRINKS:** A whole dang bar. **FEEL-GOODS:** None in particular. **HEALTH OPTIONS:** Some vegetarian options. **WIFI:** Yes.

KENNY AND ZUKE'S

Hip/Old School

A big ol' slab of New York in Downtown Portland.

1038 SW Stark Street (Downtown)

503-222-3354

kennyandzukes.com

Monday through Thursday 7 a.m. to 8 p.m., Friday 7 a.m. to 9 p.m.,
Saturday 8 a.m. to 9 p.m., Sunday 8 a.m. to 8 p.m.

(Some breakfast options available all day.

Full breakfast menu served weekdays until 11 a.m., weekends until 2 p.m.)

$14–$18 (all major cards, no checks)

Note: A newer location at 3901 N Williams, The Deli Bar, has a limited breakfast menu, as well.

I was amazed by Kenny and Zuke's even before I ate there. I heard there was a good New York-style deli downtown, so I went to check it out. Now, I was thinking about delis I had gone to in New York; I recall they were about the size of my college apartment, somewhat grimy, and filled with unpleasant people but good food.

When I saw Kenny and Zuke's, I said to myself (something like) "Holy smoked whitefish! *That's* the deli?" It's enormous, bright, clean, and well-ordered, and the people seem nice. It's like a palace compared to my deli memories. And then I saw the menu, a whopping four pages of options. The breakfast page alone made my head spin. Pastrami and eggs; salami and eggs; lox, eggs, and onions; four omelets (including, of course, pastrami, as well as the lox, cream cheese, and chives omelet); pastrami hash; corned beef hash; salmon hash; a few Benedicts on weekends; latkes; challah French toast; and maple granola.

But I've seen big breakfast menus. Kenny and Zuke's had me at the sodas. Any place that has 10 root beers, four ginger ales, five cream sodas, four colas (including Mexican Coke and Pepsi, with real sugar), six diet sodas, 17 fruit sodas, two "Others" (including Yoo-Hoo!) and seven "Premium and Rare Sodas" from places like Germany and Jackson Hole, Wyoming…well, like I said, think *palace* more than *deli*. What I think is, "I better go hiking on Saturday 'cause I'm getting some pastrami and a premium soda on Friday!"

Ah, you ask, but is it all good? Well, yes. How good depends on whom you ask—and it seems like everybody in town has an opinion. Kenny and Zuke's exists at the rare intersection of deli culture, big-time restaurant culture, and foodie culture. This means some folks get really worked up about the place, generally in a positive way.

Just about every blog in town has heaped praise on the place, usually along the lines of, "This is the closest thing to real New York pastrami and bagels you'll ever find in Portland." The *Oregonian* said of the Reuben (lunch service starts at 11 a.m., by the way), "You'll name your firstborn after it." *Willamette Week* hailed it as marking downtown coming full circle after an old Jewish neighborhood was destroyed to make way for the Portland State campus and called it "downtown PDX's first truly egalitarian new restaurant in decades," whatever that means. A writer for *Seattle Magazine* ate there three times in 24 hours. Even Matt Groening, Portland native and creator of *The Simpsons*, dropped off a sketch of Homer saying, "Mmmm, Kenny and Zuke's!"

Sure, it seems a little exorbitant. I mean, it's a *deli*, right? The prices are pretty high; the Smoked Salmon Benedict is $15.45, and challah French toast is $10.95—though you get more than a single person should be able to eat. I usually go for the pastrami hash with two eggs ($13.45), and I eat the leftovers with a couple of eggs for breakfast the next day.

Whether Kenny and Zuke's is "authentic" is entirely up to you. I shy away from opinions on this cuisine, more than any other, because I've been practically assaulted for saying nice things about Kenny and Zuke's *and* Kornblatt's. But Kenny and Zuke's is sure as heck impressive, and I recommend you check it out for yourself.

WAIT: A bit on weekends, with little room inside. **LARGE GROUPS:** Yes. **COFFEE:** Stumptown. **OTHER DRINKS:** Numi teas, milk, fresh orange juice, and a wide world of sodas. **FEEL-GOODS:** Kenny and Zuke buy local beef and make their own bagels. **HEALTH OPTIONS:** Come on, it's a deli! **WIFI:** No.

KORNBLATT'S

Old School	
"Would do just fine in New York."	
628 NW 23rd Ave. (NW)	
503-242-0055	
kornblattsdelipdx.com	
Weekdays 7 a.m. to 8 p.m., weekends 7:30 a.m. to 9 p.m.	
Breakfast served all day	
$12–$15 (all major cards, no checks)	

Whenever a place has a location for its theme—like Kornblatt's calling itself a New York-style delicatessen—I have a system to test that assertion. I call it the Memphis Barbecue Test, and it goes like this: Since I am from Memphis and love barbecue, I ask myself how a particular barbecue place would do if it were in Memphis. So, to apply this test to Kornblatt's, which humbly asserts it has the finest deli food west of the Hudson River, I invited David, a Jew who grew up in New Jersey, and Rich, who grew up on Long Island, to have breakfast with me.

I had always thought the decor might be a bit *too* New York: the autographs from Derek Jeter and Alex Rodriguez, the poster of the 1955 Dodgers, the picture of the guys eating their lunches on the beam high over the city.

On the plus side, I once had a wonderfully spastic server who kept calling me "my friend," sang loudly along with Frank Sinatra on "Chicago," and stepped outside for a smoke while saying he was "going out to lower my life expectancy." I also appreciate that the place has a glossary of deli items, most of which I can't identify, including egg cream, phosphates, blintz, kasha varnishkes, knish, nosh, kishka, kugel, lox, matzo balls, matzo brei, rugalach, pastrami, and latkes.

Rich immediately said that on appearance alone, Kornblatt's would easily fit in Great Neck, where apparently there's a large Jewish population. And David said he'd been coming here for years. So it was looking like a pass on my test already. David got the Eggs Bageldict, and the server repeated the line from the menu: "If you say it, we'll make it."

The Bageldict is a Benedict with salami (or pastrami or smoked salmon) and hollandaise on a bagel of your choice. David thought the sauce was a little light, but he also cleaned his plate, and since there was a female among us, nobody made any off-color jokes.

I got a full order of blintzes (four for $11.75), and they were light and delicious, served with sour cream and blueberry and strawberry preserves. It's best to get them if you're splitting your friend's savory dish; I was trading them for chunks of a mushroom-onion omelet, a massive but mildly flavored corned beef hash, and David's (ahem) dish.

The menu has nine omelets, ranging from basic options to, I assume, New York staples: sautéed chicken livers and onions, lox and onions, lox and cream cheese, and the Famous Mixed Deli, which is made with salami, corned beef, and pastrami and served pancake style. (Take my word: plan on taking a nap after that one!)

If that's not New York or Jewish enough for you, you can also get Matzo Brei (scrambled eggs with matzo balls) or French toast with homemade challah—and practice your pronunciation of *challah*. And for dessert, some kugel, a jumbo éclair, or some New York cheesecake. Might make you want to go home and sing along with Sinatra, too.

A wise man wades into deli culture with great trepidation, and I won't bother you with my deli preferences in our town. I ain't lookin' for a fight. I'll just say that I enjoyed eating at Kornblatt's, and the *New York Times* said that the place is "one of the truly great New York delis outside the five boroughs."

WAIT: A little on weekends at lunchtime. **LARGE GROUPS:** More than eight might be tough. **COFFEE:** Allann Brothers. **OTHER DRINKS:** Espresso, specialty sodas, egg cream, hot chocolate, phosphates, seltzer, mimosas, and Bloody Marys. **FEEL-GOODS:** You don't have to deal with too many real New Yorkers. **HEALTH OPTIONS:** Wrong place. **WIFI:** No, but "you can steal it from next door."

LAURETTA JEAN'S

Hip
Granny's in the kitchen, and all's right with the world.
3402 SE Division (SE/Division)
503-235-3119
laurettajean.com
Brunch 9 a.m. to 3 p.m. weekdays, 8 a.m. to 3 p.m. weekends.
$9–$12 (all major cards, local checks)

I walk into Lauretta Jean's, and I immediately feel transported back to a South I didn't actually grow up in. My mom never wore an apron, we didn't listen to the blues, and if there was a pie being baked, you can bet it was a simple chess pie, and it was either Thanksgiving or Christmas.

But there's a South we all dream of—or maybe it's just a simple, down-home, country life. All I know is, I set foot inside Lauretta Jean's, the door creaked, and I heard some real simple country blues, just some guy with a guitar and a harmonica talkin' about how rough life can be. A ceiling fan, wooden shelves covered with old-fashioned trinkets, pickling jars…and when you find out the place is named for the owner's grandmother, the picture is complete.

Still, this is Southeast Portland, near one of the last little pockets of light industry. (The arrival of The Hedge House, a new location for Lompoc Brewing, signals the coming of New Portland to this neck of the woods.) And on the wall was a sign reading, "To do list: Smoke weed, listen to Neil Young, split wood." So, yeah—Southeast for sure.

Basically, the décor and the feel and the whole attitude about Lauretta Jean's says, "We are about the pie." And I just love that. When I visited, the options ($4.50 a slice, $31 for a whole pie) were

Heirloom Apple, Blackberry Raspberry Streusel, Salted Pecan, Spiced Pear, Apple Brandy Blackberry, Classic Pumpkin Coconut Cream, and Chocolate Cream. Though the restaurant is nowhere near a farm or

berry patch, you get the feeling the bakers just came in from the fields with a basket of goodness, put on their aprons, and went to work.

The brunch—oh yeah, brunch. They do that, too. It's a limited menu, with biscuit-based options—four sandwiches, biscuits and gravy, biscuit French toast, and a biscuit Benedict. There's also a quiche, a cheese-veggie scramble, and granola parfait. And the place (formerly Pix Patisserie) is tiny; a group of 12 would fill it. There are a few tables outside, and cozy as it is, Lauretta Jean's is not a destination brunch place. I was on my way to a hike, and I got a nice plate of protein, a piece of pie to go, and some psychological warmth for the road.

Oh, and when I walked outside, an old-fashioned ice cream truck, recently redone, rolled by. *Good ol' Southeast*, I thought. We do like to combine the old-fashioned and friendly with the freshest and the artisan, don't we?

WAIT: Not typically. **LARGE GROUPS:** No. **COFFEE:** Water Avenue. **OTHER DRINKS:** Espresso, beer, wine cocktails. **FEEL-GOODS:** All baked goods made from scratch. **HEALTH OPTIONS:** I mean…it's pie. **WIFI:** Yes.

LE BISTRO MONTAGE

Weekend	
Still crazy after all these years.	
301 SE Morrison St. (SE/Inner)	
503-234-1324	
montageportland.com	
Weekends 10 a.m. to 2 p.m.	
$12–$14 (Visa, MasterCard, no checks)	

I have to admit, Montage cracks me up.

I can't think of a place that's more Portland—or a place that brings out such heated opinions from people. The main objections boil down to the staff being rude, the noise level outrageous, the communal seating a pain, the food mediocre, and the clientele too drunk to care. And near as I can tell, it's been that way since they opened in 1992. It's kind of like hearing people complain that Bob Dylan has a bad voice and his lyrics don't make sense.

Montage's bread and butter, as it were, is serving variations on mac and cheese to the late-night crowd. It's an enormous, loud, crowded scene around two in the morning, and its placement under the Morrison Bridge has always added a certain dingy flair. To me, it really has kind of a New Orleans feel to it, and I quit going years ago when I first gave up late nights and then gave up drinking and getting high. Maybe Montage is a phase that all of us Portlanders go through in our 20s.

Now they do brunch on weekends, and it still has a New Orleans feel to it—not a classy, Brennan's kind of feel, but an out-too-late, slept-in, need-some-sustenance-for-another-day-of-drinking feel. I tried to go there once around New Year's Day, and they were closed, with a sign on the door basically explaining they'd gotten a little carried away and needed some time off. Endeared me to them for life.

It's also funny to be in there when it's lit. Or maybe it's disconcerting, as you can clearly make out the funny tin cans pounded into the floor, as well as all the bumps and smudges usually blurred by darkness and booze. But the white tablecloths still suggest a certain (faded) elegance, and they'll still wrap up your leftovers in wacky animal-shaped foil. I don't know which server you'll get, but ours was as far from rude as could be—in fact, cute and charming in the extreme. And I've seen other online reviewers say the same.

As for the food, it's quite cheap. The priciest thing on the menu is a steak and eggs—a five-ounce flat iron with onions and bourbon demi-glace—for $10. Otherwise, there are Southern favorites like chicken-fried steak with Cajun potatoes and toast ($8.95) and a biscuit sandwich with bacon, a fried egg, country gravy, and cheddar cheese ($7.95 with onion rings). There are decadent New Orleans touches like a Rum Raisin French Toast with fruit compote and crème anglaise ($7.95). And for you Montage regulars, happy news: one of the six omelets is their popular Green Eggs and Spam (pesto, Parmesan, and tomatoes) for $7.95—formerly $6.66.

The restaurant got kudos from my friend Maria for their oatmeal, which she said didn't need sugar. That's because it's Apple Date Oatmeal and comes with French vanilla crème sauce and pecans. (Brown sugar and syrup come on the side, just in case.) And they got kudos from this Tennessean for their white cheddar grits, which come with eggs and toast for $5.95.

For our little group, consisting mainly of folks too old or restrained for the late-night scene, it was nice to go visit the place when it was safe and relatively sane. To get thoroughly stuffed for about $12 total and be able to hear each other speak was quite a bonus.

WAIT: None. **LARGE GROUPS:** Absolutely. **COFFEE:** K&F. **OTHER DRINKS:** Tazo teas, several beer, wine, and cocktail options. **FEEL-GOODS:** None in particular. **HEALTH OPTIONS:** A few things for vegetarians. **WIFI:** Yes, in the back bar.

LUCCA

Weekend/Classy
Good looks and taste, just like Italy.
3449 NE 24th Ave. (NE/Fremont)
503-287-7372
luccapdx.com
Brunch served Sunday 10 a.m. to 2 p.m.
$14–$16 (Visa, MasterCard, American Express, no checks)

After eating something like 8,000 breakfasts since launching this book, it is pretty rare that a place makes me lean back in my chair and say, "Damn." But that's what happened at Lucca.

The Crew and I hit the place at 10:30. There were six of us, so I gave a heads-up call at 10, when they opened. Was appreciated, wasn't necessary. In fact, only three other tables were occupied, two of them with groups bigger than ours. *That* doesn't happen too often, either.

Lucca is in one of *those* locations, the corner of Northeast 24th and Fremont. Seems like nothing has worked there since the original Nature's pulled out more than a decade ago. Anybody remember Aja Pacific Kitchen? Or the Dining Room? Me, neither. But Lucca has made it, going on my highly scientific sense that several people I know who are serious about food have told me they like it. Meanwhile, there are almost no lines at Sunday brunch, and I'd say the food is in the top 15 in town, based on one visit. Plus, the Italian flair really puts it in a class shared only with Accanto. (And now, a moment of silence in memory of brunch at Basta's.)

Speaking of class, Lucca is a beautiful place! The ceiling is adorned with a basket-style woven pattern, the art is subtle, the colors warm, there's plenty of light, and a side room (available for private parties) is just the right amount of set off. The staff, too, is lovely; in fact, we agreed our server looked a little like Sophia Loren. And no, we weren't drinking. (Well, not all of us.)

The menu is a true brunch, with pizza and salads in addition to fancied-up breakfast faves like French toast (with seasonal fruit and lemon-curd crema), braised beef hash with horseradish gremolata (whatever that is), and a scramble with wood-fired mushrooms, leeks, fontina, stinging nettle-pine nut pesto and spiced Yukon potatoes. They even had a pancetta and egg pizza, which we didn't order. It sounded odd at first, but really, it's bacon, egg, cheese, some sauce, bread…what's so odd? The pizzas are cooked in a (partially) wood-fired oven in plain view of the tables, and they are lovely, with a fried egg in the middle.

A couple of us got there early and shared a blueberry-lime scone that was just as buttery and flaky as could be. Then I had a frittata with goat cheese, zucchini, potatoes, apple, fennel, and arugula, and while it was among the better frittatas I've had in town, it wasn't the best meal on our table. Chela's baked French toast (really more of a strawberry soufflé with fresh cream) was amazing, and Jerry's mushroom hash had just the right mix of flavors. The coffee was strong, good, and never ran out.

Everybody agreed the place was top notch, and the word *romantic* even got tossed around. I bet in the evenings the place is even warmer and more inviting. All this, and I think I spent $15 or $16 with tip.

I think from now on, when somebody complains about lines at brunch, I will send them to Lucca—assuming they can tolerate excellent food in a beautiful place served by beautiful people.

WAIT: None. **LARGE GROUPS:** Definitely; notice is nice. **COFFEE:** Caffè Umbria. **OTHER DRINKS:** Espresso, juice, cocktails. **FEEL-GOODS:** They list a dozen local farms on their site. **HEALTH OPTIONS:** Some veggie options. **WIFI:** Yes.

MAMA MIA TRATTORIA

Weekend/Kiddie	
Kinda fancy, kinda Italian.	
439 SW 2nd Ave. (Downtown)	
503-295-6464	
mamamiatrattoria.com	
Brunch weekends from 9 a.m. to 1 p.m.	
$13–15 (all major cards, no checks)	

I am lucky enough to visit Italy almost every year, leading hiking and touring trips, and I try very, very hard to not be That Guy about Italian culture. You know That Guy: he tells you that Italians don't drink cappuccinos after lunch, that their high-speed and chaotic driving style actually makes more sense than ours, and that the word *panini* actually means sandwiches. What you really want, he says, is *un panino*.

You hate That Guy, right? So do I, yet I've said all the above things. So I tried to leave That Guy outside when I went in for brunch at Mama Mia. That Guy didn't expect to find any kind of "authentic" Italian place, but I didn't care; I was hungry and downtown and didn't want to wait for brunch. I arrived at 10 a.m., and sat right down. So both he and I were happy.

At first glance, and probably more so at night, Mama Mia looks kinda fancy. They have more than 20 crystal chandeliers and nearly 50 gilded mirrors, a whole wall of 14-foot-tall windows, and a black granite bar they call "the most comfortable in downtown Portland." That Guy seriously doubts the latter claim and has never seen a place like Mama Mia in Italy, but we were keeping an open mind.

The staff was prompt and attentive, and I had a menu plus a drink within minutes. The crowd seemed a little touristy, with no sign of slackers, hipsters, or anybody who might soon be appearing on *Portlandia*. That Guy and I were fine with this; eating in downtown places like Mama Mia and Mother's Bistro (which formerly had the same owners) is like leaving "Portland" and visiting "Downtown American City" for a while.

The menu is ~~molto grande~~ large, with nine cocktails, five four-egg frittatas, four four-egg scrambles, several variations on French toast and pancakes, five Benedict/specialties, and a Lighter Side section of granola, fresh fruit, and oatmeal. Oh, and there are six things on the kids' menu, plus enough à la carte sides to make up several meals. The Italian flare shows up in ingredients like mozzarella, Italian sausage, and "Mama Mia's Celebrated Pesto." Otherwise, it's ~~pretty generic~~ all stuff you've seen before.

That Guy, who would like you to know that Italians don't even eat breakfast, insisted we get the Mama Mia Classic Benedict, because it includes prosciutto, and other than espresso and olive oil, the best way to judge an Italian *ristorante* restaurant is to try their prosciutto. Honestly, neither of us expected much.

We were pleasantly surprised. First, the food came right out—my whole meal took about 45 minutes, though I was never rushed—and the Benedict was well done and tasty. It had—along with the prosciutto (which That Guy was underwhelmed by)—excellent spinach, a perfectly poached egg, and yummy hollandaise on their standard rosemary-Romano scone, which ~~isn't Italian in the least~~ held up well and was still firm and tasty to the end.

~~Allora~~ Look, nobody will ever confuse Mama Mia with the great ~~Italian~~ brunch places in town, but there were times during that Benedict when I really, really dug it. The ingredients were fresh and well prepared, and there were moments of outstanding taste. And how many good brunches are there downtown with no wait at all?

I suppose that's our best summary of brunch at Mama Mia: It's ~~not authentic~~ tasty, it's ~~fake~~ comfortable and friendly, and it's ~~touristy~~ very accessible. With a half-shrug and a hand held palm-up, we conclude, *Va bene, non è male.* ("It's okay, it's not bad.")

WAIT: None. **LARGE GROUPS:** Yes, with notice. **COFFEE:** Stumptown. **OTHER DRINKS:** Cocktails, Italian sodas, fresh-squeezed juices, espresso. **FEEL-GOODS:** The menu claims Mia Mia uses "only the best local products and sustainable resources available." **HEALTH OPTIONS:** Egg whites at no charge and cholesterol-free eggs for $0.95. **WIFI:** Yes.

MARCO'S CAFE

Classy
Because a village needs a nice restaurant.
7910 SW 35th Ave. (SW/Inner)
503-245-0199
marcoscafe.com
Weekdays 7 a.m. to 9 p.m., Saturday 8 a.m. to 9 p.m., Sunday 8 a.m. to 2 p.m.
$12–$16 (all major cards, local checks)

Multnomah Village really does have a small-town feel to it, and I've always thought that, like any small town, it has subtle class divisions. I don't mean animosities—the Village is hardly a place with class tension—but divisions, at least when it comes to the breakfast scene. The working-class Villagers have the Fat City Cafe, where old guys sit at the counter talking city politics, and there's an item on the menu called the Fat City Sizzle.

Now consider Marco's, where on one of my visits, the specials (written on etched glass just inside the door) were an asparagus, bacon, tomato, and spinach scramble in fennel butter topped with Asiago and an Oregonzola Egg Sandwich with bacon, Oregonzola cheese, fried egg, scallion, tomato, and herb mayonnaise on Asiago grilled Como bread. Well. And on their website you'll see a picture of chef Maurice and read about his work experience in Laguna Beach and Switzerland; he's also fluent in both French and Spanish! His wife is the pastry chef, and they've cooked together there for nearly 20 years.

Marco's has been a wildly popular restaurant since 1983, and there are some reasons for it. The food is always good, the folks are friendly, the place is clean, and the prices aren't bad for some pretty classy food.

But it is very much a Southwest Portland place: a while back they

tried to open a location on Northeast Fremont Street, and it flopped. And although I like to make some fun, I also agree with the *Oregonian*: "Marco's manages to be both nouveau and down-home at the same time."

I dragged my usual Fat City gang of fellas over there one time, and after all the jokes about whether they'd let us in and "I sure hope I don't drool on these nice tablecloths," etc., we chose among four omelets, nine egg dishes (not including Benedicts), and 12 specialties ranging from blintzes to roast beef hash to bagels and lox. Everything had a legitimate, expert touch to it, like the light but sturdy hollandaise on three Benedicts.

We were impressed and satisfied, as I always have been at Marco's. And whenever the food or feel starts to get just a bit snooty, I see the Franz bread, the packets of freezer jam, the regulars, and all the accommodations for kids, and I feel a little more at home. I do still giggle at some of the goofier touches, like the collection of umbrellas hanging from the ceiling (though they muffle the noise and are part of a charitable effort) and the quotes painted on the wall: "One cannot think well, love well, sleep well, if one has not dined well," said Virginia Woolf, whom I'm almost certain damn few people have actually ever read. And "All happiness depends upon a leisurely breakfast," said John Gunther, whom I'm certain no one has ever heard of.

I can make up a breakfast quote too: "Since today is all we have, what better way to start our lives than with a fine breakfast with good friends?" Maybe they'll put *that* up on a wall someday!

WAIT: Pretty long on weekends, with a small space inside and some cover outside. **LARGE GROUPS:** Yes, but no separate checks or reservations. **COFFEE:** Equal Exchange (organic, fair trade). **OTHER DRINKS:** Espresso, Mighty Leaf teas, fresh juice, specialty coffee drinks, cardamom tea, full bar. **FEEL-GOODS:** Solar hot water; local, naturally grazed beef; local, organic herbs and mushrooms; hormone-free milk; cage-free eggs; Monterey Bay Aquarium-approved seafood; the restaurant recycles 95 percent of its waste, donates food to charities. **HEALTH OPTIONS:** Good options for vegetarians and gluten-free folks, egg substitutes available, trans-fat-free menu. **WIFI:** Yes.

MERIWETHER'S

Weekend/Classy
Aiming for greatness.
2601 NW Vaughn St. (NW)
503-228-1250
meriwethersnw.com
Brunch weekends 8 a.m. to 2:30 p.m.
$18–$25 (all major cards, no checks)

Meriwether's looks great, it's in a great spot, the menu is amazing, and the patio out back is as nice a place as you can find to eat breakfast in Portland. It clearly aims to be a serious restaurant; sometimes that comes off as attitude ("Water is served only on request"), sometimes as aspiration, sometimes as a business plan. But it certainly doesn't lack ambition.

The location, on the site of the 1905 Lewis and Clark Centennial Expo, has hosted a few restaurants over the years, but this one seems to be sticking. The Breakfast Crew was suitably impressed by the exterior—a charming old house near Forest Park—and wowed by the amount of money obviously invested. With numerous levels of seating and a country-home feel, it's a luxurious and comfortable place to be. And there are things on Meriwether's menu (confit, frizzled onions, basil pistou) that I can't identify. And this is precisely what fascinates me: it's a place where serious dining and Portland brunch intersect in wondrous surroundings. There's also a heavy emphasis on local ingredients and sourcing; they even have their own farm up in the West Hills.

My crew was certainly impressed, and we had a fine time. Jerry, a musician, loved the musical selection. We all loved the patio, which is adorned with wrought iron, heat lamps, copper piping (from which canvas hangs in cooler weather), bamboo fencing, fuchsias, hydrangeas, hostas, and a fountain. And it's a *big* patio, with three separate areas to it, one covered and featuring year-round blooms and an Italian fountain.

We had eggs Benedict with Dungeness crab—for $20, which I suppose is fair, but just remember, this place ain't cheap; Fried Chicken and Waffles with bacon, marionberries, and sautéed pears ($18), and Lemon Crema Crepes ($13) with seasonal fruit (strawberries, on my visit) and candied lemon.

I think the same food served in a lesser location would somehow seem more impressive (and probably cost less). Regular food in this setting would drive the place out of business, pronto. Instead, it's a beautiful and impressive place with great outdoor seating and, well, pretty darn good food.

WAIT: Not bad, but reservations are recommended for Sundays. **LARGE GROUPS:** With notice. **COFFEE:** Kobos. **OTHER DRINKS:** Espresso, cocktails, sparkling wine, juice, hot chocolate. **FEEL-GOODS:** It even has its own farm. And it has a full parking lot west of the building. **HEALTH OPTIONS:** Egg whites for omelets, substitute fresh fruit for potatoes ($2), salads on the brunch menu. **WIFI:** Yes.

MEXTIZA

Weekend/New
Tasty "pieces of Mexico."
2013 N Killingsworth St. (N/Inner)
503-289-3709
mextiza.com
Sunday 10 a.m. to 2 p.m.
$14–$18 (all major cards, no checks)

I rolled into Mextiza one afternoon, late in the book research. Honestly, I was so tired of brunch that I considered not even putting the place in. But it's the sister restaurant of Autentica (see page 34), whose brunch I love, and the foodies on portlandfood.org loved it, so—even though I had already eaten a brunch that morning—off I went to North Killingsworth. Oh, how I struggle for my art!

First I drove right by the place, because I was distracted by Beaterville, which is about 100 feet to the west. Also, I thought the building I passed was some kind of auto garage or something. And I thought I saw a Pabst sign.

Turns out, no, that's Mextiza, which is frankly hideous on the outside but clean and classy on the inside: a sunny front room looking out on a patio, shiny wood tables with black chairs, a little bar on the side with a wall of bottles and a few folks enjoying a late brunch or early drink, and some cozier seating in the back. I was the only person at a table at just before 2 p.m., and all I wanted was something sweet.

The waiter dropped the menus and a water bottle with "Agave de Oaxaca" inscribed on the bottom. I opened the drink menu and immediately understood (A) why there is a wall of bottles behind that bar and (B) why I don't drink anymore. If I ever got started again, particularly on tequila, I would never get out of this place.

Maybe this isn't relevant to brunch, but Mextiza has dozens of tequilas: *tequilas blancas, tequilas anejos, mezcal, tequilas reposados* and *reserva especial.* On the next page are the cocktails, margaritas, beer, and wine. I took a breath, set the menu down, and looked at the food menu, which was thankfully only one page, with 13 items. The first, Pan Frito, would be my meal: Mexican-style French toast with pear, bacon, sea salt, piloncillo, and almendrado syrup. And welcome to Mextiza, where the drinks are plentiful, the food is serious, and even the French toast will have you asking about mysterious ingredients.

Turns out that piloncillo is compacted brown sugar (I'm sure there's more to it than that, but it's enough) and almendrado is a dessert liquor made of tequila (of course) and almond syrup. Right, I said; bring me that!

Perusing the rest of the menu, with my newfound understanding of what makes Mextiza tick, I decided that I would have to bring a Breakfast Crew of at least 13 people here, so I could taste everything. There's a pork belly sandwich with chile verde; green chile chorizo with eggs and pinto beans; fried, breaded steak with hard-boiled egg and avocado salad; a version of Benedict with fried corn-masa cakes, bacon, and huitlacoche sauce. And what is huitlacoche sauce? According to my server, "A corn truffle sauce with…some spices."

I don't think he was dodging the question; I think he was saying a combination of "it's hard to explain" and "you just have to eat it." And then he laid my "Mexican-style French toast" on me. It was a little piece of art! Three thick, rectangular pieces of golden bread in a puddle of the almendrado syrup with strips of pear all over it, tiny chunks of perfect bacon on top, and powdered sugar drizzled over the whole thing.

I looked at the waiter, whose expression I now read as, "See?" I took a bite and drifted off for a minute into whatever world is created when sweet and savory are thrown together. I looked around and wondered why nobody else was in here. And then I looked at the menu, remembered why I like brunch, and vowed that I would come back and eat my way through this place.

WAIT: None. **LARGE GROUPS:** Yes. **COFFEE:** Caffé Umbria. **OTHER DRINKS:** Oh my! **FEEL-GOODS:** "Whenever possible" they use local produce and meat as well as wild-caught fish. **HEALTH OPTIONS:** Good for vegetarians. **WIFI:** Yes.

MILO'S CITY CAFE

New/Hip/Old School
If New York was down-home...
1325 NE Broadway Ave. (NE/Broadway)
503-288-6456
miloscitycafe.com
Breakfast weekdays 6:30 to 11:00 a.m., then a fair portion of the breakfast menu during lunch until 2:30 p.m.; weekends 7:30 a.m. to 2:30 p.m.
$10–$15 (all major cards, local checks)

My friend Bob and I love getting together for breakfast early on weekdays. Sometimes we meet with the fellas down at Fat City Cafe for a boisterous round of shit-talking, and sometimes it's just the two of us, talking writing and politics and perhaps a few personal things before he goes to the insurance company and I go home to chase pennies as a freelance writer. We're professionals, slackers, creative folks, and old buddies.

For these occasions, Milo's is our default choice. It's kind of like Bob and me: professional in that it's clean and has excellent food, slackerly in that it's not a problem hanging out for a while, and friendly in that we always have the same server and often see somebody we know. In fact, the website now says, "Everyone meets at Milo's!"

To dig where Milo's stands in the Portland breakfast pantheon, you'd first have to get a handle on Northeast Broadway itself. What *is* the character of that street? Hawthorne is hippie, 23rd Avenue is shopping, Alberta is a little wacky, Broadway is...what? You've got your Elmer's Flag and Banner, Dollar Store, and tanning booths—*and* your Peet's-Grand Central-McMenamins corner at 15th, a dozen kinds of food, both discount and high-end shopping, and old-time places like Helen Bernhard Bakery a few blocks away from a conveyor-belt sushi chain. It's like a neighborhood place and a mini-downtown. And in breakfast terms, you've got your blue-collar Village Inn, your happy-wicker Cadillac Cafe, and good ol' Milo's.

Milo's is not a down-home place, mind you. The decor is sort of a sleek, stylish New York kind of thing, but the feel is both efficient, like a serious restaurant, and relaxed, like a neighborhood place. Six omelets

158

and six Benedicts feature veggies, pepper bacon, Italian and chorizo sausage, ham, and smoked salmon, and the Benedicts also offer petite tenderloin and crab cake options. Four hashes include pepper bacon, smoked salmon, and corned beef. Vegetarians need not run away, however. In addition to a veggie option on all of the above, there's granola, oatmeal, and waffles.

But Milo's makes its name on the meat dishes. The overall theory is simple. One of the owners, Loren Skogland, told the *Portland Business Journal*, "I buy really good ingredients and I don't screw them up." The article also said that the Skoglands, longtime restaurant folk, "opened Milo's in part so they could control their own hours and schedules, and chose the location, within a few minutes of their Alameda home and the grade school, in order to better juggle all the demands on their time."

All the Skogland kids have menu items named for them, and the vibe continues with Jeremy's Peanut Butter and Chocolate Waffle and the Peanut Butter and Jelly Stuffed French Toast, which is basically a big, gooey PB&J sandwich on sourdough French toast for $7.75.

And such is Milo's: unpretentious and impressive at the same time, with a subtle dash of family and friendly.

WAIT: Can be long on weekends, covered benches outside. **LARGE GROUPS:** With notice. **COFFEE:** Boyd's. **OTHER DRINKS:** Tea, sparkling water, hot chocolate, juice, beer, wine, breakfast cocktails. **FEEL-GOODS:** Nothing in particular. **HEALTH OPTIONS:** Some veggie options; no-cholesterol eggs or egg whites $1 extra. **WIFI:** No.

MOTHER'S BISTRO

Classy
Somehow both dressy and faded.
212 SW Stark St. (Downtown)
503-464-1122
mothersbistro.com
Breakfast Tuesday through Friday 7 a.m. to 2:30 p.m.,
weekends 8 a.m. to 2:30 p.m.
$13–$16 (all major cards, no checks)

If this place was called anything *other* than Mother's, I'd say the name was wrong. As soon as you walk in, you feel that combination of dress-up and old, faded comfort and class we associate with Mom. At least I do, but I was raised by a Mississippi native descended from French and Irish stock.

I ate at Mother's once with my friend Alice, who spent 10 years in Mississippi, and she said the same thing: kind of an Old South-French feel. It's by no means modern, and in places it seems like it could use a little dusting. But so could my mom's house.

We were seated by a white-clad hostess who indicated our table with that upturned hand I associate with people who've been trained in politeness, and when I looked around, I got another dose of that grown-up feel: there were women in heels and men in suits! I'd always wondered where the downtown business and tourist crowds eat breakfast, and here they were, bathed in the light of tall windows while Billie Holiday crooned through the speakers. (Downtown hotels always seem to send tourists to Mother's and Bijou Café.)

By now you may be thinking that the food is expensive and fancy. It is a little higher than in some places, but not all. On one visit I managed to spend $20 with tip, but most entrées range from $8 to $11. Alice and I shared a French-press coffee for $4.50 and got three cups out of it. At the low-cost end is organic oatmeal for $5.95 (add raisins, bananas, pecans, or walnuts for $1), and on the high is the House-Cured Lox Platter for $14.95.

What lies between is some down-home stuff. At lunch and dinner, Mother's is known for comfort food like meatloaf, macaroni and cheese, and chicken and dumplings. But there's an international flavor as well; a message on the menu from the owner explains that she's after an international sense of Mom (pirogi, ravioli, green curry), and every month there's a Mother of the Month (M.O.M.) featured in the menu with her story and some of her dishes.

Breakfast doesn't veer too far from this, with a mushroom scramble, a prosciutto-garlic-basil-provolone scramble called Mike's Special, sausage and biscuits, and all your favorite Northwest must-haves: wild salmon hash, tofu scramble, and challah French toast. I had the French toast as a side instead of the potatoes. (The substitute was "no worries," and I think they charged me $1.) I thought it was great: a little crunch on the outside, nice and soft on the inside. Alice had a portobello-spinach-Asiago scramble that was perfectly done. And yes, we cleaned our plates.

I've always found the food at Mother's to be basic, tasty, and well-done. It's never innovative or eye-popping, and I suspect we're paying another dollar or two per entrée for all that ambience and the seeming abundance of staff. Young folks think it's stuffy, foodies think it's dull, and many of the latter were shocked beyond words when owner Lisa Schroeder won Chef/Restaurateur of the Year from the International Association of Culinary Professionals during its 2010 Conference in Portland.

But Mother's seems to be full all the time, and it can't be just tourists and the suit crowd. I suppose there's always going to be interest in what Mom is cooking, even if it isn't fancy or cutting edge.

WAIT: Quite long on weekends, with some indoor seating available. **LARGE GROUPS:** Yes, but they request you make a reservation. **COFFEE:** Stumptown drip and a rotating blend for the French press. **OTHER DRINKS:** Harney & Sons teas, Oregon Chai lattes, mimosas and other cocktails, house-infused vodkas with seasonal fruits. **FEEL-GOODS:** The menu says Mother's is "committed to making your meal a warm, fuzzy experience." **HEALTH OPTIONS:** Egg whites or tofu available (for $1); gluten-free bread; and vegetarians have several options. **WIFI:** Yes, during the week.

TOP HASHCAPADE (SEE PAGE 301)

MUDDY'S

Hip/Veggie
Wait, that's a restaurant up there?
3560 N Mississippi (N/Inner)
503-445-6690
muddyspdx.com
7 a.m. to 4 p.m. Monday and Wednesday through Saturday, 7 a.m. to 3 p.m. Sunday
$12-14 (Visa, MasterCard, Discover, no checks)

I worked on this silly project of mine for, I don't know, six years before I found out Muddy's serves a full breakfast menu. Now, there could be several reasons for this: my brain is bacon-sick; new places get all the attention; they call themselves a coffee shop instead of a restaurant or café; they aren't on Facebook; or nobody has ever said to me, "You should check out Muddy's." All of those things are true, and here we start to see where Muddy's fits into the local breakfast scene.

See, I always tell people that my breakfast experiences fall first into two basic categories: memorable (for good or ill) and not memorable. This is true for setting and food. So a place might have an awesome setting and forgettable food (I think I'll refrain from naming names) or awesome food and a weird or unsatisfying setting (say…Sweedeedee). I think if you ask around town, and if you can find 10 people who have eaten at Muddy's, eight of them will say, "Yeah, it was fine." Of the other two, one will love it and one hate it.

Am I wasting time here, because I can't think of what to say about Muddy's? Kinda. Yes. I mean, I almost walked past the damned place when I was actually looking for it. It's in an old house, up a flight

of steps, with a sign that's half-buried by vegetation in summer. It just doesn't *look* like much.

Actually, once you get up there, it's quite homey and comfy. There's a broken rocking chair on the front porch, a nice garden in the front yard with a table, and inside is, well, a coffee shop with some tables. But all the tables and chairs and plates and silver are mismatched, so it's like a coffee shop with tables in somebody's house. Out back, there's a nice patio with a long picnic table and a metal one with five chairs that don't match each other or the table. It's a little…loose feeling.

When the guy I was meeting walked into the place, the first thing he said was, "Wait, this place serves breakfast?"

Yes, they do. And am I still wasting time here because the food fell into that "unmemorable" category? Absolutely. The full-page menu has lots of options for vegetarians, a dozen savories, half a dozen sweets and kids' items, and a bunch of comments that aren't as funny as they think. (I know, same could be said of this book!) I had a scramble with bacon and apples, or at least that's what it looks like from my pictures. The menu on the website is three years old, and I forgot to steal ask for one.

Okay, we should wrap this up. It's a nice place, cozy and uncrowded, you might like it, and I enjoyed my meal. Or, at least, I don't remember anything bad about it!

WAIT: Maybe a little on weekends. **LARGE GROUPS:** Not the best option. **COFFEE:** Portland Roasting. **OTHER DRINKS:** Espresso, fruit juice, sodas, beer, cocktails. **FEEL-GOODS:** Cage-free eggs. **HEALTH OPTIONS:** Small fees get you egg whites, tofu, or tempeh for eggs, and soy sausage or fruit instead of potatoes. **WIFI:** Yes.

NAVARRE

Weekend/New
Love it, hate it, what is going on?
10 NE 28th Ave. (E/Burnside)
503-232-3555
navarreportland.blogspot.com
Weekends 9:30 a.m. to 4:30 p.m.
$12–$15 (Visa, MasterCard, American Express, no checks)

Navarre blows my mind. Just trying to describe it is hard. It's definitely not what I call a breakfast place, or even a weekend brunch place. According to its website, it serves 50+ wines by the glass, offers small and large plates of food "based in Italian, French and Spanish origin," and "works with a CSA (47th Avenue Farms)…the specials are based on what is delivered that week along with the whims and interests of the staff."

It was also, according to the *Oregonian*, the Restaurant of the Year in 2009. And that's where the fun starts. For one thing, the article announcing such has disappeared from the paper's website, so good luck reading it. And the paper has since laid off both of its main restaurant reviewers—unrelated, but adding to the chaos. The award set off a frenzy of discussion on foodie websites, where Navarre had been universally written off years before, panned for inconsistent, mediocre food and poor service. A 2009 book called *Fearless Critic: Portland Restaurant Guide* also trashed it.

To all this, Navarre's fans say things like, "I love how the menu changes all the time," and "Sure, some things don't work out, but that happens if you're tied to the produce calendar, and at least they're honest. It's like having dinner at a friend's house." As a long-time admirer of the Grateful Dead, who were capable of awful nights, I recognize the outlines of this argument: it's love or hate, depending entirely on taste. The *Oregonian* seemed to be rewarding Navarre for sticking to its principles and keeping things affordable in a recession. A lot of folks think there is better, more consistent food elsewhere. It's an argument with no solution.

So, what is brunch like there? For one thing, uncrowded—perhaps because many folks assume it's fancy and expensive, and many others hate it. The décor is pretty casual, with cookbooks all over the place and jars of pickled ingredients lining shelves. You get your own coffee, and the kitchen is right there for you to watch. Again, it's like eating at a friend's house.

They bring out a menu of small and large plates, and you check off what you want. Our group took a family-style attitude, going with a large plate of six Benedicts and a host of small plates. I don't recall what we had, but I've seen reference at Navarre to things like braised greens, lentils, sautéed mushrooms, hash browns, steak and eggs, beet-and-basil salad, and a veggie scramble. Some of the stuff we didn't know about, like a leek and potato terrine, which is like a layered, compressed pie baked in a pot. *Pain d'épices* is kind of a hardy French gingerbread.

I can tell you that we all enjoyed ourselves and liked the food. I can also tell you that we might be bumpkins. And, finally, I can say that the Breakfast Crew has never said to me, "Hey, we should go back to Navarre!" But it sure is an interesting place.

WAIT: None. **LARGE GROUPS:** Reservations recommended for parties of six or more **COFFEE:** Courier. **OTHER DRINKS:** Fresh juice, mimosas, Bloody Marys. **FEEL-GOODS:** They work with a local CSA farm. **HEALTH OPTIONS:** Tons of vegetarian and vegan options. **WIFI:** Yes.

NED LUDD

Hip
Retro with a capital R.
3925 NE MLK Blvd. (MLK)
503-288-6900
nedluddpdx.com
Brunch Sunday 9 a.m. to 2 p.m.
$12–$15 (all major cards, no checks)

Going to brunch at Ned Ludd felt like a culinary adventure to me. I am not a foodie in any way—and I don't mean that in the sense of, "I reject labels." I mean that generally my reactions to food range from "it was fine" to "wow" to "not so much." And sometimes I'm a complete smartass.

So, brunch at Ned Ludd. First, if you didn't know, Ned Ludd was a guy who may have smashed some looms in the eighteenth century (no one's sure why) and whose name was adopted by the Luddite Revolution, which was an uprising against the automation of industry in the nineteenth century. How this relates to Ned Ludd, the restaurant, is that the kitchen staff does all their cooking in an actual wood-fired oven. And you can watch them do it, too.

The decor is all about wood and vintage chandeliers and mismatched old-fashioned plates and silver. You'll also find stacked wood for the oven and various pickled items in jars. It's kind of an Old West feeling, which my friend and I agreed would probably work very well in the soft light of evening. At 10 a.m. on Sunday, it looks like a little more like the inside of a Simpler Times display at a theme park. Okay, that was smartassy, sorry.

Also, there was no line whatsoever for the hour-plus we were there.

The menu, which changes often, is simple and short, with a few little twists we couldn't identify. The one on the restaurant's website wasn't exactly the one we saw but gives you some idea: note the words *frisée, confit, tartine, harissa aioli,* and *Cotija.* One on level, it's super basic, but instead of "cheese plate" it's "farmstead cheese board, accompaniments." There's a Mac n' Mornay, Pork Coppa Steak and Eggs, and Creamed Greens, Brioche Toast, Eggs. It's single-oven cooking (there must be a stove involved somewhere?) with fresh ingredients and an artisan twist. I had to ask about the coppa ham and was told something that included "shoulder muscle," so being from Tennessee and understanding "pork shoulder," I went with that one. Chris got the Polenta with Pork Gravy, and before that we had the cheese board, which came with three types of cheese (she told me, but I can't remember the names, which I hardly caught in the first place) and some yummy, grainy bread. Also pickled apples, of which a little goes a long way.

A *Willamette Week* review of Ned Ludd's dinner used phrases like "briny counterpoint" and "the blackened yet still edible tips of the allium balancing out the caramelized sweetness of the bulb with a crackly bitterness." What I can tell you is that, had you just brought out my coppa, I would have said, "Mmmm, pork chops." They were little lean steaks—thin, super tender, lightly seasoned, and damn good. They came with two simple fried eggs and good bread, no jam. Also, there was no salt and pepper on the table. Chris's polenta-and-gravy was also good, but would not be confused with Jimmy Dean sausage gravy.

She had tea, and I had coffee poured from a French press. The server was cute and friendly and did a fine job, even as I made one annoying comment after another. Who was Ned Ludd? What's farro? Is that named for Rebecca De Mornay because it's hot? The bill with tip was $43.

I guess I'm supposed to give some kind of wrap-up impression here. First, we both thought it was a little pricey for what it was. That's not a real complaint, because I understand it's a Serious Food Place, not some random diner. And yes, I can be a buffoon, but there's a part of me that says, "Wait, I split some cheese and bread, then had pork chops and eggs with coffee, and it was over $20."

And it was good: not blow-my-mind good, but good, and interesting, and there's no wait. And for what it's worth, a good friend who's a real, self-admitted foodie, and also an author, says the same thing.

WAIT: None I've seen, but they take reservations for six or more. **LARGE GROUPS:** Up 12 in winter; up to 25 in summer. **COFFEE:** Heart. **OTHER DRINKS:** Full bar. **FEEL-GOODS:** They list nearly three dozen purveyors on the website. **HEALTH OPTIONS:** Nothing in particular. **WIFI:** Yes.

NEW DEAL CAFÉ

New/Kid Friendly
The paper, the kids, the dog, not much going on.
5250 NE Halsey Blvd. (NE/Hollywood)
503-546-1833
thenewdealcafe.com
Breakfast weekdays 7 a.m. to 4 p.m., weekends 8 a.m. to 4 p.m.
$7–$10 (Visa, MasterCard, Discover, no checks)

Close your eyes and try to locate Northeast 52nd and Halsey. What's around there? What's that neighborhood called?

When the New Deal Café opened in the spring of 2006, the *Portland Tribune* said it "will be a fine addition to this rather barren (except for houses) stretch of Halsey." Barren, they said—except for houses. As if houses don't count. I mean, nothing there but…people…just…living there.

I asked the staff what the neighborhood was called, and several of us had a little conference. We knew we were east of Lloyd District, south of Hollywood, south of Alameda, north of…whatever is south of there.

"It's Rose City," somebody said.

"But all of Portland is Rose City, right?"

And that's when it hit me. The New Deal Café is the local café in a perfectly generic, maybe a generically perfect, Portland neighborhood.

As my friend Jane and I worked through our meal, chatting with table neighbors and watching kids in the play area, this perfect-Portland thing became a theme. The décor is light and airy, a combination of wood tables (cozy!) and plastic chairs (modern!) splashed in happy, cheerful oranges and yellows and greens that make the place feel like a chip off the New

Seasons block.

The place is welcoming and cheerful, with high ceilings, plenty of light, fresh pastries under the glass, folks sipping self-serve coffee and surfing the WiFi, and a high percentage of customers who seem to know the staff. There's also a nice patio and a kids' play area. And cocktails.

The seasonal menu is written on a chalkboard above the counter. Keeping things grounded are a few classic scrambles—$8.50 with potatoes and toast or biscuit—and this being Portland, they use "all natural, cage-free eggs" (egg whites and tofu are also available). The Farm has mushrooms, peppers, onions, cheddar cheese, and meat/veggie sausage or tofu. The Veggie Garden comes with broccoli, corn salsa, garlic, mushrooms, and roasted pepper sauce; the Mediterranean has basil, feta, tomatoes, garlic, and kalamata olives. French toast. Pancakes. Biscuits and Veggie Gravy. A Breakfast Sammich and a Burrito.

Then there are the progressive, good-idea side dishes, all about $3: a single pancake, some sausage, coconut or regular oatmeal, a biscuit, some potatoes, a piece of French toast…a peanut butter and jelly sandwich! You have to love a place where folks can get a PB&J for three bucks. We liked the food a lot, and it showed up quickly. The French toast was made with rustic white bread (wholesome!) and done old school: crisp on the outside and eggy throughout (Mom!).

Speaking of good ideas, at New Deal, if you're eating with Poochie, you're close to Normandale Park, which has the ever-popular leash-free zone. So of course New Deal has a daily dog treat special. Such a perfectly Portland place!

What would you expect from a neighborhood café, especially when it's in a neighborhood that's named for a city known for good ideas and being a great place to live?

WAIT: Little to none. **LARGE GROUPS:** Probably not the best place. **COFFEE:** Stumptown. **OTHER DRINKS:** Espresso, juice, Tao of Tea, beer, mimosas, kombucha. **FEEL-GOODS:** Cage-free eggs, preference for local and organic and "natural." **HEALTH OPTIONS:** Tofu, egg whites available; vegan options (ask server). **WIFI:** Yes.

OLD WIVES' TALES

New/Veggie/Kiddie

Veggie-family-wholesome goes mainstream.

1300 E Burnside St. (E Burnside)

503-238-0470

oldwivestalesrestaurant.com

Sunday through Thursday 8 a.m. to 8 p.m., Friday and Saturday 8 a.m. to 9 p.m.

$8–$15 (all major cards, checks)

When it comes to rating what the public thinks of a restaurant, it's best to approach it the way figure skating is judged: throw out the highest and lowest scores, then average what's left.

In the case of Old Wives' Tales, that venerable veggie-friendly, family-friendly mainstay at the finally-rebuilt intersection of 12th, Burnside, and Sandy, what you have left is this: a place with lots of room, a kids' play area, a quiet room in the back, a soup and salad bar that's host to a very famous Hungarian mushroom soup, a massive menu filled with wholesome cooking, dozens of vegetarian and vegan options, and food that few people consider real exciting and some consider overrated.

Even folks who like Old Wives' Tales, and there are plenty of them, use words like *predictable* and *old-fashioned*. Folks who don't like it say it lacks flavor, is overpriced, and has all the charm of a Denny's. Vegetarians and vegans seem to appreciate the diversity of choices but think the food is often better elsewhere. Do with all of that what you will.

I dined there once with the Play Group, five moms and six kids who go out once a week. When I arrived early and told the host what was coming, he said, "Great!" He actually seemed excited, then put us in a big room next to the kids' playroom, all the while telling me how wonderful it is to get the kids out for a wholesome meal. With quilts on the wall, wood tables and chairs all around, and several kids already playing in the playroom, the place did feel homey.

It is also big. If you're looking for something cozy and charming, this isn't it. If, on the other hand, there are a dozen of you or you're dining with kids, Old Wives' Tales was made for you. Also, if you like peace and quiet, make your way to the Classical Music Dining Room in back, past the restrooms.

My take on the food is the same as the place: it's just the kind of stuff a bunch of old wives would come up with. They'd want the kids to have space and the grown-ups to have peace, they'd want to use healthy ingredients but not necessarily get it straight from local farmers (too pricey), and they'd try to cater to everybody's tastes and dietary restrictions.

The Play Group gave points on the kiddie stuff: a large menu in the $1–$4 range for standards like mac and cheese, applesauce, and a PB&J sandwich. "Someone gets it," one mom said.

When we were done, there was some sticker shock (I spent $14.50 with tip) as well as agreement there had been no real *wow* dish, except maybe the pancake with a mountain of whipped cream and fresh strawberries. So although I don't give ratings to restaurants, it's safe to say that if it were in the Olympics, Old Wives' Tales would finish and get polite applause, but probably not a medal.

WAIT: Not bad; they also take reservations. **LARGE GROUPS:** Absolutely. **COFFEE:** Organic Portland Roasting. **OTHER DRINKS:** Tazo and Stash teas, espresso, beer, and Oregon wines, soy and rice milk. **FEEL-GOODS:** Natural chicken and wild seafood. **HEALTH OPTIONS:** Ninety percent of the menu is gluten-free; they handle (and label) any allergy or dietary restriction you can imagine. **WIFI:** Yes.

OLYMPIC PROVISIONS

Hip/New/Weekend
With a nod of approval from Italy.
107 SE Washington (SE/Inner)
503-954-3663
1632 NW Thurman (NW)
503-894-8136
olympicprovisions.com
Weekends 10 a.m. to 3 p.m.
$12–$14 (all major cards, no checks)

Okay, let me start by explaining the tagline above. I have this Italian friend, Silvio. Total snob about food. Or, at least, he insists that it be good and serious; otherwise he dismisses it completely. I saw him once, at a café in Greve, Chianti, almost break his plate by throwing down a spoon in disgust…after tasting the olive oil.

When I visited him once and brought along a gift of Finocchiona salami from Olympic Provisions (with garlic, black pepper, and fennel), he nodded his approval, and then ate more than usual.

Point is, Olympic does some very serious things with meat. This will be clear from the display that greets you when you enter their Northwest location, in particular. It is a bank of yumminess. Over at the southeast location, you'll likely notice first the wall of wine, even more than the flashing *Meat* sign, the hams hanging behind the window, the high ceilings, the east-facing, sun-filled windows, or the impossibly cute staff.

Both locations are a little generic looking on the outside, and really out of the way. You're unlikely to just drive by either of them, and in fact I rarely meet somebody who has eaten there. But when I think back on all the meals I ate for this edition of the book—and the number is embarrassing—the plate of food that springs to mind first, and makes me feel all warm and happy, is the Kielbasa Hash from Olympic Provisions. I'll do my best here, but really, just go get one.

Start with perfectly sized and roasted Yukon gold potatoes. Add oyster mushrooms, also perfect. Then kielbasa. Then bacon lardons. And what's a lardon? I asked the chef, Colin Stafford, the same thing, and this is what he told me: The lardon is probably the absolutely most quintessential French ingredient. It is bacon that is cut substantially thicker than you would if you were going to crisp it up for a slice of bacon—so probably a quarter-inch thick, at least. You cut it into long slabs, and you cut those slabs into perfect squares. Then you put those in the oven or sauté them in a pan until they are slightly rendered and still tender.

You want one now, don't you? But wait, there's more! We haven't even added the onion confit (cooked in butter), frisée (a slightly bitter lettuce that doesn't wilt), and a poached egg. It is…well, it was my favorite breakfast dish in 2013, for whatever that's worth. And when the woman at the next table bit into hers, she said "oh my god" loud enough for about 10 people to hear it.

And it's far from the only good thing on their menu. They do a Benedict with their own Sweetheart Ham, and also do versions with spinach, biscuit-bacon-sausage gravy, and steak and arugula. And there's a Ploughman's Platter with two kinds of salami, pork terrine, cheese, pickled egg, bread, and a glass of draught beer! There's also a "classic breakfast" with, that's right, two meats, as well as a brioche French toast with orange butter. You can add spiced apples and whipped cream to that, if you want.

In fact, you can do whatever you want. I'm leaving right now to get something to eat at Olympic Provisions.

WAIT: A little. **LARGE GROUPS:** Yes, but make reservations. **COFFEE:** Stumptown. **OTHER DRINKS:** Signature Bloody Mary, breakfast cocktails. **FEEL-GOODS:** All meats sourced locally. **HEALTH OPTIONS:** Eh. **WIFI:** Yes.

TOP HASHCAPADE (SEE PAGE 301)

THE ORIGINAL

Weekend/Classy
So much fuss about a fancy diner.
300 SW 6th Ave. (Downtown)
503-546-2666
originaldinerant.com
Weekdays 6:30 a.m. to 11 a.m., weekends 7:30 a.m. to 2 p.m.
$13–$15 (all major cards, no checks)

It doesn't seem that The Original has been open long enough for folks to say, "It ain't what it used to be." But it ain't. And that may be a good thing. They started out claiming they served "evolved American cuisine," which was kind of like saying, "Please make fun of us." At one point they had a burger on a buttered and grilled Voodoo Doughnut. There was also a lobster corn dog. And the media descended on it.

The *New York Times* called it "a super-designy restaurant that wants you to think it's just a hipster diner." The *Mercury* followed up with "gimmicky, showy, and plagued with problems." With the blood now in the water, nobody would be outdone. *Willamette Week*'s review headline was "The diner is ironic. The pain is real." And the *Oregonian* wondered, "When you make a fried bologna sandwich with shallot mayonnaise, are you actually making it something more nuanced and sophisticated than a fried bologna sandwich?"

Looking at the menu today, you might think you walked into the wrong place. Now The Original has much less "evolved" cuisine, whatever that even meant. The twists that remain are much more low-key, like a French toast named for Elvis and featuring bacon, banana mousse, and peanut butter sauce. Or the Put a (Fried) Bird On It option: add a fried chicken breast to any griddle items for $4.

It's still something of a themed place, the theme being "a diner somewhere on the road in the 1950s." I, too, was at first put off by the super-designy nature of the place, and it was obviously an expensive place to put in. I suspect maybe the restaurant is aiming for tourists and businesspeople staying at the Marriott upstairs. But that would be if you think "normal" Portlanders don't eat at themed places like this. Evidence throughout this book (see Broder and Screen Door) suggests otherwise.

Elsewhere on the menu, you'll find both a classic and crab Benedict ($12-14), a burrito, chicken-fried steak, seven omelet/scrambles, and a handful of basics like biscuits and gravy and steak and eggs. On the weekends their brunch menu adds waffles, burgers, and salads. At all times there's also oatmeal, granola, smoothies, and half a dozen cocktails.

Maybe you're wondering, what's the big deal with all that? To which I say: Exactly. Forget the goofy past and go find out for yourself.

WAIT: Only for large groups. **LARGE GROUPS:** With notice. **COFFEE:** Stumptown. **OTHER DRINKS:** Espresso, juice, shakes, malts, full bar. **FEEL-GOODS:** None. **HEALTH OPTIONS:** A few things for vegetarians and vegans; house-made gluten-free bread **WIFI:** Yes.

ORIGINAL HOTCAKE & STEAK HOUSE

Old School
Family by day, circus by night.
1102 SE Powell Blvd. (SE/Inner)
503-236-7402
hotcakehouse.com
Breakfast served 24 hours
$7–$12 (Visa, MasterCard, no checks)

Saturday, 1:15 a.m. I haven't seen 1:15 a.m. since I quit drinking. I stumble out of the Crystal Ballroom, dazed. It's finally time to go to the Hotcake House. Some things have to be seen in the middle of the night.

I pull into the lot, see a few bikers, and watch as a drunk couple staggers to a car…and doesn't drive off. Well.

My God, there's a line out the door! I join it and look around: prom kids. Another drunk couple; she's draped over him, asking if he remembers their first date. Zombie-looking dudes are coming out of the kitchen with steak and eggs, massive stacks of hotcakes, and piles of hash browns…at 1:30? Black-clad teen boys in a booth. A guy at a table telling two women about somebody screwin' him over. Every now and then he gets a little loud and profane, and the rest of the place goes quiet.

Are those three girls at the head of the line *still* ordering? I've been here 10 minutes already. My ears hurt.

There's a woman next to me in line, and an old guy ahead of us waves at me, points at me, then points at her, then *licks his lips.* She and I exchange a nervous glance.

The cashier is giving the three chicks a dumbfounded look. She isn't getting one word of whatever they're saying. I just realized one of the guys in a tux with a horrible red tie is not a guy.

It's now 1:35. I do some math: At 2:15 I'm either gonna be here, waiting for my food…or in bed after taking a shower. I bail. On the car radio, Tom Petty is singing "Breakdown," and I realize I shouldn't be awake at this hour.

* * *

Thursday, 9:30 a.m. I walk in and go right up to the counter. The specials, on sticky notes, are cinnamon rolls, Polish sausage, biscuits and gravy, and smoked pork chops. The menu, on a board under "Peter and Cheree Welcome You to the Hotcake House," is a tour of Americana: steaks, eggs, ham, bacon, sausage, beef patties, country-fried steak, waffles, hotcakes, minced ham and eggs, corned beef hash. Pretty much everything is under $10. For $9, you can get three eggs with your choice of meat or corned beef hash *and* two 'cakes or hash browns or toast!

I order the blueberry waffle ($6.75), get some coffee, and grab a seat in a booth next to a guy who's singing along with Jimi Hendrix on the jukebox while playing Here Comes the Airplane to get his little daughter to eat. I see folks involved in friendly, multitable conversations and pictures of the Little League teams the place sponsors, and it occurs to me that this is one of the few Portland places where I've seen blacks and whites eating breakfast together. The cashier is wearing a gray ponytail and tie-dyed bellbottoms.

I decide that while the Hotcake House's evening vibe is something that every Portlander should see…once….I definitely like its friendly daytime persona a lot better. Then I dig into my hotcakes.

WAIT: Up to half an hour from about 10 p.m. to 3 a.m. on weekends. **LARGE GROUPS:** During the day, sure. **COFFEE:** Self-serve Farmer Brothers. **OTHER DRINKS:** Tea, juice, milk, soda. **FEEL-GOODS:** Sometimes they have a security guard! **HEALTH OPTIONS:** Eat here during the day. **WIFI:** No.

ORIGINAL PANCAKE HOUSE

Old School	
It's like Mickey Mantle is still hitting homers.	
8601 SW 24th Ave. (SW/Inner)	
503-246-9007	
originalpancakehouse.com	
Wednesday through Sunday 7 a.m. to 3 p.m.	
$15–$20 (cash and checks only)	

Maybe it's the tiny wooden booths. Or the community table. Or the regulars who, when the place opens, have a newspaper and their favorite dish waiting on their tables. Or the traditional, shared misery of waiting in the lobby.

All I know is I'm in love with the Original Pancake House, and I'm not alone. I also know that it's not of this era. It's like the *Prairie Home Companion* of Portland breakfasts, with its old-world charm that steadfastly refuses modern trends like credit cards and good coffee. Just ask folks about it sometime; you'll either get a crinkled nose and a comment such as, "What, wait all that time and pay all that money for *pancakes*?" Or, you'll get kind of a warm-glow smile and a story about eating there with Grandpa.

Pancakes and coffee will set you back about $15 with a tip. But these aren't your ordinary pancakes (warning: highly biased remarks ahead). For one thing, there are 14 kinds: buttermilk, buckwheat, potato, sourdough flapjacks (pause here while I enjoy a warm glow), 49er flapjacks, Swedish, blueberry, bacon, banana, Hawaiian, Georgia pecan, coconut, silver dollar pancakes, and wheat germ. There are also pigs in a blanket, sourdough French toast, strawberry waffles, Danish Kijafa Cherry Crepes, and the

twin signatures: the Apple Pancake (a steaming mass of Granny Smith apples and cinnamon glaze) and the Dutch Baby (a baked bowl shape of eggy pancake pleasure with whipped butter, lemon, and powdered sugar).

Plenty of other options are on the menu—another half dozen waffles and types of meat, seven omelets, oatmeal, cream of wheat—but that's like saying *A Prairie Home Companion* has comedy sketches and musical guests. Does anyone even remember those things? I don't, and I love that show.

My friend Craig and I consider it a special occasion to go there, mainly because of the prices. But that adds a certain flair to the occasion: we're deciding where to go, then the Pancake House comes up, and we get all excited, like a couple of little kids. Deciding what to have is an excruciating ordeal for me, because half my mouth is filled with sweet teeth, and to pick one kind of pancake is to eliminate so many others. I usually get the sourdough flapjacks, which are so sweet I catch a buzz off them. Throw in a side of bacon, coffee, and a tip, and I've had myself a $20 smile-fest.

That's a lot; I don't deny it. I am also thoroughly biased and consider $20 worth it every now and then. And the OPH is a chain, but the one on Barbur is the *original* Original Pancake House, opened in 1953. From there, a chain of some 100 places has blossomed across the country. And none other than the James Beard Foundation gave it an America's Regional Classics award. You can argue with me and thousands of other Portlanders if you'd like, but I don't see how you can disagree with James Beard. Or the sourdough flapjacks.

WAIT: Nearly constant, and up to 45 minutes on weekends. **LARGE GROUPS:** With notice. **COFFEE:** Boyd's "special house blend." **OTHER DRINKS:** Hot chocolate, tea, fresh-squeezed juice. **FEEL-GOODS:** The website says it uses "93 score butter, pure 36% whipping cream, fresh grade AA eggs, hard wheat unbleached flour, and our own recipe sourdough starter." **HEALTH OPTIONS:** You don't have to eat it all. **WIFI:** No.

OVERLOOK FAMILY RESTAURANT

Old School
Working classy.
1332 N Skidmore (N/Inner)
503-288-0880
facebook.com/OverlookRestaurantLounge
Monday through Saturday 5 a.m. to 10:30 p.m., Sunday 6 a.m. to 9 p.m.
$7–$10 (all major cards, no checks, ATM on-site)

The first thing I heard about the Overlook was that it was "a place for contractors and alcoholics." Considering this remark came from a good friend who's a contractor and a recovering alcoholic, it wasn't an insult—though it hardly captures everything the Overlook is about.

When I got around to checking out the breakfast at the Overlook, two people from the Breakfast Crew showed up: Tom, who said he used to go there when he was a contractor, and R., another recovering alcoholic. Coincidence? Well, it was also the only time in the research for this book—we're talking maybe 250 meals—that professional basketball was ever discussed. The Overlook is a bedrock, working-class, fill-you-up restaurant with staff who are total pros, more food options than just about any place in town, and the ability to handle kids and large groups. And you can damn near eat yourself to death for $10.

I walked in and saw one of those classic dessert cases right inside the door. I counted 11 cakes, eight pies, two puddings, and a custard. We sat down at a table with brown–and–white coffee mugs, and above us were a Keno screen and a high-definition TV showing Fox News (this ain't your hipster, lefty Portland).

And the menu! One online reviewer joked that it was so big it had won several literary awards. Eggs Benedict, eight omelets (including a taco version), eight farm-style breakfasts, and eight specialties. Pancakes, plain and Belgian waffles, and four kinds of French toast. Two versions of steak and eggs are $9.50 (top sirloin) and $10.50 (New York Steak), including toast, jam, and pancakes or hash browns. And heck, for $2.25 they'll cover anything with their sausage gravy, thick with big chunks of sausage. I could go on.

Tom, for old times' sake, was wearing a Carhartt shirt and ordered the Monte Cristo: a triple-decker French toast sandwich with grilled ham, cheese, and egg that came with a serrated steak knife stuck through it. We called it the Sandwich of Death. I got the cinnamon roll French toast, a mess of sweetness I could barely finish. R. got the half order of biscuits and gravy and marveled that anyone would ever eat the whole one. (We teased him with, "Well, maybe if you started drinking again…")

We talked sports and jobs and women. Other diners were families, older couples, businesspeople with notebooks, somebody who may have slept outside the night before, and some kids from the University of Portland who looked like they were on an anthropological field trip. And, yes, some contractors.

Don't miss the lounge, by the way. I was there at 9 a.m. and the waiter was serving a couple of highballs to two guys watching golf on one of the many televisions. The lounge is lifted straight from the 1960s—and I don't mean the hippie 1960s, either. I'm talking about caged-in gas fireplaces with seats branching out from them, wood paneling, green seats, slot machines, and faux stained-glass windows.

So, my alcoholic friend's first report on the Overlook wasn't all wrong or all right.

WAIT: Maybe a little on weekends. **LARGE GROUPS:** No problem. **COFFEE:** Boyd's. **OTHER DRINKS:** Stash teas, milkshakes, cocktails in the bar. **FEEL-GOODS:** Uh, no. **HEALTH OPTIONS:** Egg substitute available. **WIFI:** No.

PAMBICHE

New/Hip/Weekend
Music! Colors! Options!
2811 NE Glisan St. (NE/Burnside)
503-233-0511
pambiche.com
Weekends 9 a.m. to 2 p.m.
$10–$16 (Visa, MasterCard; no checks; discount for cash)

I am one of the few people in Portland who often doesn't really get Pambiche. I have always felt underwhelmed by their food—though I completely understand that I may just be an ignoramus. In fact, there's no doubt I am, especially when it comes to Cuban food. All my "expertise" comes from the fact that I've been to Miami a couple times and eaten it there. My reaction was always a big *wow*. I love the *bistec* (steak), the sandwiches, the coffee, everything.

Then I go to Pambiche, and the bright Caribbean colors are there. The music is there. The voodoo priestess is there with her cigar. And the food makes me go…eh. Seems like it lacks zip.

Clearly, this is a minority opinion. People love Pambiche, and I don't think they're nuts for it. Although the Spanish names sound exotic, what you're often getting is a Cuban twist on something you're used to seeing: Huevos a la Cubana, for example, is a couple of fried eggs with your choice of meat (or vegetarian) plus rice, black beans, avocado, and a side of yummy, sweet fried plantains. The Torrejas con Frutas, advertised as "Cuban toast," is made with thick slices of baguette thoroughly soaked in creamy egg batter, grilled in sweet butter, topped with toasted almond slices, and served with a pile of tropical fruit. All very well done. But the capper for us was the cane syrup, made in-house. It's lighter than maple syrup in both flavor and texture, but somehow even sweeter, and it just blew our minds. Folks at our table were wondering where to get it, how to make it, everything.

Interesting and traditional Cuban dishes also abound. Pisto Manchego is a pile of chorizo, smoked ham, creole pork, shrimp, potatoes, asparagus, pimentos, and petits pois with an olive oil sofrito sauce. (A similar, meatless version, the Revoltillo a la Jardinera, features roasted peppers—but it's darn near the only option for vegetarians.) The Tamal en Hoja (creole pork in red sauce, encased in corn, yucca, and plantain masa) was a favorite as well.

But there's one thing that's becoming more and more clear to me: their sweet stuff rocks.

Start with the pastries. The best of them are the fruit-filled and sugar-coated *empanaditas*, which on any day may have mango, guava and cheese, pineapple, papaya, or dulce de leche. And we also fought over the Toronja Pound Cakes (grapefruit). Just *saying* the rest of them gets me worked up: semisweet coconut bread with ginger and pineapple, cream muffins with chunks of mango, sweet potato spiced cake with guarapo (sugar cane) icing, sweet bread filled with peanuts and baked in caramel. This lineup changes regularly, but they're all amazing. Wash them down with Café Cubano and you'll be ready to fight a revolution.

Maybe I'm just all about the coffee and sweets at Pambiche. No harm in that. It's a cool place, and having a favorite for sweets, caffeine, colors, and vibe is a good thing. Especially if it moves me toward the majority opinion—and away from being an ignoramus.

WAIT: Not bad, with plenty of cover outside. **LARGE GROUPS:** Get there early. **COFFEE:** Stumptown. **OTHER DRINKS:** Fabulous fruit smoothies and shakes, espresso, fruit juice, sugarcane lemonade, rum cocktails, wine. **FEEL-GOODS:** None in particular. **HEALTH OPTIONS:** None in particular. **WIFI:** No.

PAPA HAYDN

Weekend/Classy
Faded glory, youthful beauty.
701 NW 23rd Ave. (NW)
503-228-7317
5829 SE Milwaukie Ave. (Sellwood)
503-232-9440
papahaydn.com
Sunday 10 a.m. to 3 p.m.
$14–$17 (Visa, MasterCard, American Express, no checks)

How many times have you driven down Northwest 23rd Avenue? Hundreds? How many times have you gone by Papa Haydn and been wowed by the youthful beauty of the evening crowd? How many times has someone said to you, "That place has amazing desserts"?

Now, how many times have you actually eaten there? Did you know there's one in Sellwood? And did you know both locations serve Sunday brunch?

If you said "often" and "yes," I am convinced you're in the minority. In fact, I lived here for years before I went in there at all, and made it more than a year beyond the publishing of this book before I had a clue they serve brunch. But I am in my 40s and don't make much money. I'm pretty sure this means I'm too old for the dessert crowd at Papa Haydn and too young and poor for the brunch scene.

I went to the one in Sellwood and found it to be a lovely place with old-fashioned food and the feel of a country club. And trust me, I grew up going to country clubs. The average age of the clientele was pushing 60, the music was Sinatra and Crosby, the tablecloths were white and pressed, the staff was young and very polite, and they served quiche. They even have the nice garden patio and everything.

As for the food, I can tell you two things. One, nobody has ever said to me—and I'm known as the Portland Breakfast Guy—that I should check out brunch at Papa Haydn. Maybe that's the age thing. The other is that just about every online review I could find offered some variation of "Great desserts; otherwise forget it."

I thought the food was pretty good, actually. I had a strata, which is sort of an eggy bread pudding, like a frittata but fluffier. It had sausage and fennel in it, and we all agreed that it was tied for Best Dish with Jerry's Garden Omelet, which had a fine, smoky flavor mainly due to some mushrooms.

The rest of the menu (which changes pretty regularly) is straight-forward Portland brunch stuff: biscuits and gravy, pancakes, Dungeness crab omelet, a few Benedicts, French toast, Monte Cristo, smoked salmon omelet, and a waffle. We thought the griddle stuff didn't live up to the place's reputation for sweets. The waffle was quite firm—dry, really—but with enough syrup and fruit compote, it was decent. The accompanying fruit was not terribly fresh. Some baked goods that came out were tasty: blueberry muffin, brioche buns, a selection of cheese sticks.

All of this reminds me of visiting Grandma. She's old and sweet, but she ain't exactly cutting edge, and you like going to her place because you liked it as a kid, and you're polite toward her, so you don't men-tion—or care, maybe—that her food isn't really that great anymore. Maybe it never was. But back then you had less experience with good food, and besides, it was Grandma. And it still is.

WAIT: Maybe a little, but they take reservations. **LARGE GROUPS:** With notice. **COFFEE:** Caffè Umbria. **OTHER DRINKS:** Espresso, wine, beer, a signature Bloody Mary, and other cocktails—the Bellini is very popular. **FEEL-GOODS:** Local ingredients. **HEALTH OPTIONS:** A few things for vegetarians. **WIFI:** Yes.

PARADOX CAFÉ

Hip/Veggie	
The hippies took over the diner!	
3439 SE Belmont Ave. (SE/Belmont)	
503-232-7508	
paradoxorganiccafe.com	
Weekdays 8 a.m. to 4 p.m., weekends 8 a.m. to 5 p.m. (hours change seasonally)	
$8–$11 (Visa, MasterCard, Discover, no checks)	

I wasn't particularly kind to Paradox in the first edition of this book. I kind of covered my ass by making fun of myself and saying that I might just be an idiot. And I hung it on various friends, reporting that they all shrugged at the experience. But the truth is, I thought it was a dirty place with bad food. I just didn't know if it was me, them, or vegetarian food.

Well, now they have expanded, cleaned up, and improved on the food considerably. They also have AC and take cards, which is nice. I may still be an idiot, but I like the Paradox now.

The website used to state the cafe's philosophy as "wholesome common meals at a fair price…seasonal organic produce, organic grains, local and organic tofu and tempeh, free range eggs and hormone free meats…local co-ops…breads, sauces and desserts are mostly dairy and egg free… maple or fructose for our sweeteners." Now it just says, "Great food prepared fresh for your mind and body." Let's hear it for simplicity!

The place opened in 1993, and I suspect it was one of the first mostly vegetarian places in town. As the *Willamette Week* has said, "Customers learned to expect a little grease here, a little filth there (but) cheap and easy comfort food."

By 2013 the menu offered more than a dozen savory items plus a pile of sweets and sides. The savories include down-home options like a scramble with seasoned potatoes or brown rice, topped with steamed vegetables and your choice of one egg, tempeh, or tofu. For $1, you can also get this "curry style," which is mixed with Asian curry sauce, raisins, and toasted nuts. There's also Holy Frijoles (a tostada with chili, topped with egg or tofu), Country Comfort (a basic combo with biscuit and almond gravy), a burrito, and the Spit Fire Scramble (Mexican chipotle sausage, caramelized onions, sweet red and jalapeño peppers scrambled with seasoned tofu, and spinach, served with a dollop of sour cream and seasoned potatoes). They say they can "veganize" anything that's not already vegan.

I had the Paradox Benedict (herb and onion bread with veggie sausage and your choice of tofu or egg, topped with fresh tomatoes and "Tree Hugger hollandaise sauce," served with seasoned red potatoes), which was probably too salty but at least had some action to it, and was quite filling. The taters were awesome. My friend had the corn cake special, with bananas and walnuts in the cakes and strawberries on top. Outstanding.

By the way, neither of us finished our meal. Add two cups of coffee and a nice tip, and we got out of there for $27.

So maybe Paradox is just a little neighborhood place with a lot of cheap, healthy food, much of which happens to be vegetarian and vegan. And now that it's bigger, cleaner, and better, I'm happy to have good things to say about it.

WAIT: Medium on weekends. **LARGE GROUPS:** No more than six, I think. **COFFEE:** Portland Roasting. **OTHER DRINKS:** Ohqua teas, Columbia Gorge juices, and Blue Sky sodas. **FEEL-GOODS:** Local ingredients, free-range eggs, hormone-free meats, seasonal produce, organic Mountain Rose Herbs. **HEALTH OPTIONS:** Many dishes are vegan, vegetarian, gluten-free, dairy-free, etc. **WIFI:** Yes.

PATTIE'S HOME PLATE CAFE

Mom & Pop/Old School

Nineteen forty-seven, downtown, somewhere in America.

8501 N Lombard St. (N/Outer)

503-285-5507

facebook.com/PattiesHomePlate

Monday through Saturday 8 a.m. to 8 p.m., Sunday 9 a.m. to 8 p.m.

$6–$8 (all major cards, no checks)

Back in about 2006, when I started out to write this book, just about the first place I visited was Pattie's Home Plate Cafe in St. Johns. When I entered the first time, four guys at the counter stopped talking, looked up at me, gave me the head-to-toe, then went back to their coffee. I felt like I was on the road!

I went back in 2013 and, for some reason, thought it might have changed. After about a minute inside, I asked myself, why would it change? For one thing, it hasn't changed in the multiple decades it's been there, so why start now? And for another thing, we need places like Pattie's! Every neighborhood needs a place like this, where the staff and regulars are old friends, the food is nice and simple and cheap, and even if you've never been there you'll be made to feel welcome.

Patti's is in the middle of downtown St. Johns, and when you walk in, you couldn't be farther away from what many people think of as Portland: jogging paths, urban planning, streetcars, lattes, and so on. Some of the folks in Patti's look like they make it down to Portland only once a year or so and couldn't imagine why they'd go any more than that.

Whole families were coming in, three generations at a time. Men with

canes. Women in slippers. People speaking Spanish. A referee in uniform, and people asking which game he was working that day. Camouflage hats, flannel shirts, and Cat Diesel baseball caps.

And what they're eating is exactly what you'd expect from reading this far; just contemplate the words Home Plate Cafe. Do you need to know more? Do you expect Asiago cheese and asparagus omelets? I sure hope not. Ninety percent of the menu is some combination of eggs, sausage, bacon, ham, bread, potatoes, peppers, cheese, and pancakes.

The menu itself is very much a small-town affair, with ads for a pizza restaurant, a car parts place, and even pro wrestling! And a note for visitors: "When in St. Johns, you will want to see the St. Johns Bridge."

The food was filling and not pricey. While I ate, I watched the server greet people with lines like, "Well, it's a regular family reunion in here today!" I watched the man behind the counter cook while trading barbs with the old guys. In the store in the back, I saw wigs, yarn, picture frames, bird feeders, costumes (in March), costume jewelry, fish lures, plastic flowers, you name it.

By the way, this place even got a little media love recently. There was an episode of *Portlandia* that took place entirely in line for brunch, and Ed Begley Jr. played the owner of an ignored café that the line was forming right in front of. Well, the desired place was in Woodlawn (see Ps and Qs Market, page 202), and the "please check us out" place was Pattie's.

And you know? Sometimes I'd rather have Pattie's than whatever the latest and greatest place is.

WAIT: Can't imagine. **LARGE GROUPS:** Call ahead for more than eight. **COFFEE:** Folgers. **OTHER DRINKS:** Old-fashioned hand-packed milkshakes, juice in frosted mugs. **FEEL-GOODS:** The folks. **HEALTH OPTIONS:** Juice in frosted mugs! **WIFI:** Yes.

PETITE PROVENCE

Weekend/Classy
"Our server is from Marseilles, and he's hot!"
4834 SE Division St. (SE/Division) and 1824 NE Alberta St. (NE/Alberta)
503-233-1121 and 503-284-6564
provence-portland.com
Breakfast daily 7 a.m. to 2 p.m.
$13–$17 (all major cards, no checks)

"I would go 10 miles for these pastries; they're better than sex."

I won't divulge the name of the person who uttered that remark (her boyfriend might read this), but I will say it was typical of the Breakfast Crew's trip to Petite Provence. It was Beth who let me know that our server was from Marseilles, then added, "and he's hot!"

Yes, things got a little saucy for us at the fancy French place. In fact, just about every review I've read or heard includes something like, "The place was lovely, and my server was really cute and had a French accent."

People just seem to be in love with this place. Consider what the *Portland Tribune* had to say: "The perfect croissants are so light they nearly float; the buttery layers puff up against the flaky crunchy crust… and it's hard to get out of there without a pound cake, pumpernickel baguette or cutely decorated meringue." *Willamette Week* slipped past love and into lust, calling the croque monsieur sandwich "almost pornographic…oozing with Gruyère, butter and creamy béchamel." The *Tribune*'s writer was also smitten by the "authentically snarky French-speaking staff" and their "silky accents." I'm just sayin'.

All the pastry delights will be waiting for you right inside the door, as will gilded mirrors, gold leaf, Impressionist art, lantern-style light fixtures, and of course the fleur-de-lis motif all over the walls and tables.

But it's still an American place, with its reasonable prices, large portions, and a big menu. At the low end, around $9, are the Berry French Toast and my favorite, the Risotto Cakes and Eggs.

The menu includes two hashes: corned beef and salmon (with smoked and cured salmon and a lemon dill sauce); the best omelet is the open-faced Colette with eggs coked in basil, topped with artichoke hearts, fresh tomatoes, and mozzarella. For sweets, the Banana French

Toast comes with white-chocolate crème anglaise and candied walnuts. Crepes are available during the week only.

The items we ate almost sent us into lovers' tangles. The La Provence Omelet with sausage was perfectly light and fluffy despite being loaded with sausage; the hollandaise on the Benedicts wasn't gooey like it is in a lot of places, but "light, with some bite," as someone chuckled. My friend Cheryl had pancakes with a crème brûlée sauce that tasted like honeysuckle and had the consistency of eggnog; I shamelessly dipped my multigrain pancakes in it, and when I wanted more, I started lightly stroking Cheryl's arm.

By then, Cheryl's boyfriend was giving me a look, so I switched to other passions: a run past the pastry counter for something to go. Hmmm, shall it be the cheese brioche, the almond brioche, the chocolate croissant, the Napoleon, the meringue cookie, the mousse cake, the orange éclair...

WAIT: Long on weekends after about 9 a.m. and sometimes even during the week. **LARGE GROUPS:** With notice. **COFFEE:** Nossa Familia. **OTHER DRINKS:** Espresso, Italian sodas, lemonade, full bar. **FEEL-GOODS:** You can flirt with French cuties. **HEALTH OPTIONS:** House-made gluten-free bread; many gluten-free options. **WIFI:** Yes.

TOP HASHCAPADE (SEE PAGE 301)

PINE STATE BISCUITS

Old School/Mom & Pop

Y'all come visit and have some biscuits!

2204 NE Alberta St. (NE/Alberta)

503-477-6605

pinestatebiscuits.com

(New location planned at SE 11th and Division at press time)

Open daily at 7 a.m.—closing times are Monday through Wednesday 3 p.m.,
Thursday and Sunday 11 p.m., Friday and Saturday 1 a.m.

$8–$10 (Visa, MasterCard, Discover, no checks)

When you're talking to Kevin Atchley, one of the owners of Pine State Biscuits, it's clear that he's a restaurant guy through and through. He politely gives credit to previous mentors, compliments all his vendors, and lovingly describes the eight-month process he and his partners went through with their "chef and foodie" friends to get just the right biscuit recipe. And then he'll drop something like this on you: "See that cabinet over the door, how it's facin' the kitchen? We're gonna put a TV set in there, and y'all ain't gonna know we're watchin' ACC basketball!"

Yes, Atchley is just as much a North Carolinian as he is a Portland foodie, and he and his partners—Brian Snyder and Walt Alexander, all Pine State transplants and NC State Wolfpack fans—have given the Portland breakfast scene something it never had before: a genuine biscuit kitchen.

Take this mix of old-style Southern goodness and modern restaurant professionalism, throw in some Portland foodie sensibility, and you have Pine State Biscuits. They built a following at the Portland Farmers Market with golden Creamtop Buttermilk Biscuits served with sausage or mushroom gravy, thick-cut bacon, fried chicken, eggs, grits, and preserves. Since going brick-and-mortar, they have upgraded to Portland institution.

Such was this following that within two weeks of the "soft" opening, the (now-closed) Belmont location was already doing the same amount of business as at the market: about 500 biscuits daily; but as Atchley says, "now we won't run out." Especially since they opened another location on Alberta Street in 2010. There, they won't run out of seating, either, with about 50 seats including an outdoor section. They also intend to serve alcohol there. And as I write this in spring 2013, they are planning a new place at SE 11th and Division.

Both locations are perfectly positioned to take advantage of the neighborhood feel; Division may get a little commuter rush, like Belmont used to. Just don't think of it as a regular restaurant. Each location is designed as a Carolina-style biscuit shack, with only a few tables. The idea is to eat it quick and keep moving, or just get something to go.

So, what's in this fabulous biscuit, anyway? Of course, Atchley won't tell. But he will say there's no shortening at all. There is some butter, but all the flakiness comes, he says, entirely from the baking technique. "We decided to do something a little more health oriented. We use very, very fresh ingredients, all perishable and sourced as close to home as possible. The inspiration is from North Carolina, but the ingredients are all from right around the greater Portland area."

To further tempt us, Atchley offers sweet tea and Cheerwine (a super sweet cherry soda from North Carolina), and he occasionally features country ham. "When all the true-blood North Carolinians come in and visit with us," Atchley says, "the first thing they say is, 'When are y'all gonna do country ham?'"

Country ham is a heavily salted, cured bacon Atchley admits is an acquired taste; what he has, on occasion, is ham from Johnson County, North Carolina, which has about 40 percent the usual salt content of a "real" country ham. "It's more of a domestic prosciutto," he says. Still, to many Portlanders it will seem awfully salty; that, of course, is what the sweet tea is for.

WAIT: Long on weekends. **LARGE GROUPS:** Wait will be longer. **COFFEE:** Stumptown and MadCap. **OTHER DRINKS:** Sweet tea and specialty sodas, hand-crafted chocolate milk made by a local chocolatier, cider **FEEL-GOODS:** Everything's local and fresh. **HEALTH OPTIONS:** Does "no shortening in the biscuits" count? **WIFI:** Yes.

PORTLAND FARMERS MARKET

Buffet/Veggie

Yuppies, farmers, and old hippies—and sometimes you can't tell 'em apart.

Portland State University (Downtown)

portlandfarmersmarket.org

Saturday 8:30 a.m. to 2 p.m. March through October,

9 a.m. to 2 p.m. November and December

$5 up to whatever you want to spend (pay with cash at the booths or

use a debit card to buy tokens to use throughout the market)

My friend Julia told me somebody at the farmer's market at Portland State made good breakfast burritos. So I thought, hey, that'd be cool: get something to eat and shop for produce. I mean, that's a farmers market, right?

Wrong, by a bunch! I was there an hour before I even found the burritos, and by then I wasn't hungry anymore. That's because I had been wandering around noshing on smoked salmon, strawberries, fresh bread, jam, peas, sausage and bacon right off the grill, carrots, cherries, apples, dried apple chips, and countless kinds of cheese. And that's just what they're giving away! You could absolutely graze your way through breakfast; this is *not* the farmers market my Mississippi grandparents took me to.

The market is enchanting: the baby Thai broccoli, Yukon gold potatoes, radishes, honey, dozens of berries made into jam, spelt bread, super scrumptious Hood strawberries, various kinds of cherries. And that's not to mention all the smiling, attractive, healthy-looking people selling the stuff. I could see myself turning into one of the people I saw pulling wagons with the tops of garlic and sweet onions and five kinds of lettuce sticking out.

For $20 (I showed restraint) I bought a 16-ounce organic coffee; an orange croissant that was pure heaven (sold by people who also had an Oregon croissant with almond paste, sugar coating, and marionberries); a French toast bread pudding with praline topping, maple syrup, and fresh strawberry slices; two pints of Hoods; two pints of sugar snap peas; and three sweet onions. The Hoods didn't last the day, and the peas and onions will soon be appearing in a wok near me.

Along the way several defining moments came to me. One was walking past a divine spread of organic greens and herbs and roots with sprawling bouquets of flowers across the way and suddenly smelling bacon being grilled—and then hearing somebody say, "Ah tell ya, once ya taste this h'yer bacon, it is *ovah*, ahmon tellya. You gawn *buy* some-a that there bacon." I was smelling pig and hearing Texas, and it was hell gettin' away from that booth.

Another such moment came while admiring different types of honey and a honeycomb-shaped candle carved out of beeswax, then noticing a jar filled with little crystals of bee pollen. After I made the requisite "not as good as A pollen" joke, I asked the bespectacled fellow behind the counter what's up with the pollen. He said people just eat it, then pointed to a little card that listed the nutritional qualities of bee pollen: it's 40 percent protein and rich in free amino acids, vitamins including B-complex and folic acid, and many other wonders. And how did he get it? He puts a filter on the door of a hive that's big enough for a bee with one piece of pollen but not two. When the bee arrives, it dumps one piece so it can enter the hive. How cool is that?

Finally, there was the moment sitting near the old-timey country fiddle band, watching all the people, when my friend Jean pointed out, correctly, that about one-third of the population we could see was between the ages of 1 and 2. With all those young couples getting those toddlers out of the house, and all the locally grown food, our overall impression of the place was fertility and bounty.

WAIT: Every stinkin' year until spring! **LARGE GROUPS:** Absolutely! **COFFEE:** All over the place. **OTHER DRINKS:** Espresso, juice, tea, you name it. **FEEL-GOODS:** The whole thing. **HEALTH OPTIONS:** Ditto. **WIFI:** Who cares?

PO'SHINES

Mom & Pop/Old School
At the intersection of food, church, and community.
8139 N Denver St. (N/Outer)
503-978-9000
poshines.com
Monday 7 a.m. to 3 p.m., Tuesday through Thursday to 8 p.m.,
Friday 10 p.m., Saturday 8 a.m. to 10 p.m.
$11–$13 (all major cards, no checks)

When I first ate at Po'shines, I wrote on my blog, "I may have found my next neighborhood." Kenton, centered around Interstate and Denver, has all the markings of the "next thing": old but nice homes, pedestrian-friendly streets, parks, a Max station, and a little commercial strip of a few blocks with some empty places for businesses to set up. And it's got a couple of breakfast places.

Kenton still has that grassroots feeling, as well, epitomized by Po'shines, which is part restaurant and part nonprofit, both of them run by a church. Here's what their website has to say: *Much of our profit goes back into the cafe and to our youth training program. As a part of the Teach me to Fish Organization we provide training and counseling to youth and young adults of our community who are in need of such services as job skills, life skills and GED preparedness. All of our regular employees volunteer their time, including our Chef and our Management Staff.*

Our mission is simple: feed the community and feed it well.

When I had the CEO and manager on my podcast, it became the finest half hour of my broadcast career. They were polite and reserved until, a few minutes in, I asked the CEO (also the minister next door at Celebration Tabernacle) about the food, and when he started in about sweet potatoes, catfish, and peach cobbler, his manager and (and nephew) shook his head, smiled, and said, "Oh, we're goin' to *church* now!" From then on, those two preached the gospel of soul food.

To see what they're talking about, get the Bayou Breakfast Burrito (spinach, onion, bell pepper, mushrooms, white beans, fresh herbs, and a four-cheese blend) and add the blackened catfish. Not many places in Portland have catfish (and the Po'shines folks won't say where they get it), but when it's good, fresh, and blackened, eating it can be a religious experience. I also once had chicken and waffles: three briny full wings fried with a little something spicy in the dark crust, sitting next to a pair of sturdy waffles that held up while I was eating the chicken and after I slathered them with syrup.

You can also get grits, fried okra, a creole omelet, chocolate or blueberry or plain pancakes, cornmeal waffles, and Chef Lorenzo's Louisiana Scramble, which is hash browns, bell peppers, onions, and diced tomatoes with your choice of bacon, ham, or sausage, topped with two scrambled eggs, cheese, and country gravy. Mercy!

The Southern flair is legit (the CEO/minister is from Louisiana), and so is the hospitality. The whole time I sat there, the staff was greeting customers like old friends, and there was some kind of little meeting happening among four people at a table. (When I drove by again the next day, the same four people were sitting at the same table.) There's a small kiddie area, a couple of sofas, jazz posters on the wall, and the biggest gumball machine you'll ever see.

Plan on spending a little time when you eat at Po'shines—not that they're slow, but because you just might want to settle in for a spell and visit with those nice folks.

WAIT: Maybe on Saturday. **LARGE GROUPS:** With notice. **COFFEE:** Portland Roasting. **OTHER DRINKS:** Juice, espresso, sweet tea, sorrel (hibiscus) sweet tea, and green tea. **FEEL-GOODS:** Locally sourced meats and fresh local produce. **HEALTH OPTIONS:** Decent vegetarian options. **WIFI:** Yes.

PODNAH'S PIT

Old School/Weekend
Git yer Texas on!
1625 NE Killingsworth St. (NE/Alberta)
503-281-3700
podnahspit.com
Breakfast weekends 9 a.m. to 1 p.m.
$9–$12 (all major cards, no checks)

In earlier editions of this book, I wrote that Podnah's Pit didn't look like much, inside or out. But that was in the old location on Prescott Street; now they're in a much bigger and nicer place on Killingsworth. The menu, especially at breakfast, is as simple and to-the-point as the décor used to be. But Podnah's is a serious attempt to capture the simple, profound magic of Texas-style barbecue.

Podnah's doesn't serve much barbecue at breakfast, but here the emphasis is as much on *Texas* as on *barbecue*, and besides, barbecue isn't just a style of cooking or a sauce; it's a state of mind and a way of life. Like Podnah's Pit, it is utterly non-ornamental and is entirely about substance. I once experienced a slightly teary moment of peace at a (then Formica) Podnah's table, sipping iced tea and chewing a piece of brisket while Dolly Parton sang "Smoky Mountain Memories."

I'm not alone in this experience. Among the volumes of positive comments about Podnah's on the Internet, the one must-read is the Food Dude's rapturous soliloquy at portlandfoodanddrink.com. In describing childhood summers in Maypearl, Texas, he weaves together images of hay bales, ceiling fans, raising a calf, losing his virginity, a living room he wasn't allowed to use, "impossibly red tomatoes," and watching his grandmother make "perfect chocolate pies with a meringue that always cried a little; she said they were angel's tears."

There are no pancakes or waffles, but there's plenty of food—until the kitchen runs out. You can get biscuits and gravy for $5.50; add a couple of eggs for another $1.50. Or you can get just a biscuit with jam for $2.25 (or three for $6). The biscuits are, according to the *Oregonian*, "the best biscuits in town—at once buttery, tall, flaky and tender, with a subtle crispness around the edges." You can get them with grits, ham, and two eggs for $8.75—in fact, I recommend you do.

A little further up the fanciness scale is a yummy smoked trout hash ($9.25 with two eggs), and more basic is a taco with potatoes, egg, and cheese for $5.25. If you get the latter, add chorizo for another $1.50 and plan on taking a nap soon afterward. The house-made salsa is available on the taco, too, and isn't to be missed. There will also be the occasional pot of *menudo* (a spicy soup), *migas* (a Tex-Mex classic with peppers and cheese and tortilla), and maybe some *kolachkes*, Czech fruit-filled pastries that for some odd reason are huge in Texas. The expansion to Killingsworth brought the addition of smoked brisket to the breakfast menu, as part of Kyle's Breakfast (with two eggs, potatoes and a biscuit, $10).

Even now, sitting at my computer, I think back to a moment at Podnah's Pit. It was early on a Saturday morning, and I was there with my friend Steve, from Missouri. We were filling up before doing some work around his house. I was having the hash, and he was happily working on a burrito. We weren't talking much, because there wasn't much to say, and when Tony Joe White started singing "Polk Salad Annie," Steve half-closed his eyes, stopped chewing for a second, dropped his head a little, and started groovin'. I slouched a little deeper into my chair, felt the warmth radiating from my stomach, reached for some more tea, and let myself drift down South for a spell.

WAIT: A little. **LARGE GROUPS:** No. **COFFEE:** Self-serve Stumptown. **OTHER DRINKS:** Orange juice, mimosas, and red beer (Tecate beer mixed with tomato juice). **FEEL-GOODS:** Meats smoked in-house; cage-free eggs. **HEALTH OPTIONS:** Uh, no. **WIFI:** No.

PRASAD

Hip/Veggie	
Too much loveliness.	
925 NW Davis (NW/Pearl)	
503-224-3993	
prasadcuisine.com	
Weekdays 7:30 a.m. to 11 a.m., weekends 9 a.m. to 11 a.m.	
$10–$12 (all major cards, no checks)	

I confess that sometimes I feel a little piggish when I go to Prasad. This is despite the absolutely charming staff, who have told me they go out of their way to make folks like me feel comfortable.

Prasad, you see, may be the single healthiest spot in all of the Portland breakfast scene. In fact, it's not even of the Portland breakfast scene. It's a crossover from the world of health, fitness, and spirituality. It just happens to serve excellent breakfast food during the morning hours (as well as its lunch menu starting at nine, by the way.)

Consider their mission statement: *Prasad is an offering of sustainable organic cuisine to nourish and heal the mind, body and soul. Here to honor our earth, community and one another, we gratefully utilize the precious ingredients of dedicated farmers, fostering change to provide a future of health, love and respect for all.*

And it's in the lobby of Yoga Pearl, which means it is without question the only breakfast place in town with little signs on the tables asking you to be mindful (read: quiet) because there's yoga and meditation going on.

So, the reason I feel piggish is that I've never come anywhere near a yoga class, and my diet is more a force for world destruction than any kind of healing. Whenever I eat at Prasad, I feel like a grateful visitor in their world…and I try not to flirt too much with the beautiful young women who run the place.

In fact, I had them on my podcast; they were the only guests to ever show up drinking kombucha. The owner, Karen Pride, is a restaurant lifer who went to culinary school and by her late 20s was in Portland running a food cart at Northeast 15th and Alberta. When the old Blossoming Lotus place opened up in the Pearl, she pounced. "It's all so natural," she said on my show. "It's just the right spot, and everything happened the way it was meant to happen."

That in-the-flow attitude, combined with her travels, Eastern philosophy, and time as a vegan all show up in the menu at Prasad. Almost everything is vegan and gluten-free because she sees her role as helping people heal themselves through food.

Hence, there's gluten-free bread, from local baker New Cascadia, served with butter or jam; zucchini hummus, cucumber, and tomato; sprouts and avocado; or almond butter and fruit. There's a Chipotle Tempeh Scramble with black beans, spinach, tomatoes, carrots, zucchini, and avocado, served with green chili sauce, red rice, and toast. There's also a Chili Scramble with roasted garlic chili, chipotle tempeh, dark greens, spinach, avocado, scallions, quinoa, garlic tahini sauce, and toast. The best seller is the gluten-free oatmeal (from Bob's Red Mill) served with dried figs and currants, Brazil nuts, fresh fruit, vanilla, cinnamon, and maple syrup. I don't often get oatmeal, but I do often dream of Prasad's.

The oatmeal is indicative of how I get over feeling out of place at Prasad. It's all about relaxing, being happy, and peaceful, and eating well. Anybody can dig that.

WAIT: A little. **LARGE GROUPS:** No. **COFFEE:** Stumptown organic cold press. **OTHER DRINKS:** Foxfire and Townshend teas, ginger tea, chai, and amazing smoothies. **FEEL-GOODS:** Everything! **HEALTH OPTIONS:** Everything! **WIFI:** Yes.

Ps and Qs Market

Weekend/Hip
Look what cute things these kids are up to!
1301 NE Dekum St. (NE/Outer)
503-894-8979
psandqsmarket.com
Weekends 9 a.m. to 1 p.m.
$11–$14 (Visa, MasterCard, Discover, no checks)

I don't know if it's condescending to call a place "adorable," or if using that word implies that they aren't serious about what they're doing. I am, however, pretty sure I shouldn't bring race into anything or get into the shifting demographics of a neighborhood. And yet I can't help myself: This place used to be a black-owned soul-food place that none of my friends knew about, and now these cute young white folks have turned it into the most adorable little country-store type of place that the local foodie media is just in love with.

Now let me introduce you to brunch at the Ps and Qs Market, which is a name that implies both more and less than the place really is. It's a market, but it's the kind of small, specialty independent grocer that, so far, hasn't survived around town. (Remember when half of the New Deal Café was a grocer?) They have produce in wicker baskets, locally made chocolates, "Norwegian cow cheese" in the cooler, and fruit boxes with "Peras Argentinas" written on the side. The songs of Johnny Cash, Neil Young, Elvis, and 1950s country crooners fill the air.

They also have a long row of south-facing windows, allowing brilliant sunshine to pour through cloth curtains and onto wood tables, each adorned with fresh flowers. There are plants all over the place, and most of the hanging artwork is of vegetables and flowers. It is, in short, so damn cute that I couldn't stop smiling or taking pictures of it.

It's also a sweet little café with coffee and baked goods, and a small brunch menu on weekends. This is where the "more than it sounds like" comes in. For example, I got a beef tenderloin hash that was salty, sweet, and utterly delicious. At $10, it was the priciest thing on the menu. I also got a piece of toasted house-made bread and was offered two kinds of house-made jam: grape vanilla and persimmon.

Elsewhere on the menu, I saw biscuits and tomato gravy ($6.50), a frittata of the day ($5), and ham with fried egg, arugula, paprika, and sriracha mayo on a potato bun ($7). See? It isn't just a market. It's a neighborhood place. The other folks dining were two women in their sixties, half a dozen twenty-somethings talking about a party they attended the night before, and an old guy who didn't say a word but seemed to be a regular.

And since I can't think of anything else to say about the place—other than I recommend it, though it seems a little *Portlandia* to me—here's a semi-interesting story that took place down the street. Remember the "Brunch Village" episode of *Portlandia*, the one that took place entirely in line for marionberry pancakes? Well, the place people were waiting to get into was Woodlawn Coffee, just down the street at 808 NE Dekum. But the place in line that Ed Begley Jr. was trying to get folks into was actually Pattie's Home Plate Cafe in St. Johns, the bookstore that got annoyed at all the traffic was In Other Words on NE Killingsworth, and the chaos-ridden End of the Line was a vacant lot down by OMSI. Such is the magic of television.

I thought you might want to know this while you're waiting for your yummy food in the sunny, adorable Ps and Qs Market.

WAIT: None. **LARGE GROUPS:** Maybe. **COFFEE:** Trailhead. **OTHER DRINKS:** Jasmine Pearl tea, beer, wine, juices, mimosas. **FEEL-GOODS:** Local organic, seasonal produce whenever possible; local, natural meat. **HEALTH OPTIONS:** Most dishes can be modified to be vegetarian/vegan/gluten-free. **WIFI:** Yes.

RADAR

Weekend/New/Mom and Pop
Serious food, casual attitude.
3951 N Mississippi (N/Inner)
503-841-6948
radarpdx.com
Weekends 10 a.m. to 2 p.m.
$12–$14 (all major cards, no checks)

Many restaurant people will tell you they've had a life in restaurants, but Lily Tollefsen's life actually *started* in one. Her parents owned and lived in a restaurant in New York, and one day her dad told her she was conceived right above the kitchen. That may be an odd thing to know about a person, but she told me that story during a podcast interview, so I suppose I can share it here. Anyway, imagine hearing that as a 13-year-old girl!

In 2012, she and her husband Jonathon opened their first-ever restaurant on North Mississippi Street, with a menu he described as "a reflection of what we like to eat, places I've worked, and really my whole career over 25 years."

Summarized in two words, apparently what this charming couple likes to eat is "American Tapas." The small-plate revolution swept over Portland and its brunch scene in the wake of Tasty n Sons' massive success, so it only makes sense that super crowded Mississippi Street would have its own tapas place.

In fact, Lily says she cleared their brunch plans with the owner of Gravy up the street; apparently he not only said "yes" but added "please." Where, after all, would Gravy put more people?

Actually, before Radar had brunch, it served as a kind of waiting room for Gravy. "People would come in and get a coffee or a mimosa and keep an eye on the line," Lily said. "And we were okay with that."

Now, though, people come in for dishes like braised pork shoulder and Cotija grits with chile puree. Jonathon said it's braised for seven to eight hours and served over "real North Carolina grits, not instant Yankee grits." And I've listed this place as a "mom and pop" because there's a decent chance you'll meet Jonathon or Lilly during you brunch.

You can also get Swedish Pancakes (his mom's recipe), herbed French toast, and smoked bluefish pâté; the fish is overnighted by friends on Long Island who stuff local newspapers and other sentimental trinkets in with the fish.

Radar also offers a pretty chill environment, which isn't a coincidence. "Portland's a very laid-back place, and our brunch in particular is a very calm experience," Lily says. "Just from what I watch, people come in and sip coffee and spend an hour or two, and I welcome that. Our goal when we opened Radar was to have a place where people feel comfortable and at home."

You can relax in a cozy window table up front, at the bar, along a counter, or on the nice enclosed patio out back. And since they take reservations, you don't have to worry about any long waits, either.

So, if visiting a happening street to have a chill brunch served by nice folks who've spent their lives in restaurants sounds like a good idea, head for that cute little place down by Gravy.

WAIT: Some, but they take reservations. **LARGE GROUPS:** With a reservation. **COFFEE:** Ristretto. **OTHER DRINKS:** Full bar. **FEEL-GOODS:** Local, organic produce and meats. **HEALTH OPTIONS:** Vegetarian, vegan, and gluten-free options; chef will work with any dietary restriction. **WIFI:** Yes.

RADIO ROOM

Hip/Weekend
A big rockin' show.
1101 NE Alberta (NE/Alberta)
503-287-2346
radioroompdx.com
Breakfast daily 9 a.m. to 2 a.m.
Some brunch additions weekends 9 a.m. to 3 p.m.
$13–$16 (all major cards, no checks)

Big. That's the word I keep coming back to when I think about breakfast at Radio Room. It's a big place. Big menu. Big portions. Big patio. *Two* big patios, in fact—one downstairs with a fire pit, and one upstairs with a pretty big view.

I gathered some of the Crew there one sunny Saturday, and at first we were a little thrown off. Is it a restaurant? A bar? An outdoor party? Well, yes. And it has a definite rock and roll theme, including a picture of the Ramones on the men's room door. Rock on!

We saw families in the restaurant, hipsters in the bar, and people with paint all over them on the patio. Wait…what? Turns out the Color Run had happened that day in Portland; apparently you go for a run and people throw colored powder all over you? That would be two things I know nothing about. But it did add a whole new level of, well, color to our visit. Radio Room has plenty of room for all of this.

The heated upstairs patio has a nice view out over the rooftops of the Alberta area, and we even saw a couple that had found enough space in the corner to get a little snuggly. The place is like an environment unto

itself. And the 21-and-over bar has its own life, with Microbrew Mondays, Top Shelf Tuesdays, and Happy Hour from 3 to 6 daily.

And then there's the menu! They have about a dozen breakfast items available all day and night: a lox plate, burrito, biscuits and gravy, scrambles, challah French toast, even a vegan hash with mushrooms, potatoes, shallots, garlic, tofu, grilled asparagus, frisée, nutritional yeast, roasted garlic oil, and fresh herbs. We were just commenting on the number of things in that item when we caught a glimpse of somebody's biscuits and gravy. *Holy pig fat* was that big!

(The weekend menu adds three Benedicts, pancakes, a handful of cocktails, and a Bloody Mary bar. Oh, and they have a special menu for groups for 10 or more.)

We all ordered, and when each member of the Crew had given me a sampling of his or her order, we had a big enough plate feed somebody else. Seriously, what they sent out for three could have fed four, maybe five. I think I was still working on my Boss Hogg Benedict (with melted brie and crispy bacon) two days later.

And how was it? Um, big. Look, nobody is likely to claim that Radio Room has the best food in town, or maybe even the neighborhood. Also, I've had way too many breakfasts for many of them to really stand out. And their claim of having "Portland's most excellent espresso bar" is, well, a pretty big claim.

But it was fun, and they have every right to go big. I'll tell you what Radio Room certainly is: clean, comfortable, friendly, line free, outside, breakfast-all-the-time, boozy, and big. And if you happen to really dig the food, it will rock your world.

WAIT: Sometimes on Sunday. **LARGE GROUPS:** Good choice; give them a heads-up, though. **COFFEE:** Red E. **OTHER DRINKS:** Full bar, Foxfire tea, fresh-squeezed juices, sodas. **FEEL-GOODS:** None that that they tout. **HEALTH OPTIONS:** Some vegetarian and gluten-free options; substitutions available. **WIFI:** Yes.

RAVEN & ROSE

Weekend/Classy	
Grand history, architecture, and dining.	
1331 SW Broadway St. (Downtown)	
503-222-7673	
ravenandrosepdx.com	
Weekends 10 a.m. to 2 p.m.	
$16–$21 (all major cards, no checks)	

One thing that has happened since I've been writing this book is that downtown has become a really happening place for breakfast and brunch.

It used to all there was downtown was Mother's (page 160) and Bijou (page 46), plus some hotels (page 258). Or you could go over to the Pearl. Lately, of course, the food-cart revolution has taken over the streets of the central city, with something close to 100 carts open weekdays, quite a few of them doing breakfast (page 264).

And then an occasional existing, classy restaurant like Raven & Rose comes along and decides to do brunch.

It's a beautiful building, and even from the outside it's clearly a mix of old and new. In this case, "old" means 1883, when it was first built as the Ladd Family Carriage House. The Ladds were a big deal in Portland—William Ladd owned the Oregon Iron and Steel company—and their estate covered several blocks in this area.

The "new" is that in 2007 the building was moved (!) to make way for new construction, then brought back and renovated into a beautiful, luxurious, LEED-certified place that used original interior materials and now returns kitchen scraps to local farms for livestock feed.

Inside, there's a nice little nook by the front windows, set off from the rest of the dining room. There's a bar with seating for 10, a big table in front of the fireplace, and seating for another 70 spread out in a spacious layout. Clearly, somebody spent a lot of money in here!

Upstairs is truly impressive; there's another bar, and a pool table, and a soaring ceiling with exposed rafters. It's called the Upstairs Rookery and is open five to midnight Monday through Saturday, with a small-plate and dessert menu.

At first glance, the menu reveals Irish, British, and Southern influences, with corned beef hash, black and white puddings, croque madame, biscuits and gravy, and shrimp and grits. Then you notice the little twists, like stewed tomato and chard in the shrimp and grits, or spinach, mustard and crème fraîche on the hash. They call it "classic farmhouse cookery," but I never saw a farm that eats this well.

We started with a basket of donut muffins—basically, muffin batter formed into donuts and fried, then rolled in cinnamon and sugar. Then I decided to get something out of my ordinary, the Rabbit and Biscuit, with creamed spinach and a poached egg. It was sexy looking and tasted awesome, though we did crack a few too many jokes about the cute (and tender!) little bunny who died to make it happen.

Another highlight was the asparagus hash, with mushrooms, poached egg, and the same mustard-potato-spinach-crème-fraîche combo on the corned beef hash. Two people got this one and really liked it. Then there was the Croque Madame, which is just a Croque Monsieur (a ham and cheese sandwich, dipped in egg batter and fried) with an egg on top—in this case, the cheese was Gruyère, and there was also béchamel sauce. Let's just say it wasn't light eating! It was damn good, though.

The Crew had a fine time with all of this, and we were totally knocked out by the setting and decorations. Really a beautiful place, inside and out, and I only recall one person not being thrilled with their meal. I should also say that when the bill came, it seemed a little high. I am sure that restaurant owners will howl at this, and talk about fine ingredients and staff effort, and that's all true, I'm sure. I also assume that somebody (us) has to pay for all the work done in this place.

It was a really good meal, but I also know that I had a leg of rabbit, an egg, a biscuit, some creamed spinach and a cappuccino…and I paid $20 before the tip. Do with this as you will, but I do recommend you check out the beautiful and tasty Raven & Rose.

WAIT: None. **LARGE GROUPS:** Yes, but reservations preferred. **COFFEE:** Spella. **OTHER DRINKS:** Lots of brunch cocktails. **FEEL-GOODS:** "Relationships with local farmers and producers." Their own eggs. **HEALTH OPTIONS:** Not a lot for vegetarians. **WIFI:** Yes.

BREAKFAST IN BRIDGETOWN

REDWOOD

New/Classy
Swedish past, Southeast present.
7915 SE Stark St. (SE/Outer)
503-841-5118
redwoodpdx.com
Brunch Wednesday through Sunday 9 a.m. to 2 p.m.
$14–$16 (Visa, MasterCard, Discover, no checks)

It's not like I always know every single thing that goes on in the world of Portland breakfast, but when I come across a completely new brunch place that I've never even heard of, it still throws me off a bit. I mention this because Redwood opened, in January 2013, to very little fanfare and a couple of so-so reviews. It just kind of…appeared…and right down the street from a super popular place, the Country Cat.

I tried to rally the Crew to go check it out, and everybody was indifferent. I told them Montavilla is a cool neighborhood, like its own little downtown on the other side of Mount Tabor, and they shrugged. I told them I looked in, and it's a beautiful place. Nothing. Then I told them the owner/chef ran the kitchen at Broder for years, and several of them signed up immediately.

It was a sunny, warm Saturday when we rolled in to the sparsely crowded place, and Montavilla was in fine form: Folks walking around with their kids and dogs, shopping and sipping coffee and waiting for a noon movie. We settled into Redwood's pleasant dining room and immediately decided the decor was just what you'd expect from a new Portland place called Redwood: dark, red-stained wood, black metal furnishings, and cast-iron light fixtures. It seemed well built

for both soft-lit evenings and sunny Saturdays.

The menu came out, and I immediately saw an opportunity to crack a joke. Next to the Huevos Rancheros was a word I didn't know—*escabèche,* or pickled jalapenos—and the notation *$9 (tongue + 2)*. "Damn," I said, for just two bucks I can get tongue on my huevos!" And we were off.

I do feel the need to crack a joke when I'm in a place claiming to serve "upscale comfort food" with a menu that sends me looking for a dictionary. "Comfort food" is right up there with "fusion" and "hangover food" in often-used, nearly meaningless restaurant phrases. But Redwood didn't seem too "upscale," anyway. My roasted pork shoulder hash was only $10, and the priciest item on the menu was, strangely, the Oatmeal Waffles with two eggs, bacon, and maple syrup for $12. Other menu items included a Breakfast Sandwich with the same pork plus eggs, rouille, arugula, and chili vinegar on ciabatta ($10), Chilaquiles ($11), a Pan-Seared Trout Hash with rémoulade ($11), a couple of scrambles, two different fritters, and a seasonal oatmeal crisp. I had to check Wikipedia, but rouille is "a sauce that consists of olive oil with breadcrumbs, garlic, saffron and chili peppers," and rémoulade is "very much like tartar sauce."

We thought the food was excellent, my hash a fine combination of crunchy and soft, salty and smoky and sweet, with what Michelle of the Crew called a "spicy citrus back note." I would never say such a thing, but she was right. Her oatmeal waffles, meanwhile, stayed perfectly crisp to the last bite. The staff was lovely and prompt, and getting in and out of a Southeast Portland weekend brunch in less than an hour and under $15 each was quite refreshing.

If nothing else, Redwood's brunch may play the role of Interurban or Radar to Mississippi Street's Gravy: It's the nice place with a good brunch right down from the long lines at Country Cat, and even though its main emphasis seems to be on evenings, it's a fine alternative for brunch, too.

WAIT: None. **LARGE GROUPS:** Sure, with notice. **COFFEE:** Stumptown. **OTHER DRINKS:** A whole page of cocktails, plus beer and wine. **FEEL-GOODS:** None they brag about. **HEALTH OPTIONS:** Some options for vegetarians, not much for vegans. **WIFI:** Yes.

THE ROXY

Hip/Old School

"Forget fancy and healthy."

1121 SW Stark St. (Downtown)

503-223-9160

theroxydiner.com

Tuesday through Sunday, 24 hours

$10–$13 (Visa, MasterCard, Discover, no checks)

I have a "little brother" from Big Brothers Big Sisters, and one morning I offered him the choice of three downtown Portland breakfast places. I said we could go fancy cool hotel (Urban Farmer), Mexican/healthy (Isabel's), or old-school diner with a huge menu (the Roxy). I don't know what I expected from a 13-year-old. Off to the Roxy we went.

Now, I know that going to the Roxy during the day is like going to the 24-Hour Hotcake House during the day. What you really want is the late-night scene (see below for more about this). But I am old, my little is young, and neither of us does late nights. So it wasn't a shock when we were the only people there at 9:30 a.m. on a Wednesday.

The first thing he was taken by was the collection of famous-people signed photos: Some he knew (Bill Clinton), some he didn't (Bo Diddley). All of them either ate there or met the owner, except for David Bowie (unknown to my little) and Elvis (well-known, not understood). A lot of them appeared to be musicians and comedians who probably stumbled in after doing their shows; this being the only 24-hour place on the west side.

Anyway, his attention quickly went to the various other oddities in the place: the crucifix over the jukebox, the plants growing out of old toasters, the leopard-skin-pattern chairs and purple tables. I was just thinking that it was a slightly odd place to bring a 13-year-old, when the waiter walked over with menus; he was wearing a shirt that said, in very large letters, "PORTLAND FUCKING OREGON." Nice.

The fun continued on the first page of the menu, the FAQ. I am glad he didn't ask me to explain stuff like:

Q: Why do I have to buy something to be in here?
A: Because 25% of zero makes a shitty tip.

Q: Why don't you have cherries?
A: Because there are no virgins at The Roxy.

They have some funny names for basic breakfast combos. We both ordered off the page labeled "Herkin' Big Pancakes and Arrogant French Toast." He got Pancakes and Pig Meat (two buttermilk 'cakes and bacon, $8), and I went with Too Snobby To Even Look at You French Toast (three slices, two eggs, two sausages, $9.75). Out came our very own pitcher of weak, awful coffee and a baby bottle filled with cream.

While we waited, I went into the bathroom, which has to be one of the great ones in Portland. It is a festival of graffiti and old newspapers. My little went in there, too, and I was really glad he didn't ask me to explain the condom machine.

Out came the food, and it was a tasty, rich version of your basic breakfast food. The bacon was thick and crisp and yummy, the sausage had just a little kick, and the pancakes and French toast were perfect expressions of Generic American Breakfast.

Thoroughly satisfied, I paid our bill ($27 with tip), and off we went, back into the sunshine, to face the mall for some holiday shopping. There was now one other table occupied.

"I like this place," he said.

"Me, too," I said. "Who needs fancy and healthy?"

PS: You need to read about the late-night scene at the Roxy, but I'm not the one to write it for you. A while back, the website pdx.eater.com posted an amazing journal of the night shift at the Roxy, written by Suzanne Hale, the owner of the place. It includes lines like "The professional alcoholics are smart enough to eat *before* drinking." Really, go to their site and search for her name. It almost made want to quit writing about restaurants.

WAIT: Only late-night on weekends. **LARGE GROUPS:** During the day. **COFFEE:** Panache. **OTHER DRINKS:** Espresso, Italian sodas, milk, sodas, juices, tea, chai, Monster energy drinks. **FEEL-GOODS:** (Shaking my head.) **HEALTH OPTIONS:** (Still shaking my head.) **WIFI:** No.

SANBORN'S

New/Classy
Real cooking, real casual.
3200 SE Milwaukie Ave. (SE/Powell)
503-963-8000
sanbornsbreakfast.com
Wednesday through Sunday 8 a.m. to 2 p.m.
$10–$16 (Visa, MasterCard, Discover, no checks)

Wherever I go in my role as The Breakfast Guy, I get The Question. In fact, the only time I *didn't* get it was when I bet somebody I would. The Question is, of course, What's your favorite breakfast place?

I always punt and say there are a lot of them…and the person asking gives me a look that says, "I know.…But what's your favorite place?" I fumble around internally, looking for a place that (A) is really, really good, (B) run by cool people, and (C) probably unknown to the asker of The Question. I do like to seem like an expert.

That's why Sanborn's is usually one of my first answers. It isn't really my No. 1 Favorite Place, but it's way up there. And I must not have much pull, because I've been talking it up for years, and they still have manageable waits, even on weekends.

So, how does this sound? You slide into a comfy booth in a spacious, natural-light restaurant. A pleasant server (one is the owner's daughter, who runs the front-of-house staff) brings you a French press of coffee (that's a $5.99 option; a regular cup is $1.99) and hands you a menu full of delicious-sounding meals at perfectly reasonable prices, with half orders available on everything except potatoes.

It's heavy on baked goodies, with six kinds of pancakes ranging from $4 to $10: buttermilk; buckwheat; sourdough (from a genuine 1847 Oregon Trail starter); blueberry with powdered sugar and blueberry compote; blue corn; and potato with diced green onion and egg, served with sour cream or house-made applesauce. This doesn't count the *eight* variations on German Pancakes, including the German Pancake with whipped butter, lemon, and powdered sugar; the Apple Pancake with sliced apples caramelized in sugar and cinnamon; seasonal pancakes; and the Mango Pancake with sliced mango caramelized with sugar, ginger, lemon, and orange peel.

There's also a French Toast and two kinds of waffles.

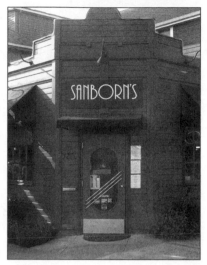

Oh, I'm sorry, did you want some protein? There are a bunch of House Favorites (corned beef hash, biscuits and gravy, and so on) as well as a Build-Your-Own Omelet section (any two ingredients in a three-egg omelet for $12, another $1 each for more ingredients); I once got one with chorizo, feta, and peppers. There were 15 other ingredients to choose from, and you can get the same deal in a scramble for $10.

What came out was as surprising as the rest of the experience: a massive omelet in which the eggs had been whipped, then stuffed with the ingredients, folded over, and baked. The first time I ate this, I was stunned. And soon I was stuffed.

Sanborn's is also casual and friendly. And it's not crowded. And it's across from the Aladdin Theater. Any more questions?

WAIT: Up to 45 minutes on weekends. **LARGE GROUPS:** Up to 20, with notice. **COFFEE:** Bridgetown. **OTHER DRINKS:** French press coffee and Foxfire teas; hot cider, fresh-squeezed juices, milk, mimosas, sake cocktails. **FEEL-GOODS:** None that are touted. **HEALTH OPTIONS:** Egg whites available on scrambles. Veggie sausage an option. **WIFI:** No.

SCKAVONE'S

Weekend
Still there, still in the family.
4100 SE Division St. (SE/Division)
503-235-0630
sckavones.com
Weekends 8 a.m. to 2 p.m.
$11–$13 (Visa, MasterCard, no checks)

Since I am the author of a breakfast guidebook, there are two questions I get all the time, neither of them easily answered. One is what's my favorite place, and the other is where a person can go for brunch without a long line.

I am somewhat ashamed to admit that whenever I answer either one, I always forget about Sckavone's. In fact, I'm willing to bet that unless you live near the place, you don't even know it exists. And now I know why: The folks who run it like things that way.

It's been open since 2006, and yet I rarely run into anybody who's been there. It's just a little neighborhood place with, as the website says, "No pretense, just really good food served by nice people in a great space."

It's a space with a great history, as well. Nick Sckavone came from Italy to Southeast Portland in 1908. He led a labor action against the *Oregonian* at age 15, and at 17 he formed a club of neighborhood baseball teams; there's a field in Westmoreland named for him. In 1930, he opened a drugstore at Southeast 41st and Division, and in 1980 his grandson took it over.

It still has every bit the look and feel of a neighborhood place—and the original counter—as well as the complete absence of a wait when I visited on a Saturday at 10 a.m. We left close to 11, and there was still no line. I once asked the owner about this lack of a crowd, and he said it was just fine. Sckavone's, he assured me, wants nothing more than to be a little neighborhood place with good food.

We tried the corned beef hash (crispy and excellent, eggs poached just right), the smoked salmon Benedict (good sauce and fish, muffin still crispy), and the French toast, which really was more like apple pie, with cream-cheese icing and cinnamon and chunks of apple. It wasn't really French toast, as far as I'm concerned, and it was too big to finish, and too intense to have solo, but it was good. If you have a group of four or more, have everybody get something savory and get one order of the French toast as the table sweet. I think if you ate the whole thing, you'd have to run around the block to burn off the energy…and then take a nap.

Other folks had omelets, including a veggie with a big chunk of avocado on it. Portions were large, coffee was good, we all agreed the food was excellent, and seven of us got out of there for about $85 with tip. Actually, I think one person didn't order, so it was the usual $12 or so per person, with coffee and tip.

I really had no idea about this place, until I noticed it from the #4 bus one day. But if you're looking for a combination of comfort, a chilled-out vibe, and quality, check out Sckavone's. It's just your basic neighborhood place, and it has been for 80 years. Kind of makes a guy want to move to the neighborhood and sit at that counter all the time.

WAIT: None that I've seen. **LARGE GROUPS:** Yes, with notice. **COFFEE:** K & F. **OTHER DRINKS:** Tea, Italian sodas, milkshakes, floats, full bar. **FEEL-GOODS:** None they tout. **HEALTH OPTIONS:** Veggie sausage. **WIFI:** Yes.

SCREEN DOOR

Weekend/New/Classy	
Southern soul meets Northwest style.	
2337 E Burnside St. (E Burnside)	
503-542-0880	
screendoorrestaurant.com	
Brunch weekends 9 a.m. to 2:30 p.m.	
$10–$18 (all major cards, no checks)	

I was all ready to make fun of the Screen Door. I'm from the South, you see, and when a restaurant outside the South calls itself Southern, I tend to load up the sarcasm cannon. Waiting for my friends at the Screen Door, I saw Swiss Chard and Bacon Frittata, Goat Cheese Scramble with Roasted Red Peppers, and Bananas Foster French Toast on the specials board. "Good luck finding any of *that* in the South," I thought.

Maybe it's not a Southern place, in the stereotypical sense. It's a Portland restaurant with a Southern theme. And, as it turned out, that was just fine with all of us.

Still, the sarcasm cannon almost went off when I saw something called Garden Grits, with spinach, mushrooms, caramelized onions, and provolone, and Farm Grits with ham, poached eggs, and provolone. I thought, "That's not how you do grits!"

I emailed this news to some of the prime Southern ladies in my life. Below are some of their responses.

My mom, Marjorie, in Memphis: "Well child, I just can't imagine all these names they thought up for grits! Cheese grits is a standard brunch dish here, but with cheddar, for Pete's sake! If I ordered regular grits—which a menu would never need to say, 'cause grits is grits—I would just put a heap'a butter on it. Mercy!"

My sister-in-law, Lela, in Memphis: "Having been born in Alabama, raised in Tennessee, and schooled in New Orleans, I've yet to meet the self-respecting grit that would interact with provolone."

My sister, Lucy, in Maryland: "Provolone is great on a turkey sandwich but definitely *not* on grits. I may have left the true South, but there are just some things you don't fergit." (Yes, she typed *fergit*, but she was going for the effect. I think.)

Dee, a family friend in Atlanta: "All that gussied-up grits on the menu is just for those poor Northwesterners who don't know any better."

So, the South didn't exactly rise up in favor of this grits thing, nor for Screen Door's Praline Bacon Waffle, which is very sweet and covered with pecans. And I didn't have the heart to tell the ladies about the blackened tofu scramble.

But I had to email everyone back and say, "I hate to tell y'all, but this place was *good*, and the regular side grits have cheddar in them." Indeed, the Breakfast Crew was entirely impressed, from my Fried Oyster Benedict to the waffle smothered in fruit and whipped cream to the Alabama Scramble with ham, green onions, and pimento cheese. The menu is full up (as my grandma would have said) with modern twists on old faves: cilantro-lime crema on the migas and vegetarian mushroom gravy on biscuits.

Two objections come through in most of the Crew's reactions to Screen Door: the place is way too loud, and it feels a little overpriced. There's also the line, which frankly is obscene. But here's something you might not know: At the opening time of 9:00 a.m., they take reservations at a few tables for parties of six or eight. Just get everybody there on time, or it's the back of the line for the lot of you.

I have long since accepted that Screen Door is an awesome Southern restaurant. And there's no feeling of power like walking past that line with five friends to get me a steaming bowl of fancied-up grits.

WAIT: Legendary; no cover outside and a tiny area inside. **LARGE GROUPS:** Up to 12, with reservations, at 9:00 a.m. **COFFEE:** Stumptown. **OTHER DRINKS:** Fresh juice and a wide range of cocktails. **FEEL-GOODS:** Some produce and meats from local vendors. **HEALTH OPTIONS:** Some organic ingredients. Vegetarian friendly; tofu for $1.50 or egg whites for $1. **WIFI:** No.

SEASONS AND REGIONS

Weekend
It's all about the fish.
6660 SW Capitol Hwy. (SW/Outer)
503-244-6400
seasonsandregions.com
Breakfast weekends 9 a.m. to 2 p.m.
$12–$16 (all major cards, no checks)

Seasons and Regions is a restaurant that practically nobody in the Portland breakfast scene has ever heard of. For one thing, it's on Southwest Capitol Highway, hardly the center of our culinary world. Since breakfast is served only on weekends, it's hardly the signature offering. If you were to drive by, you would probably think, "Gee, it looks like an old Dairy Queen or something." And that's precisely what it was; the drive-through window is still there, in fact.

So, what is served? Well, a lot of the breakfast classics with one big variation: seafood. Even on the weekend brunch menu, the bounty of the sea dominates. There's Crab Cake Benedict, Nova Scotia Benedict with house-smoked salmon, and Hangtown Fry with fried Willapa Bay oysters, eggs, bacon, spinach, and mushrooms topped with freshly grated Parmesan. There's Smoked Salmon Hash, Smoked Salmon Scramble, and the all-out Tillamook Scramble: three eggs scrambled with salmon, bay shrimp, Pacific cod, mushrooms, onions, spinach, tomatoes, and Tillamook cheddar. The prices are downright reasonable, as well: the Tillamook Scramble is only $8.90, and has been for a while.

Seasons comes off as a semiserious place. And that's not a slight: the website boasts "Fresh Northwest seafood and shellfish, transformed into

world class creations and served by friends." Many of the patrons are local regulars. There's a full bar, and the food falls somewhere between diner and cutting edge. They have down-home stuff like the Mexican

Chorizo Breakfast Burrito and an apple waffle, and "fine-dining" stuff like garlic-Parmesan cream sauce on the Florentine Benedict and Northwest Omelet. Just about everything comes with rosemary potatoes (crispy outside, soft inside); light, fluffy rosemary scones; or both.

As you may imagine, a former Dairy Queen is not exactly an architectural must-see. I happened to eat there with three women (not braggin', just sayin'), and they said it "looks like a dude decorated it." Trivial Pursuit cards were on the unfinished wood tables along with salt and pepper shakers shaped like slot machines. Grapevine-shaped lights hung from a black ceiling that said *evening dinner*, but the yellow walls said *daytime cheery*. Faux picture windows "looked out" at lovely scenes that were not Capitol Highway. A year-round outside seating area is covered by a tent and has overhead heaters.

The owners (two dudes, by the way) met while working at McCormick's Fish House & Bar in Beaverton, and critics would say Seasons is just a local version of that chain. In a 2002 *Portland Business Journal* story, the owners said they aim for a wide breadth of options based on what's currently available, so you'll see a revolving menu and different specials depending on the time of year.

My friends and I enjoyed our meal, especially because we didn't have to wait at all on a Saturday morning. Seasons and Regions seems to put more effort into dinners, but there's a lot to be said for a down-home, laid-back breakfast place with tons of options, fresh seafood, and just a hint of fanciness without being over-the-top expensive.

WAIT: Perhaps a little; feel free to call 30 min. ahead. **LARGE GROUPS:** Yes; reservations available; one check policy. **COFFEE:** Organic Seattle's Best. **OTHER DRINKS:** Kobos espresso, mimosas, Bloody Marys. **FEEL-GOODS:** Most ingredients are local, including some from the owners' farm. **HEALTH OPTIONS:** Egg substitutes available; gluten-free and vegetarian menu now available. **WIFI:** No.

SEN YAI NOODLES

Hip
An outpost of an Asian empire.
3384 SE Division (SE/Division)
503-236-3573
pokpoksenyai.com
Weekdays 8 to 11 a.m., weekends 9 to 11 a.m.
$12–$14 (Visa, MasterCard, Discover, no checks)

For years, the one breakfast niche not being served in Portland was Asian. Why, you couldn't get a good bowl of *jok* for love or money in this town! Then our local empire-maker, Andy Ricker, he of the obsessive devotion to Thai food, saw the vacuum and filled it, according to his nature.

Ricker, who owns Pok Pok and several other places, opened Sen Yai in 2013, at the corner of Division and 34th. It is now one of 437 restaurants on SE Division. That's an exaggeration, I admit, but looking out the windows of the #4 Trimet bus, I watched as we passed Genies, the upcoming Pine State Biscuits, Los Gorditos, Detour Cafe, Ford Food and Drink, Sunshine Tavern, the new St. Honore, Little T American Bakery, and Blue City Biscuits. Right across the street from Sen Yai is Roman Candle Bakery, which has some breakfast items. And had I gone as far as SE 42nd, I would have passed Xico, Tom's, and Sckavone's. And those are just the *breakfast* places!

Sen Yai is a bright, fun little café specializing in noodles. In fact, the name means "big noodle." The art features veggies, kitchen utensils, and farming scenes, and the whole vibe is a little playful. He said when he opened it that he wanted it to be like a breakfast nook in the mornings.

They were playing some very bouncy, strangely appealing Asian pop music when I went in, which the waiter said came from a playlist created by Ricker. I tried to SoundHound one of the songs, and it completely whiffed. My friend Jen, author of *The 100 Best Places to Stuff Your Faces*, bested me by going to Shazam and finding it was a crooning love song (I assume) called "Arai Gaw Dai." It's funny to hear cheesy pop music when you can't understand what they're singing, so you pay more attention to the music and production.

The same is true for breakfast; when it isn't at all what you're used to, you pay more attention. And at Sen Yai you find tasty, unique treasures. The breakfast menu is pretty limited but does include some morning classics from Asia: jok, rice soup in pork bone broth, and coddled eggs in a glass. Jen got the noodle soup, Kuaytiaw Naam Kai, and had her choice of noodles, described as "wide, thin, very thin, whole wheat, and ramen."

Jen went with wide noodles, because the waiter said they're made "right down the street" at another Ricker establishment. It came with chicken, bean sprouts, green onions, Chinese celery, and fried garlic.

I got the jok, or congee, which is basically rice boiled forever until it turns into a smooth, ricey-tasting porridge. From there, it's all about what you put in it; at Sen Yai the choice is "bouncy pork" (no explanation given) or seafood, neither of which tells you much. I went with seafood and still couldn't tell you which critter it was. Nor do I care.

Waiting on the table were four containers of spices: Thai chile, serrano, Thai pepper, and sugar. Also, a shaker bottle of white pepper and one of Maggi sauce. We both really thought he said *maggot*, but in our defense, we were both game, too. Maggi sauce is like soy sauce but with no soy; it's also a Nestle product and was invented in Switzerland.

My jok was really good, and such a nice break from the usual break- fast. I found it similar in texture to cream of wheat, but with a nice rice taste, and with the spices you can take it in whichever direction you want. Just beware the serranos!

Whenever things got too hot for us, we could always take a break with the crullers and *sangkhaya*, a rich coconut custard. Neither was too sweet, but compared to my ever-spicier jok, they were perfect. I even finished off Jen's last one, so I think we're dating now, or something.

Back at the bus stop, I was admiring Ava Gene's and thinking that Southeast Portland ain't what it used to be. Then a skateboarder sat on the ground next to the bus sign and lit a joint. I felt much better.

WAIT: No. **LARGE GROUPS:** With notice. **COFFEE:** Pour-over Stumptown. **OTHER DRINKS:** Beer, wine, Steven Smith teas, drink- ing vinegars, full bar, and lots of odd-sounding Thai drinks. **FEEL- GOODS:** None. **HEALTH OPTIONS:** Limited options for vegetarians and vegans. **WIFI:** Yes.

SIMPATICA DINING HALL

Weekend/New/Classy
A serious place—and seriously good.
828 SE Ash St. (SE/Inner)
503-235-1600
simpaticapdx.com
Sunday 9 a.m. to 2 p.m.
$13–$16 (all major cards, checks)

Most of us diners are aware of only the normal world of restaurants—the ones with signs outside, private tables, and food that's familiar. But there's another world of restaurants. It's a parallel universe of experimentation and innovation, and it's on a higher plane, like the New York fashion world is to the local mall. Most of us eat in the mall; the Serious Food People eat in New York.

Simpatica Dining Hall is of the Serious Food World, and it was born in a Portland restaurant movement that is simultaneously innovative and old-fashioned: family-style suppers featuring the creations of highly trained chefs and made from local ingredients. It started as invitation-only suppers among friends served in backyards or local restaurants. Three of the guys (two are owners of Viande, a specialty meat company) created a catering company that eventually started hosting events in the basement of the long-lost Pine Street Theater. This is Simpatica, where reservations-only fixed-menu dinners are served a couple of nights a week, along with brunch on Sundays.

Still, you sort of have to know where it is. A small line forms outside the nondescript building (with only a small sandwich board announcing its presence) just before 9:00 a.m. every Sunday, with people doing crosswords and reading magazines to kill time. Much of the seating is still family-style, so if you're a party of two, you'll probably be seated across from each other and next to another party. This leads to much cross-party conversation and menu discussion.

Despite the mildly underground vibe, it is a very serious restaurant. But neither the prices nor the attitude is worrisome. And, keeping to the old-is-new spirit that makes family dining from local farmers something revolutionary, the menu at Simpatica is really just all your breakfast favorites, a little fancied up and done very, very well. I had French toast, for example, with a smoky orange marmalade and chantilly cream. At one point I was wiping up a combination of real maple syrup, cream, and marmalade with a piece of bacon, and I officially reached the top of both the fat intake scale and, not coincidentally, the pleasure scale. Another time I had a crab cake Benedict, and after one bite actually felt sad that it would have to end.

Other offerings I have seen on the ever-changing menu include a classic Eggs Benedict with ham; crepes filled with butternut squash or bacon, asparagus, and crème fraîche; an andouille and prosciutto hash; and lunch items like a much-raved-about cheeseburger and a Philly cheesesteak sandwich. All the meats are outstanding, as you would expect from guys who own a meat company; vegetarians will probably have to stick to the sweet stuff.

We counted four servers who stopped by our table at some point, all efficient and thoroughly knowledgeable about the entire menu. Substitutions were easy, and when other friends happened in and joined us, their orders were taken, and somehow the food all arrived together.

Among the many pleasures of living in Portland, one has to count the existence of young folks like those who run Simpatica.

WAIT: Can get long; get there when it opens if you're in a hurry. **LARGE GROUPS:** Tough. Reservations for parties of four or larger, maxed out at 20–25. **COFFEE:** Stumptown. **OTHER DRINKS:** Foxfire teas, cocktails. **FEEL-GOODS:** Everything is local. **HEALTH OPTIONS:** A few options for vegetarians. **WIFI:** No.

SLAPPY CAKES

Kiddie/Veggie
"Let them eat—and cook their own—cakes!"
4246 SE Belmont (SE/Belmont)
503-477-4805
slappycakes.com
Monday through Thursday 8 a.m. to 2 p.m.,
Friday through Sunday 8 a.m. to 4 p.m.
$11–$13 (all major cards, no checks)

If you live in or near Portland, there's almost no chance this is the first you'll hear of Slappy Cakes. I can't think of a place that got more buzz when it opened, and for a simple reason (which you probably already know about): You cook your own pancakes there. And you can get a Slappy Screw, but I'm getting ahead of myself.

I suppose the owners figured "cook your own" was about the last niche available in the Portland breakfast pantheon, so in 2009 Slappy Cakes opened in a neighborhood that didn't already have a breakfast joint, and the fire was lit.

It's a gigantic space, actually an early-twentieth-century garage, and they filled it with a combination of orange and fuchsia that puts you somewhere between art deco and the cheesy '70s. They also scored a collection of amazing twisted orange vases at an estate sale.

Giant paintings of pancakes add to the festive air—as does an outrageous cocktail menu, all made with locally distilled spirits. This is where you'll find the Slappy Screw, with Lovejoy Vodka, organic orange juice, and house-made ginger syrup. It's one of seven cocktails that, along with several champagne-based "sparkles" and a few Bloody Mary variations, are all available from opening time at 8:00 a.m. One owner came on my radio show and said they sell "whiskey for breakfast" mainly to nurses getting off the graveyard shift. Uh, right.

There is a kitchen-created menu here (chicken-fried steak, huevos rancheros, a few Benedicts, etc.), which answers a common question: why the hell would I pay them so I can cook my own pancakes? Well, they'll cook them if you like, but what's the point? Anyway, you're paying them to provide the batter, do the prep work, and clean up.

And it really is fun to cook the 'cakes on each table's Japanese teppa-nyaki grill (made in Germany, by the way). The staff spreads rice bran oil on the griddle, and you order (for $5 or $6) a little eight-ounce squeeze bottle filled with one of five batters: buttermilk, ginger, vegan whole grain, gluten-free, and a rotating seasonal option; I've seen peanut butter, carrot-cardamom, and pumpkin. Yes, I've been in a few times. And yes, you can make your cakes in whatever shape you want.

Then there are the mix-ins, which are $1 or $1.50 each. It's a heck of a list, with variations on chocolate, butterscotch, fruit, nuts, and creations such as lavender honey, lemon curd, and orange ginger marmalade. And that's just the sweet stuff! The savory list includes bacon, sausage (regular or veggie), peanut butter, cheddar/blue/goat/vegan cheese, roasted mushrooms, and chopped scallions. Organic maple syrup is $2.

The best plan seems to be to order one or two batters—either as an appetizer or just as the sweet alternative—and get something savory from the menu. Nobody seems too impressed with what the kitchen creates, and nobody seems to care, either. I think that's because they're too busy cooking their own pancakes and maybe enjoying a Slappy Screw.

WAIT: Crazy long and kid-inundated on weekends. **LARGE GROUPS:** With notice. **COFFEE:** Stumptown. **OTHER DRINKS:** Espresso, Foxfire Teas, Columbia Gorge organic juices, beer, wine, cocktails. **FEEL-GOODS:** Local, seasonal, organic produce, plus a garden out back. **HEALTH OPTIONS:** Gluten-free batter and plenty of stuff for vegetarians and vegans. **WIFI:** No.

STEPPING STONE CAFE

Hip/Mom & Pop

Northwest Portland really does have a neighborhood place!

2390 NW Quimby St. (NW)

503-222-1132

steppingstonecafe.com

Monday and Tuesday 6 a.m. to 7 p.m.,

Wednesday and Thursday 6 a.m. to 10 p.m.,

Friday 6 a.m. to 3 a.m., Saturday 7:30 a.m. to 3 a.m., Sunday 7:30 a.m. to 10 p.m.

$10–$14 (all major cards, no checks)

My first apartment in Portland was on Northwest Quimby Street, back in 1996. I had just stumbled into town from a fishing season in Alaska, and on one of my first lonely mornings, I started walking toward Northwest 23rd Avenue, the only street I knew. On the way I passed a little corner diner with five people sitting in it. I heard laughter and smelled bacon. I couldn't resist.

I walked into Stepping Stone Cafe and immediately found myself taking, and then giving, a bunch of crap from the guy working there. I was fresh off a fishing boat, more than capable in such pursuits, and I immediately fit in. For the next six months, until my fishing money ran out and I had to move to a hovel in Southeast, I ate at Stepping Stone several times a week, and the legendary, cranky staffer became something of a friend—until one day, according to published reports, he relapsed into his drug habit and was banned from the premises.

Those were different times, and today Stepping Stone is friendlier, although the official motto remains: You eat here because we let you.

I make it back to Northwest often, and Stepping Stone still feels like my local place. Yes, even fashionable Northwest has a little neighborhood diner. It's not flashy like Meriwether's or sophisticated like Besaw's. It's just a diner, and has been for more than 50 years, since the block across the street (now townhouses) hosted a garage for the streetcar.

The menu is probably similar to what the old streetcar guys ate: chicken-fried steak, ham, Tillamook cheddar, five scrambles, and 10 omelets, although they probably didn't have sundried-tomato-basil-chicken sausage or an omelet with spinach, portobello, feta, and artichoke. The menu has also expanded to include three kinds of French toast, Belgian waffles, and cheese blintzes. The cinnamon sweet roll is still insane (they used to joke that if you eat 10, you get a free angioplasty), and now it's been sliced up for French toast.

There's still a slight edge of funkiness about the place, like the dismembered action-hero dolls that move up and down when the doors open, and the chain-pull toilet in the men's room, where a Help Wanted sign hung for years. But it's also extremely down-home, with checkered tablecloths, red vinyl chairs, immensely charming booths, and pictures of friends (called Stepping Stoners) on the wall.

You won't see high-heeled ladies sipping mimosas; more likely a musician just waking up and doing a crossword or, god bless him, some hungover, stoned kid in a corner booth staring blankly into his coffee.

I'm not that kid anymore, but I still feel at home at Stepping Stone. And now that it's become entirely cruelty-free, you can too.

WAIT: Long on weekends, almost entirely outside. **LARGE GROUPS:** Yes. **COFFEE:** Portland Roasting special blend. **OTHER DRINKS:** Cocktails, great milkshakes, hot chocolate, cocktails, and beer. **FEEL-GOODS:** Nothing jumps out. **HEALTH OPTIONS:** One tofu scramble; veggie sausage. **WIFI:** Yes.

SUGAR MAMA'S CAFE

Old School	
Southern-style belly bombs.	
320 SW Alder St. (Downtown)	
503-224-3323	
Daily 7 a.m. to 3 p.m.	
$12–$14 (Visa, MasterCard, no checks)	

For much of 2013, I rented an office in downtown Portland, and across the street was a breakfast place trying to open. It was the new location of Sugar Mama's Cafe, and it turns out their delays—while officially having to do with plumbing and other mundane things—was like the Manhattan Project of Portland breakfast places. That is, behind those papered windows, these people were building belly bombs!

They've been open since that summer, and I've been in twice now to check out their Southern-style food and what they claim to be, yes, the best biscuits and gravy in town—a claim that seems bold until you continue on to "best meatloaf on the planet."

They already had me with these gut-busters, but when I walked by on a Friday, I knew I was in trouble. A sign in the window said *Cinnamon Roll Friday*. I walked no more on that morning.

Yes, every Friday these folks serve up variations on the cinnamon roll. The specials board on my table ran through the selections: classic; toasted pecans with house-made caramel; bacon-maple; French toast with fruit, maple, or bacon; and cinnamon roll bread pudding.

I don't think there's any Portland breakfast place that is as obviously family-run as this one—especially since Johnny B's closed. When I walked in, I found a woman at the counter wearing an apron and eating her breakfast—the same woman who seems to always be there. I assume this is "Mom," as the other folks working there all seem to be related. When I said something to the waiter about the size of one cinnamon roll, he said he's struggled with weight all his life "from eating this food." He's been my waiter all three times, by the way, and on one occasion he said of some dish, "If anybody can cook it, my mom can!" Mom apparently likes to bake, as well, judging from the always-stuffed pastry counter, even when it isn't Cinnamon Roll Friday.

Feeling all Southern, I decided on one occasion to get the biscuits and gravy. I don't know about "best in town," but only because I refuse to go on some kind of a biscuits-and-gravy tour of the city. I rather enjoy being alive and hope to see the age of 50. But these were darn good, with biscuits that stayed firm without being too hard, gravy that was thick and creamy and peppery, and actually just about the right-sized portion. Nice job, Mom!

One another visit I got the "Memphis Morning," which is creamy polenta with greens and two eggs. I grew up in Memphis, and back home we call 'em cheese grits, but I guess now it's polenta?

The grits polenta was nice, the greens done just right, and the eggs… well, they were eggs. Over medium, just the way I like 'em. Another time, still in my Memphis groove, I got the pulled pork and sweet potato hash, with yams, apples, onions, and bacon—because, you know, the plate obviously needed some bacon added to it!

I followed up both of those meals with a Nashville Nap.

The old location, closer to PSU, had a little more of a down-home feel to it—by which I mean it was small and semidingy. I am probably supposed to say that was more "authentically Southern," but that's crap. They upgraded to a bigger, nicer place, even if it does have an odd combination of pale green walls, blue ceiling, and purple piping. They still have cute salt and pepper shakers.

All in all, Sugar Mama's is a fine and homey addition to the downtown Portland breakfast scene. It's not the best place in town, but it serves a niche that downtown didn't have before: a comfy, cozy home-style place where you can always get a table, you'll recognize your server and host, and they will straight up drop a belly bomb on you, whenever you like.

WAIT: None. **LARGE GROUPS:** With notice. **COFFEE:** Basic. **OTHER DRINKS:** Tea. **FEEL-GOODS:** Come on! **HEALTH OPTIONS:** Still with this? **WIFI:** No.

SWEEDEEDEE

New/Hip
"It always works out."
5202 N Albina Ave. (N/Inner)
503-946-8087
sweedeedeepdx.tumblr.com
Monday through Saturday 8 a.m. to 4 p.m., Sunday 8 a.m. to 2 p.m.
$12–$14 (Visa, MasterCard, no checks)

One weekend I had a chance to eat brunch at Sweedeedee, in North Portland. It's an insanely cute little place, and I had heard many good things about the food. Jen Stevenson, of *100 Best Places to Stuff Your Faces*, said something like "favorite place ever."

Well, it couldn't be more Portland, from the screen door to the pies, the wood floors to the jars in windows, the iPad register, the pickled carrots, and the young folks running it. Adorable little place.

And it is little, like with twenty-something seats, tops. And herein lies the rub, for my money. We got there and got in line to order, but all the tables were filled. It seemed odd to place an order when there's no place to sit, but I was told, "By the time your food comes out a table will come up. It always works out."

For the record, that did happen. But…

Maybe I'm just being grumpy. But why take my order if there's no place to sit? Why create the anxiety of me (along with many others) standing around, waiting for food, while vulturing over tables? There's also no designated waiting area, so you're literally hovering over others while they eat.

Meanwhile, you take what tables you can. I saw a party of four crammed around what should be a two-top. I saw someone standing at the counter, with their plate between her two seated friends…what's the point? Why not seat us, then take our order? We'll wait. On the other hand, it *does* seem to work out, so maybe it's genius.

All right, like I said, a table opened up, and we grabbed it, with three other parties hovering around. End of complaining. More or less.

What came out, a while later, was two little plates of perfectly matched breakfast heaven. They, like the place, were adorable! I got the corn cakes with eggs, bacon, and greens. Why more restaurants in Portland don't offer a little sweet-and-savory variety plate like this is beyond me.

My friend got a breakfast plate with bacon, egg, salad, cheese, pear, bread, and marmalade. All delightful. I would tell you more about the menu, but there wasn't one to steal ask for, and they have cute animal videos on their website instead of their menu. Oh, Portland.

The bacon was perfectly crisp, my eggs were just as I like 'em, and in short everything was yummy — except for the logistics. Jen complains about this, as well, so I think it isn't just me. We were there on a Sunday around nine, and it was packed. Not sure what it's like during the week.

So, the bottom line: cute place, great food, hassle seating. Or I'm an old fart. I just have to figure out a way to keep going to Sweedeedee.

WAIT: Yes, and it's awkward. **LARGE GROUPS:** Hell, no. **COFFEE:** Extracto. **OTHER DRINKS:** Tea, kombucha. mimosas, wine, beer, sparkling water. **FEEL-GOODS:** Local ingredients. **HEALTH OPTIONS:** Anything can be made vegetarian; some vegan options. **WIFI:** No.

TASTY N SONS/TASTY N ALDER

New/Hip
A long, fine journey continues.
Tasty n Sons: 3808 N Williams (N/Inner)
503-621-1400
Tasty n Alder: 580 SW 12th (Downtown)
503-621-9251
tastyntasty.com
Daily 9 a.m. to 2 p.m.
$10–$15 (Visa, MasterCard, American Express, no checks)

The short version of this story is that a guy with a lot of restaurant experience lived in a neighborhood that didn't have a breakfast place, so he opened one. But saying John Gorham has a lot of restaurant experience is like saying Michael Jordan played basketball. And calling Tasty n Sons a breakfast place is like calling U2 a band.

So here's a little more background. Gorham grew up in a restaurant family and always wanted to be a chef; he was working in kitchens before he finished high school. He then hit the road, working the kitchen circuit—golf courses, ski resorts, etc.—and did some traveling in Europe. He worked at the landmark Cafe Zenon in Eugene in 1993, where he discovered the joys of buying direct from farmers. He also knew a Malaysian woman married to a Chinese man who opened a casino in western Africa, and he helped open a restaurant there while also working as a pit boss in the casino. He is, by the way, a great storyteller.

In the late '90s, he wound up in Berkeley and in the extended family of Chez Panisse chefs; he helped open an Italian place there, then came back to Oregon in 2001, where he opened another Italian place, Fratelli. But soon after that, his long-time desire to run his own place started to blossom, and he got a chance to buy Viande, the meat counter inside City Market on NW 21st. He did that in partnership with Ben Dyer, who he'd worked with at Zenon, and since neither one wanted to run a meat counter, they together started a Sunday evening supper club (served at Bridges Cafe) called Simpatica—now housed on Southeast Pine Street and described elsewhere in this book.

Still with me? I love these kinds of restaurant stories. Turns out Simpatica's most popular nights were the tapas meals, and in fact *USA Today* called their tapas night "the No. 1 meal in the world," for whatever that's worth. That, Gorham says, was it; he sold out, bought a ticket to Barcelona to study tapas kitchens, and came home to start Toro Bravo. The lesson, as he put it on my podcast, was that "family style was the way to go. Please bring it all at once, put in the middle of the table, and we're gonna feast."

And *that* is what happens at Tasty n Sons. It was the culmination of a local genius's career up to that point. (He has since added a tapas cookbook called *Toro Bravo* and Tasty N Alder downtown.) The menu changes regularly, based on what's in season and what the crew feels like cooking; when I asked him to describe the food, the first thing he mentioned was the chocolate-potato doughnut with crème anglaise. He also mentioned the yams with toasted cumin, glazed in maple syrup. And the frittata with (when I asked) fava beans, olives, confit green beans, caramelized onions, and feta, served in the cast-iron pan.

I could go on. But you need to go on over there. Get a crew together, feast, and be glad you're in John Gorham's hometown.

WAIT: Crazy on weekends. **LARGE GROUPS:** Yes, and they take limited reservations for parties of six or more. **COFFEE:** Water Avenue. **OTHER DRINKS:** Steve Smith teas; fresh-squeezed orange, grapefruit, and cranberry juice; soda; wine, beer, and cocktails. **FEEL-GOODS:** Local ingredients abound. **HEALTH OPTIONS:** Vegetarians and vegans could do well. **WIFI:** No.

TIN SHED GARDEN CAFÉ

New
What was once "pioneering" has gone massively mainstream.
1438 NE Alberta St. (NE/Alberta)
503-288-6966
tinshedgardencafe.com
Breakfast daily 7 a.m. to 3 p.m.
$11–$13 (Visa, MasterCard, no checks)

If you're fairly new to the Alberta Street scene, you might not remember the Clown House. You might not remember when Last Thursday consisted of folks sipping cocktails and walking from one art gallery to another. Or when the idea of a restaurant with mushroom-rosemary gravy, and a motto about energy traveling through food, was considered something new and perhaps weird.

But that was the world the Tin Shed entered in the old days of about 2001, when for a lot of people, this and one or two other restaurants were the main reason to go up there. Now Tin Shed is so mainstream, and the lines are so long, that I already hear people wonder why you'd wait that long for that food. Times have certainly changed.

Once you get inside—and it will be an hour or more on weekends—the feel that's always struck me is grown-up hippie, or as a fellow former Southerner put it, "kinda weird, but good." He was referring to the Brie and green apples on top of his Sweet Chix scramble (with chicken-apple sausage, sweet onion, basil, and roasted red peppers). But he might as well have been talking about the light fixtures with forks on them, the artwork, or even some of the people eating breakfast. The crowd is Alberta Arts + late-rising horn-rimmed hipster + just-bought-a-house

 young adult, all watched by curious tourists from other parts of town (or, now, other towns) coming over to check out "goofy Portland."

Tin Shed is a monument to what has happened on Alberta. As late as the

mid-'90s, Alberta was a place that showed up on the local news every month or so—with police lights flashing. But it was cheap to live there, so artists moved in. Then came coffee shops, galleries, and the Last Thursday art walk. Eventually, people started noticing all the cheap, older houses around the neighborhood.

Flash forward a few years. Folks are sitting in the Tin Shed's garden patio eating French toast made with sweet-potato brioche; scrambles with portobello mushrooms, sun-dried tomatoes, spinach, and goat cheese; and the Tim Curry: tofu, roasted garlic, yams, zucchini, mushrooms, and sweet onion in a coconut-curry sauce served over a bed of spinach and topped with avocado.

Flash forward a few more years, and Guy Fieri appears on their website, for heaven's sake.

And then there's the potato cake. It's what the place is known for, and as a signature, it's an appropriate choice. The Shed potato cake is somewhere between hash browns and potato pancake—golden brown outside, soft in the middle, semimashed and semistringy—and served by the hundreds each day, either as a side (with sour cream and green onions) or underneath a scramble with bacon and eggs and cheddar, or sausage and gravy, or spicy sausage, peppers, onion, and eggs. Mmm.

In other words, the signature potato cake is just right: it's got variety, it's unique, and folks line up for it, kinda weird or not. And that's all you need to know about Tin Shed.

WAIT: Long, mainly on weekends, mostly outside. **LARGE GROUPS:** One big table seats eight. **COFFEE:** Their own Tin Shed Blend from Portland Roasting. **OTHER DRINKS:** Steven Smith teas, espresso, cocktails. **FEEL-GOODS:** Free-range eggs, and for a small fee you can get pure maple syrup. **HEALTH OPTIONS:** Vegetarian, vegan, egg whites, tofu. **WIFI:** No.

TOAST

New/Mom & Pop
One man's quest, a neighborhood's gain.
5222 SE 52nd Ave. (SE/Outer)
503-774-1020
toastpdx.com
Brunch daily 8 a.m. to 2 p.m.
$9–$20 (all major cards, no checks)

The way Donald Kotler sees it, every neighborhood needs a great breakfast place. So when he and some old restaurant friends wanted to open a place, it made sense to do breakfast in his own Woodstock neighborhood. Apparently, the neighborhood agreed: the day Kotler opened Toast in August 2007, a 45-minute line lasted for two hours. It's been hopping ever since.

Kotler's other goal was to keep it simple—on the menu and in the space. "We wanted to take food and bring it back to its simplest form, not overprocessing it or covering it with overly lemony hollandaise sauces, but letting the true flavors of the food stand out on their own," he told me on my old podcast.

Toast's appearance is also clean and simple, with bamboo tables and comfortable chairs. The room's history is a little more interesting: it used to be Bad Ass Video, purveyor of porn, and the name lives on in the Bad Ass Sandwich (fried eggs, bacon, goat's milk cheese, and field greens on toast served with a potato *rösti* for $9).

One more thing about the space ties in with Kotler's plan for the food: Toast is *small*—what you can see is all there is—meaning food can't be kept for very long. So everything is fresh, and much of it (like jams,

peppers, baked goods, and sausage) is made in-house. He's even got some herbs growing out back.

A lot of the food is from local farmers and vendors (ask to see a list of suppliers), and Kotler has created a menu that is, as he puts it, more brunch than breakfast. You can get mac and cheese at 8:00 a.m., for example—and it will be serpentini pasta with cave-aged Gruyère cheese, Mornay sauce, and herbs. Well! And there's beer and half a dozen cocktails. You'll find granola (called Hippies on Parfait) and oatmeal, and a pork belly hash served over squash, brussels sprouts, sweet potatoes, and fresh herbs drizzled with crème fraîche and topped with a sunny duck egg. You can get a hanger steak and eggs, several Benedicts (including one with tempeh), and granola-crusted French toast with whipped vanilla bean crème fraîche with local pear and apple marmalade.

Portions and prices (averaging $20 for mains) are quite reasonable, and everything I've had was tasty—never flashy, never awe-inspiring, but there's a lot to be said for fresh ingredients cooked well. What has always set Toast apart, for me, among Portland breakfast places, is their treatment of vegetables. Veggies here are fresh, abundant, and cooked perfectly. And the vibe, as you might expect from such a local place, is extremely welcoming and friendly. (I'm also a sucker for anyplace that welcomes you with a little scone of the day.)

Toast is wide open not only to changes ("We want to be a restaurant that says *yes,*" says Kotler) but also to suggestions: at first there was no bacon on the menu, but enough diners said they wanted it that there's now nitrate-free bacon.

What else would you expect from your little neighborhood brunch place?

WAIT: Can get long on weekends. **LARGE GROUPS:** Call ahead. **COFFEE:** Courier. **OTHER DRINKS:** Tazo teas, beer, wine, cocktails, juice. **FEEL-GOODS:** Everything's fresh, local, and natural; many organic ingredients. **HEALTH OPTIONS:** Cascade Farms Natural pork; tofu scrambles available on request. **WIFI:** Yes.

TOP HASHCAPADE (SEE PAGE 301)

TRINKET

New/Hip	
Cozy, comfy, nonthreatening.	
2035 SE Cesar E Chavez Blvd. (SE/Hawthorne)	
503-477-4252	
trinketpdx.com	
Daily 8 a.m. to 3:30 p.m.	
$14–$18 (all major cards, no checks)	

I guess we needed another Southeast brunch place, right? That what I thought when Trinket opened up on SE 39th Ave.—I mean, Cesar Chavez Blvd. in 2013.

It was at that time in the book-writing process when I hate breakfast, hate writing, and wish new places would stop opening up. So I was a tough sell. But as soon as I walked in, I liked the place. It's small, with dark wood and comfort-inducing touches like half curtains in the windows, an antler chandelier, and what look like old-fashioned plates from an estate sale or something.

A friend had told me I had to get a pistachio roll, and I try to follow instructions. Also, I always get whatever a place offers in the realm of baked + sweetness + nuts. This was a little $2 sweetheart, served on an old-timey plate.

I munched that while waiting for my friends. This was on a Thursday, and only three tables were occupied at 9:30. They are brunch-only, with breakfast and lunch items on a small menu, available 9 to 4 every day but Tuesday. The staff was lovely, and the place has its own little parking lot. So getting there and getting settled is easy and pleasant.

There were only three pure-breakfast options on the menu, plus a couple of waffles; the rest was lunch items. And, being a good Breakfast Crew, we got all three breakfasts! We do what it takes to report on Portland brunch.

The fall sausage hash came with parsnip, carrots, sausage, potatoes, onions, and two sunny-side-up eggs ($10). I had a taste and thought it was good, but not as good as my Benedict, with poached duck eggs, Canadian bacon, hollandaise, and an English muffin. Jenny, who ordered the hash, said later it was "not overly remarkable, but tasty."

The Benedict is the priciest breakfast item on the menu, at $13, and it was good. I'll go with "not overly remarkable," in fact. It was all well cooked, and I do like duck eggs, but it seemed to lack "pop," which I look for in a hollandaise. You might get it and think it's awesome; this kind of thing comes down to taste. The hash browns were fantastic, though—or, should I say, just the way I like 'em, which is crisp on the outside and soft on the inside.

The other thing we got to see, briefly, before it was consumed by a hoggish Crew member, was the polenta with steamed eggs and kale ($9). Apparently, it's a layer of creamy polenta, and mixed in are onions, garlic, mushrooms, and chili. I asked Hoggy for her take on it:

"Tasted better than it looked. In general, I prefer kale with more green, i.e., not overcooked, but it did have a soft texture that was similar to the polenta. The polenta was not as firm as in some restaurants, but soft and creamy on the tongue, more along the lines of grits. Happy for any veggies to be offered with breakfast."

On the menu when we visited, there were also a granola with fruit and two waffle options: sweet (apples, honey, cinnamon, and whipped cream) and savory (onion, bacon, thyme, and goat cheese).

Trinket's people, the setting, the location, the presentation…all solid. I wonder if the food will get more exciting as they go, but for right now, if somebody said, "Let's go to Trinket," I'd say *heck yeah*, and I'd try that savory waffle!

WAIT: Maybe on weekends. **LARGE GROUPS:** Up to 12, with notice. **COFFEE:** Extracto. **OTHER DRINKS:** Fresh-squeezed juices; a whole "spirits" menu. **FEEL-GOODS:** Ingredients locally sourced, organic, and seasonal whenever possible. **HEALTH OPTIONS:** Vegetarian, vegan, and gluten-free friendly; small-plate breakfasts available. **WIFI:** Yes.

UTOPIA CAFE

New/Hip/Veggie
Grown-up hippie, or hippie grown-up?
3308 SE Belmont St. (SE/Belmont)
503-235-7606
Breakfast weekdays 7 a.m. to 2 p.m., weekends 7:30 a.m. to 2:20 p.m.
$9–$14 (Visa, MasterCard, no checks)

"Not as hippie as I expected."

That's the first line in my coffee-stained handwritten notes from a trip to Utopia. I don't recall whether it was good news or bad. I guess I was expecting something a bit more airy from a place in Southeast Portland called Utopia.

I was probably just being cranky. When I entered through the very cool old-timey screen door, though, I saw a long black bar, Formica tables, lovely wood floors, high ceilings, fused-glass art on the walls, and faux stained glass. It was all very clean and modern, and not a bit rustic. "This is nice," I thought—as if *hippie* and *nice* couldn't possibly coexist. Just being cranky, I'm sure.

Out came the menu, and it was pure Portland: eight scrambles ranging from Garden (with goat cheese) and no-egg Tofu (with tomato, onion, zucchini, mushroom, basil, and garlic) to the Baja (with chorizo) and the Camp (with bacon, mushrooms, and red and green peppers). And they'll sub tofu for eggs or meat for no charge.

I was eating with two women who called themselves the Candida Sisters because they both had issues about eating sugar and wheat, and they had no problem finding stuff they could eat. And substitutions were easily made.

So here's the thing about Utopia. The first time I went, I came home with no notes at all; chalk that up to being distracted by eating with two women. The second time, I was in the neighborhood and wanted to try the Brioche French Toast. It was amazing and bountiful. I wasn't really in "work mode," so I still didn't have good notes on the place. The next time I got the Bacavo Scramble with bacon, tomato, avocado, and blue cheese crumbles. It, too, was amazing. Again, I took almost no notes.

For some reason I could not get a handle on the Utopia Cafe. So I decided to see what other writers had to say. Among all the Internet praise, I found this from the *Portland Mercury*: "There's no angle on the Utopia Cafe. It's not a good place to take Grandma, it's not great for a date, it's not healthy, it's not vegan, it doesn't have great ambiance and they don't allow dogs. It's just really good food."

So it wasn't just me! Then I found this in the *Willamette Week*: "Utopia offers a breakfast dish I have never seen before, and it strikes a very satisfying note: hot wild rice…a mix of long gray and black grains, thoughtfully served with raisins, hazelnuts, and brown sugar."

Really? Utopia has that? Well, I dragged out the menu, and, by golly, it does. It's past the From the Griddle section, which explains why I never made it that far. I also saw Fried Cornmeal, cooked on the grill and served with warm syrup. Somehow I missed that, too. Clearly, I need to go back—a pattern I have no intention of ending.

WAIT: Pretty long on weekends, with some space inside but little cover outside. **LARGE GROUPS:** Yes, but no split checks for parties of five or more on weekends. **COFFEE:** Portland Roasting, Utopia Blend. **OTHER DRINKS:** Espresso, Kobos loose-leaf tea, juice, milk, soda. **FEEL-GOODS:** Lots of organic stuff. **HEALTH OPTIONS:** Plenty of vegetarian options as well as egg substitute and egg whites available for a small charge. And they can make any scramble vegan. **WIFI:** No.

VERDE COCINA

New/Weekend
Beautiful, tasty, healthy, and fresh.
6446 SW Capitol Highway (SW/Inner)
503-384-2327
Daily 9 a.m. to 3 p.m.
524 NW 14th (Pearl)
Weekends 9 a.m. to 2 p.m.
(503) 894-9321
verdecocinamarket.com
$12–$14 (all major cards, no checks)

Surprises were the order of the day when I went to Verde Cocina in the Pearl. The out-of-the-way location was new, for one thing. After they started in the Portland Farmers Market and expanded to a location in Multnomah Village, Verde Cocina popped up in the Pearl—but on NW 14th by Glisan. It's like the outskirts of the Pearl, over by the highway and some of the last commercial printing outfits in the neighborhood.

Pleasant Surprise No. 2 occurred when I sat right down—that's right, no line, in the Pearl, on a weekend. Then came Pleasant Surprise No. 3, the menu. That's where you really see the essence of Verde Cocina: the beauty of simplicity, of fresh ingredients, and yes, of a fantastic, healthy, and line-free Portland brunch, served in the Pearl District.

I went with the chilaquiles, because for me they kind of define a Mexican place. But we should stop at the word "Mexican," because some of you might still be tortured by this idea of Mexican food that places like Muchas Gracias have laid upon us: you know, a mushy semistew of refried beans, pale-red rice, sour cream, and some kind of meat. Yuck.

No, this is something else entirely. The defining aspect of Verde Cocina's food is a big pile of fresh, yummy, roasted vegetables. In fact, they call it Veggie Mountain, and it appears on everything. Consider the chilaquiles, which Wikipedia defines as, more or less, fried tortillas with salsa or mole poured over it, all of which is simmered for a while before meat, eggs, and maybe beans are added. I know, it sounds like Muchas Gracias, but plenty of places around Portland serve a kick-ass chilaquiles at breakfast or brunch (Autentica and even Veritable Quandary come to mind).

At Verde Cocina, it's not even a stew—more like a pile of fresh goodness. All the traditional ingredients are there, but with a Verde Cocina twist: a mountain of carrots, yellow squash, zucchini, onions, and kale. Its website talks about how the chef looks for fresh vegetables daily (everything is sourced locally), so you never know which flavor of mountain you'll get.

My companion for the day, writer/editor Martha Wagner, is gluten-free and had recommended this place. (In fact, she wrote the gluten-free chapter that appears on page 281.) She got their take on Huevos Rancheros, which has been rendered lame at so many other places. Here, it's eggs on a tortilla with white beans, the same veggie mountain I had, and a little dusting of fresh Cotija cheese.

Pleasant Surprise No....whatever I'm on...came when I bit into my chilaquiles. It took me a second to figure out what this amazing sensation was, coursing through my mouth. I finally realized: it was the taste of fresh corn! The tortillas in this dish (gluten-free, by the way) just exploded on my tongue. It's like I'd forgotten what fresh corn tastes like—and it's great, by the way.

I used to have a "lovely assistant" named Elisa, who contributed to my blog for a while. She actually met the owners at the Hillsdale location and explained where this whole pile-of-fresh-veggies thing comes from: "Chef Noe Garnica is from Guanajuato, Mexico where he grew up farming and practicing sustainable living with his large family. His wife, Anna, is from California, where she grew up surrounded by agriculture in her rural town. Together, they have striven to offer the richness of the Northwest with Mexican flair and flavor. And they have succeeded!"

Indeed they have. *Vamonos a la Verde Cocina!*

WAIT: Not usually. **LARGE GROUPS:** No more than eight; call ahead. **COFFEE:** Nossa Familia. **OTHER DRINKS:** Tea, agua fresca, kombucha, beer, wine, cocktails. **FEEL-GOODS:** All local produce and products. **HEALTH OPTIONS:** Vegetarian, vegan options; 100 percent gluten-free menu; will accommodate food allergies. **WIFI:** Yes.

VERITABLE QUANDARY

New/Classy/Weekend
Old-style class, new-style cuisine.
1220 SW 1st Ave. (Downtown)
503-227-7342
veritablequandary.com
Brunch weekends 9:30 a.m. to 3 p.m.
$15–$20 (all major cards, no checks)

Portlanders have been eating at VQ for almost 40 years. The place is also a visual anchor, perched near the end of the Hawthorne Bridge, and it's been a popular lunch, dinner, and happy hour hangout for a generation or two. There's also been a long-running question: just what kind of place is it?

Is it a serious restaurant that wants to compete with the city's finest? Is it a casual lunch hangout? A happy hour where lawyers and downtown corporate types hit on one another? A tourist spot? A fancy bar? The answer to all seems to be *yes.*

My feeling is this: let's say there are three very general levels of restaurant. The low-end places are the cafés and diners of the world. The high-end places inspire foodie conversations about the presentation of the *osso buco* or the subtle mix of flavors in an *amuse-bouche*. And then there's an area in the middle, whose inhabitants are trying to find a balance between casual and fine dining. I put VQ up at the top of this midsection, where your Benedict with house-smoked pork loin is $15 and your Spicy Prawn and Pork Belly Hash is $16.

I am probably overthinking this thing. And overwriting it. It just seems like, to foodies, VQ is a small step below their usual haunts, and to the

other 80 percent of people, it's a fancy place that makes a fine start for a special cultural evening downtown. I do know that my good friend Mindie Kniss, the most frequent guest on my podcast, says VQ is her favorite place in town.

The staff, which trends to young and cute, is everywhere and extremely helpful. The seating options include a dark, elegant bar; a light, airy dining room with tall windows; the famed flower-adorned patio; and a super cool wine cellar with one table for about eight.

The menu is grounded in everyday breakfast tradition, but with foodie twists—and prices. For example, I once saw a sausage-and-egg plate that was actually house-made Italian sausage, two local unpasteurized eggs, potato cakes, and "Peppers & Onions Agro Dolce tossed with fresh Mozzarella, Arugula, and Basil." When I went with my friends Bob and Judy, none of us knew what Agro Dolce was, and for $14 we decided we could get something else anyway.

Bob got the Benedict, on house-made English muffins with house-smoked pork loin, and he loved it. Judy had the Chilaquiles with Manchego, which the menu said was tortillas with chile sauce and scrambled eggs, guacamole, and crème fraîche. She also loved it. And I think it's the typical VQ brunch dish, because (a) it was really good, (b) it looked and sounded fancy, and (c) it could also, accurately, have been called Breakfast Nachos.

Now, am I saying VQ is trying to be something it isn't? The thought has occurred to me. Am I saying it is a serious restaurant trying to "keep it real"? I'd say that applies as well. What it seems to boil down to, though, is that whatever you're looking for in a slightly upscale brunch, it's probably a good idea to check out VQ, especially in nice weather, as they have a darn fine patio as well.

WAIT: Tends to form later in the morning. **LARGE GROUPS:** Yes, especially if you can get the wine cellar room. **COFFEE:** Stumptown. **OTHER DRINKS:** Full bar, espresso, and fresh-squeezed juices. **FEEL-GOODS:** Plenty of local ingredients and only local unpasteurized eggs. **HEALTH OPTIONS:** A few vegetarian options. **WIFI:** Yes.

VITA CAFE

Hip/Veggie/Kiddie

A veggie palace, a local hangout, a Portland institution.

3023 NE Alberta St. (NE/Alberta)

503-335-8233

vita-cafe.com

Breakfast daily 9 a.m. to 3 p.m., weekends 8 a.m. to 3 p.m.

$9–$13 (Visa, MasterCard, local checks)

When my college roommate was visiting from Dallas, Texas, he brought his wife, their three kids, his mom, and his wife's parents. The group collectively became known simply as the Texans.

My friends wanted to know how the Texans were liking Oregon, where I was taking them, and so on. And since they like to eat organic whenever possible, I knew before they came to town that I'd take them to Vita Cafe, a monument to what "my" Portland is all about: healthy food, community, grassroots neighborhood development, hipsters, hippies, leisurely breakfasts, outdoor dining, and local-sustainable-organic-vegetarian-vegan food.

The first charming moment came when the eldest Texan, after watching some of the human traffic stroll by on Alberta, asked me sincerely, "Paul, where does a woman with tattoos get a job?"

It may be that nothing like Vita Cafe or Alberta Street has ever happened in Dallas. The menu at Vita is a vast array of mostly vegetarian and vegan dishes. I wanted the Texans to see that organic, vegan food can be both good and filling. They pored over the menu, expressing surprise at tasty-sounding dishes like a Greek, Mediterranean, Mexican, or Italian scramble, asking me, "And it's *vegan*?" It is, if you get it with

tofu or tempeh instead of with free-range eggs.

Then they asked what tempeh was, as well as tofu, jicama, miso, and TVP. And how you get milk from rice or soybeans. I didn't know, actually, but it's all explained in the Food for Thought section of the menu, which brings me to another of Vita's endearing qualities: it is by no means an elitist place. It's practically an advertisement for a food movement that doubles as a kid-friendly restaurant and neighborhood hangout. There's a full bar and happy-hour specials, and kids eat for a buck daily from 5 to 7 p.m. There's even a bocce ball court on the sprawling patio.

The best-known breakfast dishes are the corn cakes (including Mexican and Thai versions), the "Chicken" Fried Steak made with tempeh, and my favorite, the Tofurky Florentine, which is English muffins topped with slices of Tofurky, spinach, vegan hollandaise (warning: it's brown), and either eggs or tofu. I'm not a vegetarian by any means, but I feel right at home at Vita; in fact, my favorite dessert in town is the super-sweet (and also vegan and wheat-free) carrot cake.

For me, the lasting image is sweet and wholesome. Late in the meal, with the kids romping on the patio with the not-too-hot sunshine streaming down, one Texan asked another with a slight grin, "How's your fake food?" Without even looking up from her rapidly emptying plate, Texan #2 just mumbled and gave two thumbs up.

WAIT: A little on weekends, mostly outside. **LARGE GROUPS:** Yes. **COFFEE:** Stumptown. **OTHER DRINKS:** Smoothies, fresh juices, tea, full bar. **FEEL-GOODS:** Free-range, sustainable, local ingredients; 1 percent of sales is donated to local social and environmental groups. **HEALTH OPTIONS:** Everywhere! **WIFI:** Yes.

WEST CAFE

Weekend/Classy/Veggie
All things to all people?
1201 SW Jefferson St. (Downtown)
503-227-8189
westcafepdx.com
Sunday 10 a.m. to 2 p.m.
$12–$14 (all major cards, no checks)

I go to the Unitarian church in downtown Portland, and West Cafe is right down the street. I've seen it for years, and the only people I ever knew who ate there were Unitarians. I always wondered: if nobody ever tells me, the Breakfast Guy, about a place that serves breakfast, what does that mean?

Well, here's what I think: if breakfast places were churches, the West Cafe would be Unitarian.

Understand, I love the Unitarian church. Yet there are some funny things about it, and Unitarians often make fun of themselves. For one thing, they are always trying to explain—to themselves and each other—who they are and what they believe. They are a little bit churchy, with a choir and a pipe organ, but real low-key, polite, non-flashy, and open to nearly everything. For example, the church hosts Buddhist meditation group and occasional pagan services.

And the West Cafe is…well, start with the name. What does that mean? Does it project anything to you? Northwest means something, Southwest means something, but just West? Next up is the decor. It's a perfectly nice place, a little bit fancy but not trying to wow you. It's… comfortable, aiming for class.

Reviewers have used phrases such as "a little something for almost every taste," "a long list of healthy creative entrées," and "sophisticated American food," whatever that means. Even their website says it's "simply inspired" and "casual but comfortable." In fact, the restaurant once had a contest on their Facebook page to come up with a name for their cuisine!

Next up is the crowd, which is slightly older than average— certainly when compared to, say, Cricket Cafe. The menu is a true brunch, with six starters, 11 breakfasts, 11 soups and salads, and a dozen or more sandwiches and wraps. Breakfasts range from the basic, like a skillet scramble, to the fancier, like poached eggs with crab meat and a roasted garlic-tarragon aioli. From "skillet scramble" to "tarragon aioli" pretty much covers everything—kind of like a Christian church with Buddhists in it.

As for the quality of the food, it's also non-flashy, non-wow, safe, and welcoming. And yes, I just said it wasn't particularly great. Then again, it wasn't bad. Most of my group thought our food was well-done but uninspired. For example, we joked that the French toast was just like Mom made—literally.

The best things I tasted were the oatmeal pancakes (with a berry salad, candied hazelnuts, and dark, rich maple syrup) and a wild mushroom, spinach, chèvre, and caramelized onion tart from the starter menu. The one bite I had of that tart was the highlight of the meal: like how the minister at my church occasionally says something that makes me look around at people as if to say, "Did a preacher just say that in church?"

So I'd say that if you're looking for a welcoming, friendly, community-oriented church to attend, check out the Unitarians. And if you're downtown on a Sunday looking for a decent brunch with no line, check out West Cafe.

WAIT: Yes, when two nearby churches let out at 11 a.m.; best to arrive earlier. **LARGE GROUPS:** Yes. **COFFEE:** Portland Roasting. **OTHER DRINKS:** Numi teas, juice, mimosas, Bloody Marys. **FEEL-GOODS:** None they tout. **HEALTH OPTIONS:** Numerous veggie and gluten-free options. **WIFI:** Yes.

WILD ABANDON

Hip/Veggie/Weekend
Mmmm, red velvet!
2411 SE Belmont St. (SE/Belmont)
503-232-4458
wildabandonrestaurant.com
Weekends 9 a.m. to 2 p.m.
$12–$15 (all major cards, no checks)

Six of us once tried to come up with the theme of Wild Abandon. The mural on the wall says either *Greek bacchanalia* or *Druid ritual*. The dark red tones say *New Orleans.* The sculpted hands holding candles on the walls say *freaky.* The old-school country music says *honky-tonk.* Somewhere we sensed a thread in there; we just couldn't put a finger on it.

Then Michael, the owner, told us he calls the place "garage sale baroque." *That* was it! He explained that back in the '70s, his grandmother had a basement filled with frosted Mexican lights—he assured us that Grandma's was "*the*'70s basement"—and that was the feel he was going for. He got it. In fact, one of Grandma's original lights is on the right as you walk out to the big, beautiful patio. Look for the hole in the back, where Michael accidentally hit it trying to toss a spoon into a bus tray.

He also said the building was the original home of Montage before that restaurant moved to its funky home under the Morrison Bridge. So the theme kind of continued, we thought. Before that it was a barbershop, and before that, Michael said, it was (no lie) Ginger's Sexy Sauna. Some guy once told Michael he had lost his virginity on the premises.

Michael calls himself "an old restaurant hand" and has given his

funky-feeling place a selection of old-fashioned breakfasts and a casual ambience. Basic omelets and scrambles run about $8–10, three Benedicts (spinach, ham, and salmon) average $10, and vegetarians and vegans will find several options. In fact, Wild Abandon offers a Vegan French Toast made with soy milk, soy butter, and real maple syrup.

The Old Fashioned French Toast, like the restaurant, had a little something we couldn't put our finger on; we thought it might be rum, fitting the theme, but Michael said it was orange juice. I guess we were just getting carried away. By that time our conversation had turned to a wacky combination of humanism, Alaskan fishing, our server's tale of coffee sampling (known as "cupping") to get the blend just right, and my trivia contest to see if anyone else could tell Marty Robbins from Hank Williams and Hank Snow.

Like the mood, we thought the food was just right: the Benedicts had a little crunch to the muffins, a light sauce, and some bite in the spinach. I had to defend my French toast from inquiring hands. There's a little Mexican flair to the menu, as well: Richard's Chilaquiles is an egg scramble with peppers, onions, cheddar, and fried tortilla strips, all topped with black beans, salsa, sour cream, and cilantro. Both come with or without chorizo, as does the breakfast burrito.

Mexican food, Marty Robbins, Grandma's basement, freaky hands holding candles, down-home food, cocktails, red velvet…. I'm telling you, there's a theme in there somewhere. I guess we'll have to keep going back to nail it down completely.

WAIT: Seldom. **LARGE GROUPS:** Yes, with notice. **COFFEE:** Bridgetown special blend. **OTHER DRINKS:** Stash teas, beer, wine, cocktails. **FEEL-GOODS:** None in particular. **HEALTH OPTIONS:** Garden sausage, soy products (including tofu), and an entire vegan section on the menu. **WIFI:** Yes.

XICO

Weekend/New/Classy	
What is Spanish for "holy crap, this is good"?	
3717 SE Division (SE/Division)	
503-548-6343	
xicopdx.com	
Brunch Sunday 10 a.m. to 2 p.m.	
$15–$18 (all major cards, no checks)	

Xico sits at the intersection of two huge trends that have hit Portland in the last few years: the spread of some seriously good Mexican food, and the explosion of restaurants along Division Street.

It's also a diversion from trend in this book. Namely, I have included them even though they only serve six brunch items for four hours a week. That boils down to four words: Pork Belly Carnitas Hash.

When I told the Crew we were going to check out a new Mexican place, I had to answer a few questions. No, I said, this isn't a place with breakfast burritos, and it's pronounced "chee-co." Also, I had to lay down one law: Nobody orders or touches the pork belly carnitas hash but me.

From the outside, the restaurant looks small and, frankly, a little confusing. It has nice big windows and plants in pots on the sidewalk, but also a multicolored neon sign that kind of clashes with the otherwise simple scene. Inside are plastic green chairs sitting at shiny metal tables with a faux marble pillar holding up hanging plants and flowers all over the place. I found it confusing, but strangely nice. I also know less of fashion and design than I do of nuclear physics.

But this is part of the evolution of "Mexican restaurant" on the Portland scene. I don't know exactly when we started getting places like Autentica (see page 34), Mi Mero Mole, Trebol, Mextiza (see page 156), and Xico, but it wasn't that long ago. And I'm darn happy about it. So was the Crew when we ordered a bowl of guacamole and chips, and out came the most beautiful little display of fresh, thick, and crisp corn chips served with a guacamole bright in appearance and taste. According to the menu it's molcajete guacamole, and I neither know nor care what that means. I could have eaten a gallon of it with those chips.

There were enough of us to order the whole menu, so we went for it. The Sopes Florentine (which doesn't sound Mexican) was their version of a Benedict, but the hollandaise was poured over masa cups, sautéed kale, and poached eggs, and you can add house chorizo as well. The Huevos Rancheros came with bacon, tomato, and jalapeno salsa. But everybody's favorite was the hot cakes and fruit compote, which doesn't sound like much but was

made with fresh-ground corn masa dough and topped with seasonal fruit, whipped cream, and mole spices. That's when somebody wanted to know how you say "holy crap, this is good" in Spanish.

Oh, and the pork belly carnitas hash, braised and fried in chili, with tomatillo-avocado salsa? Um, yeah, I don't recall. Nothing to report there at all. Like I told the Crew, just forget about it. There is no pork belly carnitas hash.

There are also no desserts, especially sopaipillas rolled in cinnamon and sugar and served with *dulce de leche* and chocolate-coconut sauces, nor a sweet potato pie parfait, nor hot drinking chocolate.

Mmm, hot drinking chocolate…

WAIT: Rarely, but they take reservations. **LARGE GROUPS:** Yes, with notice. **COFFEE:** Beans from Oaxaca, Mexico, roasted by Flying Goat. **OTHER DRINKS:** Horchata, hibiscus tea, cocktails, wine and beer, and (mmmm) drinking chocolate. **FEEL-GOODS:** None they tout. **HEALTH OPTIONS:** Many dishes can be made vegetarian; most of the menu is gluten-free. **WIFI:** No.

ZELL'S CAFÉ

New/Classy
Relaxed elegance, Portland style.
1300 SE Morrison St. (SE/Belmont)
503-239-0196
Weekdays 7 a.m. to 2 p.m., Saturday 8 a.m. to 2 p.m., Sunday 8 a.m. to 3 p.m.
$10–$14 (Visa, MasterCard, Discover, no checks)

Ah, back at Zell's. It's a weekday lunch, nothing like the weekend breakfast madhouse. I'm halfway through one of my two soft, buttery, and free scones, sipping apple cider, and soaking in the light that's streaming through tall windows and over the café's luscious wood tables, chairs, and bar. It's an old pharmacy, drawers and soda fountain still intact, so folks have been sitting here in the sun for many a year.

I'm feeling rather savory today, and since I'm solo, there won't be any sweets. Well, other than this homemade raspberry jam and orange marmalade on the table. So I'll have to pace myself and leave some of that for the last few bites of my scone. I want some substance, which sadly rules out the French toast with honey oat bread, and the ridiculous German pancakes, for which I shall now have a moment of silence. Man, Zell's just cries out for a group of friends!

So let's check the specials. Today the German pancakes come with hot rhubarb or strawberries. (A buttermilk waffle comes with the same.) An asparagus-prosciutto-Asiago scramble: hmm, don't care for asparagus in the morning. Avocado-bacon-tomato omelet? Don't care for avocados that much. Portobello-spinach-tomato-Asiago omelet? Getting warmer. Reuben scramble with pastrami, eggs, Gruyère, and Dijon mayo on rye with potatoes and kraut? Good gosh, that's our early leader! A gingerbread waffle with Oregon strawberries and whipped cream? See, that's not fair! I'd have the best 15 minutes of my life eating that, then need a nap. Why can't somebody else be here to order it so I can have a bite, or seven?

No, it's a savory day. Back to the menu. Two Benedicts, one with baked salmon. A salami scramble, an imported Gouda and ham scramble, a smoked wild salmon scramble. I'm getting depressed. I pick one; I eliminate all the others! Huevos rancheros, Greek omelet, corned

256

beef hash. Wait: Gorgonzola-mushroom-thyme omelet? Folks, we have a winner! And, of course, two seconds after I make my decision, here's the server to pour water and take my order. Complete pros here, every time.

Now to just sit back and take it in. Moms are out with their kids. The two ladies by the window are clearly old friends. The couple by the register is definitely a first date. The group by the door is some kind of work team. The guy at the counter is just doing scones, coffee, and the paper. The clatter of dishes, the creaking wood floor, the subdued chatter of the crowd, the jazz—everything is in balance.

And bang-o, here's my food! A wrap-style omelet, just browned on the outside, some Gorgonzola oozing out the side. I take a bite and mmm, perfect. Somehow, it's firm and soft at the same time. The potatoes are lightly seasoned, and some smaller pieces got just a little crispy. Again, everything in balance.

Back and forth between the savory omelet, the crunchy potatoes, the sweet cider, the view, the sun, and the music. I manage to save one last little buttery bite of scone, too. I reach for the jam, at peace.

Mmm, I love Zell's.

WAIT: Long on weekends, with a padded bench inside and some cover outside, as well as coffee and heaters. **LARGE GROUPS:** Possible (the earlier the better), but would add to the wait. **COFFEE:** Kobos. **OTHER DRINKS:** Kobos loose-leaf tea, espresso, mineral water, Italian sodas, cocktails. **FEEL-GOODS:** They request that everyone refrain from using cell phones! **HEALTH OPTIONS:** Tofu or egg whites available for $0.50; Morning Star patties and soy milk available; gluten-free bread, muffins, and pancakes. **WIFI:** No.

THE DOWNTOWN HOTELS

Looking for breakfast or brunch downtown? Wigged out by the lines? Check the hotels. Seems like no locals ever think of them, but I've never seen a wait at any of the hotel restaurants. They run a little bit on the high-end and fancy side, but whatever; splurge sometime, or just beat the crowds and chill with the tourists.

Some of these places probably deserve their own chapter here, and a couple have had them in past editions. But to save space in this edition, I've tossed all of them into this roundup.

GRACIE'S (HOTEL DELUXE)

729 SW 15th Ave.

hoteldeluxeportland.com/eat-drink/gracies

Brunch weekdays 6:30 a.m. to 2 p.m., weekends 8 a.m. to 2 p.m.

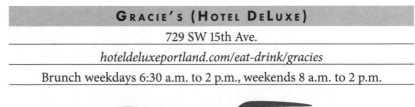

TOP HASHCAPADE (SEE PAGE 301)

This is some serious, old-fashioned fanciness here. The website even brags about it: "With soaring ceilings and an abundance of elegance and style, Gracie's exudes Hollywood glamour." They don't mention the impossibly high booths, the velvet curtains, the chandeliers, the mirrors, the gold details, the white columns, the marble tabletops…you get the idea. As you might also imagine, it ain't cheap, with four Benedicts from $14 to $16, a Hangtown Fry at $15, and orange juice at $4.50. But the food is good, and the atmosphere better. They also get credit for bringing back— even if only in name—the Thiele's Original German Pancake, from a longtime restaurant at NW 23rd and Burnside that closed in the early '90s. Be sure to check out the 60s-vintage Driftwood Room lounge, too.

THE DOWNTOWN HOTELS

H50 BISTRO AND BAR (HOTEL ROSE)

50 SW Morrison St.

h5obistro.com

Breakfast daily 6:30 to 11:30 a.m.

From the high style of Gracie's, we move on to the much more modern H50, where the bar and lounge area feel like some kind of retro Jetsons scene, and the food presentations are oh-so-stylish. The menu items are standard, but with little twists, like French toast made with Grand Marnier custard-soaked challah bread ($11), or a smoked-salmon hash with avocado puree on the side ($14). Also impressive, in taste and appearance, is the NY Steak and Eggs, six slices of tender steak sitting next to a cute little pile of potatoes and two perfectly round fried eggs. The restaurant is a quiet space and, perhaps best of all, has a front-row view of Tom McCall Park and the Willamette River. (Note: Just as we went to press, the Hotel 50 turned into Hotel Rose; this might mean some changes for the restaurant, as well.)

THE HEATHMAN RESTAURANT AND BAR (HEATHMAN HOTEL)

1001 SW Morrison

heathmanrestaurantandbar.com

Breakfast weekdays 6:30 to 11 a.m., brunch weekends 9 a.m to 2 p.m.

Portlanders are aware there's a restaurant in the hotel, especially on a night when there's a show at the Schnitz next door, but most of us, and certainly most of the crowd I run with, consider it a place for the rich and the out-of-town. And with good reason: it's pricey ($14 for corned beef hash, for example) and just a wee bit stuffy. But there's a reason the Heathman has been doing things its way since 1927; it works! I used to wait for my parents to come to town, but now I splurge once a year and feel like a grown-up. I mean, anybody can have chicken-fried steak all over town, but sometimes you want "John's biscuit-crusted Double R Ranch NY steak" and eggs. I don't know who John is, and I don't care. It's an awesome plate of food, and should be. It costs $21.

THE DOWNTOWN HOTELS

IMPERIAL (HOTEL LUCIA)

400 SW Broadway

imperialpdx.com

Breakfast weekdays 6:30 to 11 a.m., brunch weekends 8 a.m. to 2 p.m.

It's pretty rare that the opening of a restaurant in a hotel creates big excitement in the Portland food scene, but Imperial pulled it off, because of one name: Vitaly Paley. Probably the biggest-name chef in town, Paley has won a James Beard Award *and* Iron Chef, and been in every cooking-related magazine you've ever heard of. If you want to see what he's up to at Imperial, go on a weekend; that's when, like most of these hotels, the menu is a little more ambitious. The Brown Butter Beignets will kill you, as will either Benedict (they vary daily) and the Pastrami Hash. It's a real brunch, too, with lunch items from a wood-fired grill. I also really enjoy their occasional artisan take on the Pop-Tart.

NEL CENTRO (HOTEL MODERA)

1408 SW 6th Ave.

nelcentro.com

Breakfast weekdays 6:30 to 10:30 a.m., Saturday 7:30 to 11:30 a.m.,
brunch Sunday 8 a.m. to 2 p.m.

Like Imperial, Nel Centro got some news buzz when it opened because of the guy who opened it. David Machado made his name with Pazzo, Southpark, Vindalho, and Lauro, and now he's back in the kitchen at Nel Centro (which, by the way, is Italian for "downtown.") For what it's worth, this is my favorite downtown hotel brunch, and you can possibly take the "hotel" out of that. Machado calls it the *cuisine of the Riveria,* which apparently means things like poached eggs on griddled polenta with cured pork loin and sage hollandaise ($13) or an Oregon bay shrimp, roasted pepper, basil, and goat cheese omelet ($13). It's a beautiful, modern place with a view of a pretty amazing courtyard, complete with gas fire pits, a bioswale, and a "living wall." All this in what used to be a Days Inn!

THE DOWNTOWN HOTELS

THE PALM COURT (BENSON HOTEL)

309 SW Broadway

bensonhotel.com

Weekdays 6:30 to 11:30 a.m., weekends 6:30 to noon

Of all these hotel breakfasts, this one feels the most hotel-y, if you know what I mean. It's really just a set of tables in the corner of the lobby—but what a lobby! I don't know if the Benson is Portland's finest hotel, since my budget runs more in the Travelodge range, but this hotel feels classy and elegant and every bit of its 100 years of age. As for the Palm Court, well, it offers a lot of options, like five Benedicts (spinach, mushrooms, Canadian bacon, lox, crab) and an impressive array of granola, yogurt, smoothie, and pastry options. I got a waffle with strawberries and whipped cream for $10, and it was fine. But boy, did I feel rich and important just being in that hotel!

PAZZO RISTORANTE (VINTAGE PLAZA HOTEL)

627 SW Washington St.

pazzo.com

Breakfast weekdays 7 to 10:30 a.m., brunch weekends 8 a.m. to 2:30 p.m.

Since we're humping David Machado's leg, here is the Italian place he founded way back when. It has since been taken over by one John Eisenhart, who studied under Mario Batali and spent a year cruising around Italy, learning to cook. Again, weekend brunch has more going on than weekday breakfast, but the blueberry-polenta pancakes ($13) are worth stopping in for, as is the Parma prosciutto, spinach, and Parmesan cheese scramble ($14). On weekends you can also choose from lunch items, as well as breakfast additions like beef short rib hash ($15), steak and eggs ($14), and eggs Florentine with spicy salami ($15). Pazzo is located at one of the busiest intersections in all of downtown, making its brick-and-wood interior particularly comforting.

THE DOWNTOWN HOTELS

RED STAR TAVERN AND ROAST HOUSE (HOTEL MONACO)

503 SW Alder St.

redstartavern.com

Breakfast weekdays 6:30 to 10:30 a.m., brunch weekends 8 a.m. to 3 p.m.

I used to lust after this place while waiting at the bus stop out front, and no wonder: with leather and brass tacks and high ceilings and little lamps on the tables, it exudes a kind of classy old Western vibe. Turns out they have some interesting things on the menu, especially on weekends. I love the Smoked Salmon Scramble with shaved fennel, red onion, capers, smashed red potatoes, and poppy seed crema ($14). Another favorite is the Red Flannel Omelet with smoked Wagyu brisket, molasses barbecue sauce, goat cheese, and scallions. Sure beats the heck out of waiting on that bus!

THREE DEGREES (RIVERPLACE HOTEL)

1510 SW Harbor Way

503-295-6166

threedegreesportland.com

Weekdays 7 to 10:30 a.m., weekends 8 a.m. to 2 p.m.

My dad has this expression about "the better the view, the worse the food." I don't think it's always true, and anyway, I should clarify he meant exterior views, not views of the other diners. Some places have good food and good views (and usually high prices…not to mention hot staff and diners), and some places are like Three Degrees. I know, harsh. I got a chilaquiles that was basically a pile of tortilla strips with some shrimp tossed in, a little white cheese, and a fried egg on top. About as exciting as it sounds. The guy I ate with had an eggs Benedict that defined "generic," though for the record he enjoyed it, and I cleaned my plate. The weekend brunch has a bit more going on. But: sitting in that dining room, you might think you're at a yacht club in the Caribbean, such is the sprawling view of the boat basin at Riverplace. So, I don't know, maybe you'll dig it. Might just go for a drink instead.

URBAN FARMER STEAKHOUSE (NINES HOTEL)

525 SW Morrison St.

urbanfarmerportland.com

Breakfast weekdays 6:30 to 11 a.m., brunch weekends 6:30 a.m. to 3 p.m.

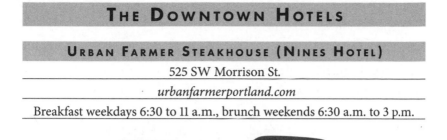

TOP HASHCAPADE (SEE PAGE 301)

There are a lot of "wow" elements at Urban Farmer. They hollowed out the middle of the old Meier and Frank Building, so you're sitting with seven floors of empty space above you, and skylights above that. They have big video screens showing clips of the Fremont Bridge and other Portland sites. They have gigantic booths covered with cowhide. Then you get the menu and realize how much they stress local ingredients and farm-to-table dining. There's a frittata of seasonal vegetables, foraged mushrooms, and aged Tillamook cheddar ($12), for example. Also a Dungeness crab omelet with grilled onions, bacon, wild mushrooms, and herbed hollandaise ($16). There's even a dash of novelty; you can play a Pac-Man-type game on their website for free brunch. I'm serious.

THE BREAKFAST CARTS

Disclaimer: You want to drive yourself nuts? Try keeping up with food carts! They open, they close, they move around, they don't keep their posted hours, they close for weather.... I mean, God bless the food cart owners; I hold nothing against them and admire them all. I'm just saying, if you want to get breakfast at a food cart in Portland, I strongly suggest you check out their Facebook page or Twitter feed right before you go—if they have one. I'll do my best to keep up at breakfastinbridgetown.com. You might also check the fantastic foodcartsportland.com.

Here are the breakfast carts I knew about as of press time at the end of 2013. Just don't expect them to be open when I say they are or serve what I say I had!

BRUNCH BOX
SW 5th and Stark
503-477-3286
brunchboxpdx.com
facebook.com/brunchboxpdx, @brunchbox
also a restaurant (see page 56)
Weekdays 8 a.m. to 8 p.m., Weekends 10 a.m. to 4 p.m.

People think I'm kidding when I say you can get a burger with American cheese, bacon, ham, Spam, a fried egg, lettuce, tomato, grilled onions, ketchup, mustard and mayo—on two grilled cheese sandwiches instead of buns. But I kid you not; it's called the Redonkadonk, and while it isn't a breakfast thing at all, it gives you some idea of how Brunch Box approaches food. Another example: The OMG breakfast sandwich has bacon, ham, Spam, American cheese, and a fried egg, which you can get on Texas Toast if you'd like. Add sausage, and it's the OMFG.

THE BREAKFAST CARTS

THE BIG EGG

4233 N Mississippi Ave.

thebigegg.com

facebook.com/thebigeggportland, @thebigegg

Wednesday to Friday 8 a.m. to 1 p.m., weekends 9 a.m. to 1 p.m.

Just a couple of random special sandwiches this little wondercart has offered: House-made sweet potato apple butter, caramelized onions, grilled Black Forest ham, Gorgonzola, baby arugula, ad medium farm egg on grilled brioche. House-made carrot marmalade, smoked ham, escarole, Tillamook sharp cheddar and scrambled farm egg with fresh thyme on grilled brioche. Their sandwiches are good, and the pod at Mississippi Marketplace is so cool that every time I go up there I think, "Why in hell am I not here all the time?" They only problem is, they run out of stuff and take a break in the wintertime. Good for them, but check their Twitter feed before you go.

BLUES CITY BISCUITS

4262 SE Belmont

503-490-7500

facebook.com/BluesCityBiscuits, @bcbiscuits

Friday to Sunday 9 a.m. to 2 p.m.

They've got Memphis food; I'm from Memphis; we're in love. Just the names on the menu get me going: Jerry Lee Lewis, Isaac Hayes, Ruby Johnson, Booker T, Ma Rainey. Then the ingredients! Sausage gravy, collard greens, molasses, pecans, sweet tea, black-eyed peas… black-eyed pea gravy! Are you *kidding* me? They've got big ol' biscuit sandwiches, soul food, and shrimp and grits. 'Nuff said. Y'all get on down and visit the cart, now, hear?

THE BREAKFAST CARTS

BRIDGETOWN BAGELS

NE 52nd and Sandy

503-268-2522

facebook.com/bridgetownbagel, @bridgetownbagel

Weekdays 7 a.m. to 1 p.m., weekends 8 a.m. to 2 p.m.

Since I grew up semi-Presbyterian and in the South—not Jewish or in New York—I'm not one of the bagel snobs who patrol this city. But this cart made my day twice in the same day. I was headed out for a research trip on my hiking book, *60 Hikes Within 60 Miles of Portland*, so I started with a Three Little Pigs (ham, sausage, bacon and an egg), which I got on a sesame bagel. (They have six other bagels to choose from, and you can make your own sandwich or choose off the menu.) I also got a super yummy lox sandwich with cream cheese, onions and capers to go. I was full and happy as I headed for the trail—and my trail lunch made the other hikers sick with envy, but it made my day complete.

DC VEGETARIAN

430 SW 3rd Ave.

503-317-4448

facebook.com/dcvegetarian, @dcvegetarian

Tuesday through Friday 9 to 11 a.m.

This mainstay cart has been in the pod along SW 3rd between Alder and Stark for years, and their small breakfast menu is really just a collection of five sandwiches, all on white rolls or Dave's Killer Bagels, with various combinations of tofu, vegan or dairy cheese, avocado, tomato, roasted-red-pepper sauce, and homemade meat substitutes playing the role of sausage and bacon. With all of them at $3 or $4 (plus additions like spinach, carrots, onions, and sprouts for 25 cents) this is a quick, tasty little treat, especially if you're vegetarian, vegan, or dairy-free. (However, they don't have gluten-free bread, last I checked.)

THE BREAKFAST CARTS

THE EGG CARTON

SE 52nd and Foster

503-758-5549

facebook.com/EggCartonPDX, @eggcartonpdx

Monday, Thursday and Friday 8:30 a.m. to 2 p.m.,

Saturday and Sunday 9 a.m. to 2 p.m.

If I showed you the menu from this place, you wouldn't think it came from a cart. They have three Benedicts—classic, vegetarian, and Hot Momma, with spicy sausage and a Sriracha kale chip—but the sandwiches are what it's all about. On my visit, there were seven of them, with the signature being the Famous FoPo Cristo, with fried egg, chunks of bacon, cheddar, spicy mustard, and strawberry jam between two pieces of French toast dusted with powdered sugar. The Egg Carton is located in a cart pod on Foster with several other carts, covered seating, and a coffee bar.

FLAVOURSPOT

2310 N Lombard and 810 N Fremont

503-289-9866

facebook.com/FLAVOURspot

Weekdays 8 a.m. to 2 p.m., weekends 9 a.m. to 3 p.m.

If I was a food writer, I'd probably say something lyrical here about a balance of savory and sweet, about textures mingling, or something. Instead, I'll just say that whenever maple, sausage, and waffle get together, I am in. Same thing for Black Forest ham and smoked Gouda cheese. And peanut butter and mallow fluff. Or whipped cream cheese with organic raspberry jam. I think you get the idea. These guys more or less dropped a waffle bomb on this city in 2007, accelerated the cart movement, and still crank 'em out with style, smiles, and good coffee.

THE BREAKFAST CARTS

FRIED EGG I'M IN LOVE

3207 SE Hawthorne and SE 43rd and Belmont

friedegglove.com

facebook.com/friedegglove, @friedegglove

Roughly 9 a.m. to 3 p.m. every day but Monday

I'll tell you what I'm in love with: pesto. I basically quit reading when I saw the first sandwich on the menu, which is their "signature sandwich," the Yolko Ono: fried egg, cart-made pesto, Parmesan, and a hand-pressed, cart-made sausage patty. There are more rock and roll names, like the Yolko Zeppelin (a double-everything Ono), the Egg Zeppelin (a Zep with Secret Aardvark aioli), and more variations on egg, bread, veggies, sauce, and meat. Everything is served on toasted sourdough from Portland French Bakery (they do have gluten-free bread available), and it's all one perfect bite of *mmmmm* after another.

GAUFRE GOURMET

SW 9th and Alder

gaufregourmet.com

facebook.com/TheGaufreGourmet, @gaufregourmet

Weekdays 9 a.m. to 5 p.m., Saturday 10 a.m. to 5 p.m.,
Sunday 10 a.m. to 3 p.m.

There are carts, then there are cart pods, and then there's the food cart Mothership. The entire block between 9 and 10th, Alder and Washington, and even up Alder a way…it's all food carts. And somewhere in there is this little treasure of a waffle cart. But "waffle cart" doesn't quite get it. In fact, "waffle" doesn't get it. Gaufre (that's French for waffle) makes their waffles from brioche-style dough, not batter, and chunks of pearl sugar are folded in right before baking. The result is a dense, chewy waffle with a sugary glaze, upon which they put, for example, goat cheese mousse, honey-roasted pistacchios, and balsamic caramel sauce. And if you want maple bacon, screw Voodoo Doughnuts and *allons manger une gaufre!*

THE BREAKFAST CARTS

GF CHEF

NE 52nd and Sandy

gfchefpdx@gmail.com

Wednesday to Saturday 8 a.m. to 7 p.m., Sunday 9 a.m. to 5 p.m.

From what I can tell, something like 7 percent of people are either gluten-intolerant or have Celiac disease. But somewhere around 2012, I think, "gluten-free" began to mean "healthy" to a lot of people. So it's no surprise that there are many GF carts around town. This one, in Rose City Food Park on Sandy (where you can also find Bridgetown Bagels, as well as bathrooms, an ATM, covered seating, and a fruit & vegetable stand), has a remarkable lineup of GF foods, including waffles, biscuits, scones, and gravy. In fact, their motto is "Real food, gluten-free." I got a tasty, filling biscuits and gravy and a cup of Nossa Familia coffee (they also have espresso), sat in the heated tent, and wouldn't have known I was going gluten-free had they not told me.

NOURISHMENT

NE 46th and Sandy

Tuesday through Friday, 7 a.m. to noon.

Saturday at the market (*hollywoodfarmersmarket.org*)

When I told the guy making my burrito that I had read about his cart on foodcartsportland.com, he said, "When did that happen?" Um, three months ago. And why doesn't Nourishment do anything online? Because they don't have to. They have been at Hollywood Farmers Market, cranking out breakfast, since 2005. In 2013 the owner found a fire-gutted Airstream trailer and fixed it up into perhaps the most attractive cart in town, with wood paneling and tin-man-style vent covers and flags, and even planted bamboo on each end. It looks a little Hobbit-like. The breakfasts—in the form of burrito, bowl, or chilaquile—all start with cheesy scrambled eggs, potatoes, black beans, tomatillo salsa, and sour cream, then you can add lamb chorizo, collard greens, or bacon. There's also a vegan option, and rotating specials are featured.

THE BREAKFAST CARTS

PERIERRA CREPERIE

SE 12th and Hawthorne

facebook.com/perierra, @perierra

Daily 8 a.m. to 3 a.m.

I love taking visitors to Cartopia, the big pod where Perierra lives. They're still thinking taco trucks, or whatever, when they (A) dig the scene in the pod, with 8 or 10 carts, covered seating, a fire pit, and so on, then (B) check the crepe menu. How about Gorgonzola, fresh Anjou pear, walnuts, and wildflower honey? Not what you expected? How about two eggs, cave-aged Gruyère, cremini mushrooms, spinach, and freshly ground nutmeg? Or the classic sweets, like lemon and raw sugar; Nutella and banana; and semisweet chocolate, prosciutto, and sea salt? There's also a moment when I trade glances with the dudes in admiration of the cuties always making the crepes, but if I stress that too much my sweetie won't let me go there anymore. You should, though—morning (chill) or night (party time)!

SMAAKEN WAFFLES

6238 SW Capitol Highway

503-688-8214

facebook.com/pages/Smaaken-Waffles

Daily 8 a.m. to 2 p.m.

Smaaken, if you're wondering, is Dutch for tasty. While waiting for your waffle, you can learn other things, like how to describe the taste of your coffee using a Coffee Tasting Wheel, or the advantages of roasting coffee (as they do) with hardwoods. Honestly, I didn't catch any of that, because I was so busy admiring the creation of my waffle with homemade spiced apples, whipped cream, and caramel sauce. The local, organic coffee was outstanding, as well. They have gluten-free, vegan waffles, but I didn't catch those, either. This cart's in a funny place—basically, the driveway of Wilson High School, aka Hillsdale Food Park—but it has covered picnic tables and a few other carts. Well worth a stop.

THE BREAKFAST CARTS

YOLK

SE 48th and Woodstock

facebook.com/yolkpdx

Monday, and Wednesday through Sunday, 8:30 a.m. to 1:30 p.m.

From the owners of Toast (see page 238) comes this bright-yellow cart on SE Woodstock. It serves the same kind of stuff you'd get at Toast, with an emphasis on simple meals that stress fresh ingredients and beautiful vegetables. I loved the Mary *Had* A Little Lamb, with ground lamb over roasted potatoes, braised greens, and summer squash, tossed with mint and herbs, topped with a sunny-side-up duck egg. But the best is The Breakfast, which is, well, whatever they say it is. You pay $11 and get what they give you, no subs, no allergies, diets or "I'm free of." Sure, it's a book about breakfast in Portland, but we occasionally venture out, right?

OUT ON THE ROAD

Get mad if you want, but I have mostly skipped right over the suburbs. I don't know why, I just did. It's my book.

Here's an introduction to some of my favorite places to stop for a bite when headed to or from mountain, lake, trail, or beach. I am usually discovering more of them, so keep up with my travels at breakfastinbridgetown.com.

22ND STREET STATION
2337 22nd Ave., Forest Grove

Years ago, when my girlfriend lived in Forest Grove, we used to go to this funky, weird, homey little place. My favorite memory was eating some of the best pork chops I ever had (granted, I was madly in love), then mixing some of her custard-stuffed French toast and syrup with my eggs and gravy and pork-chop juice. I decided I had created a new element for the Periodic Table, with the symbol Mm. This is small-town kitsch all the way, with model airplanes hanging from the ceiling, a model train running around the walls, an owner/waitress who will probably call you "hon," and no Internet presence at all. I'm not even sure of the hours! It's also hard to find and cash-only.

AMELIA'S
105 NE 4th Ave., Hillsboro

ameliasmexicanfood.com

Sweetie lives in Hillsboro now, and we've enjoyed going on little culinary road trips around Washington County. At least we did, until we found Amelia's, and now our tour route is basically Indian for dinner or Amelia's for breakfast. Though it might not sound like it, it's a Mexican place, and an extremely colorful, friendly one at that. Some of the dishes you've had or can imagine: huevos con chorizo, huevos rancheros, and so on. But how about Huevos al Albanil Rojos, which is scrambled eggs with onions in a red guajillo sauce with avocado slices? (There's also a Verde version with green tomatillo sauce.) Even more interesting is Napoles Con Huevos, or cactus with onions, cilantro, and red peppers. *Vamanos,* sweetie!

OUT ON THE ROAD

BABICA HEN CAFÉ

15964 Boones Ferry Rd., Lake Oswego

babicahencafe.com

Even after reading about it on their website, I have no idea what the name of this place is all about. Apparently, it's named for a hen statue from the owner's grandmother's kitchen? The first person who told me about it (raved, actually) had to write it down for me. It's kind of a weird-looking place, too: kind of blocky and low, with cement chunks in the landscaping. (It used to be La Provence.) It does have its own parking, though. Oh, and the food is actually awesome. They have seven different waffles (savory and sweet) and a bunch of other options, including rarities like Mexican spiced prawns over polenta with red chili sauce and Cotija cheese, and smoked salmon quinoa cakes with a beet and arugula salad.

BOB'S RED MILL

5000 SE International Way, Milwaukie

bobsredmill.com

I'm sure you know Bob's products. But if I told you their headquarters in Milwaukie had a restaurant, you'd assume it had a lot of baked goods. And you'd be right, of course. But I don't think any human can comprehend the *range* of milled products that come out of this 325,000-square-foot place until you go down there, wander through the aisles of flours and grains and who knows what, marvel at the reams of information they offer, and then sit down with a bowl of steel-cut oats or muesli with vanilla bean yogurt or granola. It's an amazing cross between modern, high-tech efficiency and down-home, closed-on-Sundays Americana. And then you should take a tour of the mill, which cranks out 260,000 units daily. "Grain Guides" offer tours on weekdays at 10 a.m.

OUT ON THE ROAD

CAMP 18

42362 Highway 26

camp18restaurant.com

Camp 18 is located about…well, 18 miles before 101. You have probably driven by it and thought it was a logging museum. It is. It's also a restaurant with outrageous portions. It's an excellent way to feed up for, or recover from, a hike to nearby Saddle Mountain. But mainly, it's a monument to the logging industry and to wood carving. They have all sorts of machinery and photos, a Loggers' Memorial, hand-carved doors that are four and a half inches thick and weigh 500 pounds, and a central rafter that's 85 feet long and 25 tons—one piece of wood! So put away your liberal anti-logging bias, go wallow in history, and chow down.

CHAR BURGER

745 NW Wanapa St., Cascade Locks

You could *not* open a place like this today. Forget the purple goo on the marionberry pancakes; I think the PC Police would burn you down if your mascot was a little naked feather-headed Indian boy named Chief Char. But this place has been open for 50 years and is a monument to the old days. By that, I mean the arrowheads and gun collection and logging photos, and also the food. It ain't fancy. Or even good, really. They've got a pizza omelet on which I still await a report. There's also a Sunday Buffet ($17.95, reservations required, 10 to 2) with beef, chicken, salmon, seafood, link sausage, bacon, fettuccine, Belgian waffles, biscuits and gravy, to-order omelets, and a fruit and dessert bar. All this, and probably the best view of any place in this book. Somebody bought Char Burger in 2013, so maybe they'll make the food better to go with that view.

COLUMBIA GORGE HOTEL

4000 State Frontage Rd., Hood River

columbiagorgehotel.com

When most of us folks under 60 think about Hood River, we picture kids on windsurfers and snowboarders, drinking Full Sail beer. This place is more like grandma having Sunday dinner. It dates back to 1921, with a little break for new owners in 2008 and 2009, and its website claims it entertained "movie stars like Clara Bow, Rudolph Valentino and Shirley Temple (and) presidents like Roosevelt and Coolidge." Now its main attraction is a seven-course Sunday brunch ($28, 9 to 2, reservations strongly recommended). They still do the famous thing with "honey from the sky" by drizzling it from arms-length onto a biscuit, they still have a waterfall and an amazing view, and they still play jazz for an older, well-dressed crowd.

COMMUNITY PLATE

315 NE Third St., McMinnville

communityplate.com

Unless you're into wine or live near the place, you might not know that McMinnville is becoming quite the little food town. It's kind of the Oregon Wine Country hub, and the wine people (A) appreciate good food and (B) have money to spend. Where those factors come together, good restaurants appear. Community Plate is a light-filled, wood-floor, family-seating kind of place that takes food seriously. During the week, it features a pretty basic menu, with pancakes, granola, oatmeal, quiche, a hash, biscuits and gravy, and so on. On the weekend they add lunch items like a chop salad and hand-cut fries, as well as a daily soup and burger. Everything is really good, and I love the feel of the place. It's on the very busy main street in town, and it's a perfect start to a yummy day in the country.

OUT ON THE ROAD

CRESCENT CAFÉ

526 NE 3rd St., McMinnville

503-435-2655

See, McMinnville again! Like Community Plate, this place is all about taking local ingredients and doing serious things with them. This is the slightly more formal option for McMinnville breakfast—the servers even wear ties on weekends!—but I don't care if they wear overalls, as long as they keep serving brandied orange French toast on house-made bread. Weekends can get crowded, and since they don't have an Internet presence, and they rotate many menu items, it's hard to say how long you'll have to wait or what you'll be able to eat. But it's popular for a reason, and I think you should make a weekend of it down in "Mac," then see for yourself why foodies are running down there for meals.

HUCKLEBERRY INN

88611 E Government Camp Loop Rd., Government Camp

huckleberry-inn.com

I confess a deep and abiding love for this place. Whether it's huckleberry pancakes before a hike or huckleberry pie after, it almost doesn't feel like a day on Mount Hood unless I sit down at their wooden booth or counter and load up on carbs. They also have a fine old-school cheeseburger. And the place used to be the Greyhound station, which meant a whole different level of people-watching. In an ever-growing and modernizing Government Camp, "the Huck" is an old-time institution. They put huckleberries in ice cream, pie, pancakes, bon bons, lip balm, tea, preserves, and milkshakes. They also make their own donuts and have the largest pile of butter you'll ever see. See if you can find it. They do have rooms, as well, starting at $90 for a single; there's also a 14-person dorm for $185.

OUT ON THE ROAD

JOE'S DONUTS

39230 Pioneer Blvd., Sandy

joes-donuts.com

All right, I said no donut places in the book. Whatever. Not only that, but I've never even *had* a donut at Joe's, the place you've driven by at the far end of Sandy, with the red and white cinder blocks. Wait: is an apple fritter a donut? I don't know, and I don't care. I just know that even for a sugar addict like me, that apple fritter is a limit-pushing orgy of sweetness. A third of the way through one, I am in heaven. Two-thirds, I'm thinking about leaving the rest for after the hike. After a kind of blackout, I suddenly have no more fritter, my head is spinning, and my ears are ringing. People have all kinds of strong opinions about Joe's, but I do recommend the place, at least once. Well, I recommend the fritter.

LA PROVENCE BOULANGERIE & PATISSERIE

16350 Boones Ferry Rd., Lake Oswego

provencepdx.com

Dang, what a place this is! It's like a palace in here, with eight heat lamps covering the front patio, heavily lacquered tables (carved with the restaurant's logo), black wicker chairs, track lights aimed at paintings of French scenes, and a gleaming pastry counter full of magical, fanciful treats. This, by the way, is the mothership to the two Portland locations of Petite Provence (see page 190) as well as one in The Dalles, of all places. There's nothing petite about this one, which opened in 2012. The menu features a salmon hash with lemon-dill sauce; risotto cakes and eggs with bacon, asparagus, mushrooms, red onions and basil; eggs Provençal with pesto; a bunch of omelets; and a Bread Pudding Souffle with egg custard, apricots, goat cheese, and apple crème anglaise. I say again: *Dang!*

OUT ON THE ROAD

MARK'S ON THE CHANNEL

34326 Johnson's Landing Rd., Scappoose

marksonthechannel.com

What do you really know about Scappoose? You pass through it on the way to Astoria, and if you're a kayaker you know all about Scappoose Bay. But breakfast? Well, there's a boatyard just off the main branch of the Columbia called McCuddy's Landing, and in that boatyard is a restaurant open from March through November. It sits on a dock and serves a nice weekend brunch, with (as you might imagine) a lot of seafood. But mainly, it's in a world of salty smells, the breezes, the soft clanging of rigging, the gentle bobbing of the water, and the immediate connection between stepping off this dock onto that boat and sometime later stepping onto any dock anywhere in the world. Whoops, sorry, I'm back now. Good food, nice folks, great setting, and heck, you can get there by boat!

OTIS CAFÉ

1259 Salmon River Hwy., Otis (at the coast)

otiscafe.com

It's hard to think of a place with a size-to-reputation ratio to match the Otis. It got written up in the *New York Times* in 1989—that story is still up on the wall—and they've been media darlings ever since. They're also loved by regular folks, who try to out-write each other with childhood memories, odes to the small-town diner, and gasps at the portions. Mainly, the tiny café (it's been there since the '20s) is known for its German potatoes, a pile of hash browns topped with green onions and white cheddar cheese. It's $5.50 for a softball-sized pile; $7.25 for a football; $1.25 each for sausage, vegetable, ham, bacon, and mushrooms; and 75 cents each for "as many eggs as you please." Also, check out the molasses toast and all the various pies. And be sure to visit the tiny bathroom; you weave through the kitchen and wait in the room where they bake the pies. That is some good stuff back there!

OUT ON THE ROAD

SKAMANIA LODGE

1131 Skamania Lodge Rd., Stevenson (Washington)

skamania.com

First, though I wish it were different, this isn't a place for people with a mania for ska music. If the management had any sense, and maybe less class, they'd schedule a Ska Mania festival. Instead, what they offer is a Sunday Champagne Brunch (9 to 2, reservations suggested) that is an epic eating experience: eight starters, eight salads, a build-your-own omelet station, a carving station with five meats, seven entrées, and a plethora of desserts. It's a spectacle. It's also $34.95 for adults, plus tax and gratuity (kids are around half that). You'll want to make reservations, go for a big hike in the Gorge beforehand to earn it, and find a spot for a nap afterward.

STONE CLIFF INN

17900 S Clackamas River Dr., Oregon City

stonecliffinn.com

I guess there are two things you're supposed to know about this place. I am required by the Writer Borg to tell you that some scenes of some *Twilight* movie were filmed here, that the beautiful actors ate here, and that this is exciting. What I really want you to know is that this is a beautiful place, a massive log-cabin-style restaurant with a patio overlooking the Clackamas River, and a Sunday brunch with four omelets around $9, steak and eggs for $12, three Benedicts ($10-14), pancakes with or without berries, marionberry French toast with mascarpone cheese and crushed hazelnuts for $9, and some outrageous desserts. In other words, considering the setting and the nice drive up the river to get there, it's a pretty sweet place to get brunch, whether you're heading to or from a hike or just feel like getting out of town for a bit.

OUT ON THE ROAD

TIMBERLINE LODGE

27500 E Timberline Rd. (on Mount Hood)

timberlinelodge.com

I have my own name for the breakfast buffet at Timberline: the Hiker Hoedown. It runs from 7:30 to 10 on weekdays, and until 10:30 on weekends, and it's $14.95. During any of those hours from July until October, look around for scruffy, perhaps still-filthy, people behaving somewhat strangely. Chances are, they have been out on the Pacific Crest Trail for a few days or weeks, and you might see them worshipping at the orange juice machine, pacing back and forth in front of the waffle iron, making architectural wonders out of bacon and sausage, and generally making the most of the "all you can eat" feature. Otherwise, you'll be eating breakfast in a 1930s-era lodge at an elevation of 6,000 feet on Oregon's highest mountain. Last I saw, among the nonbuffet options were an Artisan Bacon Sampler ($14) and a Jam Tasting with vanilla-buttermilk biscuits ($5.95). Highly recommended.

GLUTEN-FREE

I asked Martha Wagner, a local food writer who is gluten-free, to wander into the world of gluten-free dining and come back with a report. Here is her introduction to what GF means, what to look for at restaurants, and some breakfast places you might want to check out. All of them, by the way, are also covered elsewhere in the book.

You can find out more about Martha and follow her writings at martha wagner.com.

Whether you are a full-out omnivore or a devotee of a particular dietary regimen—vegan, vegetarian, low-fat, low-carb, anti-inflammatory, Paleo, or otherwise—you probably know people who follow a gluten-free diet. And you might want to know where to take them for breakfast or brunch. You may also wonder what the heck the gluten thing is all about. Help is on the way in this chapter!

To get scientific for a moment, gluten is a protein found in wheat, barley, and rye. It provides dough with elasticity and strength. A boon to bakers, it's also harmful to nearly two million Americans with celiac disease, an autoimmune disorder that damages the small intestine. Millions more people, such as myself, have a sensitivity to gluten that can cause a wide range of unpleasant symptoms. Some people are allergic to wheat alone. Others are saying no to gluten because avoiding it makes them feel better or helps them lose weight.

Food fads are so common that public understanding and acceptance of gluten-free eating has been mixed. Nevertheless, a growing number of restaurants are making menu and recipe changes, and even the prestigious Culinary Institute of America teaches chefs gluten-free cooking techniques. Some restaurants are offering gluten-free toast and perhaps a gluten-free pancake or muffin for breakfast. Others have changed their menus to offer more dishes that typically need no gluten—think hashes, tacos, huevos rancheros, and cornmeal polenta with sausage or veggies.

Challenges for restaurants go beyond what's on the menu. An article in *Food Arts* magazine in December 2012 discusses issues such as cross contamination of gluten-free food in pans and deep fryers and "hidden flour" in sauces and garnishes that may not be apparent in menu

GLUTEN-FREE

descriptions, as well as the need for restaurants to train staff to understand and respect the needs of gluten-free eaters. People with celiac disease are safest eating out at restaurants that are 100 percent gluten-free.

QUESTIONS TO ASK

As a gluten-free eater and a knowledgeable cook, I've become accustomed to asking lots of questions when I eat out. More and more servers are well-informed about what's going on in the kitchen, as they should be, and can advise you in detail about the menu. It's easier on both customers and staff when there's a separate gluten-free menu or a menu with GF symbols. Unfortunately, you can't always trust a menu. I ordered a combination breakfast—eggs, potatoes, biscuits, and gravy— at a restaurant that uses GF symbols on its menu, only to learn from a server after I finished eating that the meal *could be* made gluten-free by substituting rice for the biscuit. Lesson learned—tell your server what you need.

The smartest dining out approach for gluten-free eaters and the people who care about them is to keep in mind some basic tips.

My tips for navigating the uncertainties of gluten-free dining out are based in part on advice from a national guidebook, *The Essential Gluten-Free Restaurant Guide* (Triumph Dining):

- Talk to the right person about your dietary needs. Call ahead to ensure that a restaurant has gluten-free items or even a special menu, or check its website menus before you go. If there is a language barrier on the phone or at the restaurant, it's even more important to talk with the right person.
- Check menus for GF symbols and substitution options, such as rice or salad instead of bread. Ask if you can order a sandwich with a bed of lettuce instead of bread.
- Tell your server which grains you can and can't eat. Some people who eat gluten-free can eat rolled and steel-cut oats without a problem, and some restaurants serve gluten-free oats.
- Celiac disease is not an allergy, but you can use the word if you think restaurant staff may not be taking your needs seriously.

- Make it easy for your server. You probably know more about eating gluten-free than they do, so scout a general menu for selections that are likely to be gluten-free and present them as possible choices that your server can confirm with kitchen staff.
- Double check. When you order *and* when your meal is served, confirm with the server that everything on your plate was prepared gluten-free and that any condiments offered are also gluten-free. Take nothing for granted if you want to be safe rather than sorry.

LET'S EAT!

Keeping in mind these tips, you can probably find gluten-free choices at many restaurants that do not have a special menu or menu symbols identifying such options. Below are some of my favorite spots for gluten-free breakfast and brunch. Though I'm not a vegetarian, I prefer a menu that shows some veggie love—by featuring kale, spinach, and peppers, for example, not just a pile of potatoes. A small pile of taters is fine, preferably sautéed or oven roasted. Some restaurants fry 'em. Ask, if you care!

BIJOU CAFÉ
132 SW Third Ave. (Downtown)
503-222-3187
bijoucafepdx.com
Breakfast weekdays 7 a.m. to 2 p.m., weekends 8 a.m. to 2 p.m.
$14–$17 (all major cards, local checks)

A Portland institution, Bijou offers a broad menu, good service, and a straightforward vibe. There are no gluten-free symbols on the menu, but the staff knows its stuff and the gluten-free options are plentiful: seven omelets, four hash dishes, a tofu scramble, plus several unusual salads for brunch.

Extra points for: Locally sourced food. A menu that covers the basics as well as more sophisticated fare, such as achiote-braised pork, poblano peppers, and hominy with an over-easy egg.

GLUTEN-FREE

BUMBLEKISS

3517 NE 46th Ave. (NE/Fremont)

503-282-6313

bumblekisscafe.com

Breakfast Monday, Thursday, Friday 8 a.m. to 2:30 p.m.;

weekends 8 a.m. to 3:30 p.m.

$13–$16 (all major cards)

This adorable café does a good job with a large menu that ranges from egg Benedicts to scrambles (eight of them) to pancakes to tacos (bacon or smoked salmon). Thick and chewy gluten-free blue corn pancakes or rice bread can be subbed for English muffins. I like the Kayla, which pairs sautéed kale with potatoes that are topped with poached eggs and slivers of Havarti cheese.

Extra points for: Ample veggies. Knowledgeable staff. Lovely patio.

GENIES CAFÉ

1101 SE Division St. (SE/Inner)

503-445-9777

geniesdivision.com

Breakfast daily 8 a.m. to 3 p.m.

$9–$14 (all major cards)

A large menu and lots of choices for vegans and gluten-free folks makes Genies a good pick, except for busy weekend hours. Tasty gluten-free English muffins add a dollar to the cost of a Benedict, and Genies has five on the menu. Gluten-free whole-grain toast (also locally made by Jensen's) can be ordered with the omelets, scrambles, and a breakfast sandwich. Specialty egg dishes without gluten include corned beef or smoked turkey hash, black bean hash, and huevos rancheros.

Extra points for: Locally sourced food and house-made sausages and cured meats. Helpful staff.

GLUTEN-FREE

HARLOW

3632 SE Hawthorne Blvd. (SE/Inner)

971-255-0138

harlowpdx.com

Breakfast daily 8 a.m. to 2 p.m. (3 p.m. on Sunday)

$10–$15 (all major cards)

Harlow is the new sister restaurant to Prasad (see below) in the Pearl. An extensive, appealing, mostly vegan menu is 100 percent gluten-free, with start-the-day options ranging from oatmeal or quinoa pancakes to huevos rancheros to various hearty scrambles with eggs or "smokey" tempeh, vegetables, toast, and choice of rice or quinoa. Beverage options are dizzying, from dozens of smoothies and fresh-made juices to kombucha, health elixirs, several cocktails, and numerous tea and coffee drinks. Can be noisy. Orders need to be placed at the counter.

Extra points for: Locally sourced food and drink, prepared with skill and visual appeal, too.

HELSER'S ON ALBERTA

1538 NE Alberta St. (NE/Alberta)

503-281-1477

helsersonalberta.com

Breakfast daily 7 a.m. to 3 p.m.

$10–$15, with $5.95 specials before 9 a.m. weekdays (all major cards)

Breakfast prices keep creeping upward, so the weekday specials at Helser's are a welcome find. Gluten-free specials include a tasty grilled polenta and black bean cake with two eggs surrounded by a flavorful creole sauce, and two eggs any style with maple sausage and sautéed Yukon potatoes. The rest of the menu is large and varied.

Extra points for: Large beverage menu, from cappuccino to cocktails. Knowledgeable staff.

285

GLUTEN-FREE

PRASAD

925 NW Davis (NW/Pearl)

503-224-3993

prasadcuisine.com

Breakfast weekdays, 7:30 to 11 a.m., weekends 9 to 11 a.m.

$12–$15 (all major cards)

I love Prasad, but the vegan fare and the hip vibe may not be everyone's cup of chai. The small café shares space with a yoga studio, and orders are placed at the counter. Breakfast choices include gluten-free oatmeal, two tempeh scrambles with gluten-free toast, and a raw veggie Bravo Bowl. After 9 a.m., options expand to include salads with names like Shiva and Bliss, two soups (raw or hot), and five hearty one-dish bowl entrées, most of which feature rice or quinoa topped by a choice of raw and/or cooked veggies and one of five sauces. The vast beverage menu is similar to Harlow's (see above).

Extra points for: Locally sourced food and drink, organic produce delivered by bike (really!), knowledgeable staff.

VERDE COCINA

6446 SW Capitol Highway in Hillsdale (SW/Outer)

503-384-2327

verdecocinamarket.com

Breakfast daily 9 a.m. to 3 p.m.

524 NW 14th (NW/Pearl)

503-894-9321

Brunch weekends 9 a.m. to 2 p.m.

$14–$25 (all major cards, checks)

"Farm-to-fork ingredients with Mexican flair" is how this family-run restaurant—which began at area farmers markets—bills itself. Picture heaping piles of sautéed fresh veggies, plus locally sourced eggs and meats, thick corn tortillas prepared on-site, and house-made sauces and salsas. Specialties include chile rellenos and Gringas con Molé, rolled corn tortillas filled with a bean mash and fresh pork or veggies topped with house-made molé sauce.

Extra points for: Entirely gluten-free menu. Many vegan and vegetarian options. No chips or other fried food. House-made agua fresca, Mexican hot chocolate, beer, wine and cocktails.

THE SECOND CUT:

Other restaurants worth considering for weekend brunch include Equinox (N/Inner) and Pambiche (E/Burnside). For brunch as well as weekday breakfast, consider Tin Shed Garden Café (NE/Alberta), Vita Café (NE/Alberta), Besaw's (NW) and Marco's Café (SW/Inner).

RESOURCES YOU MIGHT FIND USEFUL:

*   glutenfreepdx.com
*   See reviews of local breakfast/brunch restaurants and food carts with gluten-free options.
*   glutenfreeliving.com/basic-diet.php
*   Easy-to-digest dietary information from *Gluten-Free Living* magazine.
*   *Portland Monthly* did an excellent gluten-free guide in their January 2014 issue. Look for it online at portlandmonthlymag.com.

EARLY-BIRD PLACES

Most places in this book open somewhere between 8 and 10 a.m. But what about you early risers? Heck, what about you *hikers*? I know you're out there, because I'm one of you, and sometimes we want something to eat before we head for the hills.

So here, sorted by location, is a list of places that open sometime before 7:30 a.m. on at least some days.

Place	Location	Page
Mother's Bistro	Downtown	160
Original, The	Downtown	174
Roxy, The	Downtown	212
Sugar Mama's Cafe	Downtown	230
Doug Fir Lounge	E Burnside	84
Beaterville Cafe	N/Inner	40
Muddy's	N/Inner	162
Overlook Family Restaurant	N/Inner	180
Po'shines	N/Outer	196
Helser's	NE/Alberta	110
Pine State Biscuits	NE/Alberta and SE/Division	192
Tin Shed Garden Café	NE/Alberta	236
Milo's City Cafe	NE/Broadway	160
New Deal Café	NE/Hollywood	168
Bridges Cafe	NE/MLK	52
Cameo Cafe East	NE/Outer	66
Gateway Breakfast House	NE/Outer	98
Stepping Stone Cafe	NW	228
Byways Cafe	Pearl	58
Fuller's Coffee Shop	Pearl	96
Cricket Café	SE/Belmont	74
Utopia Cafe	SE/Belmont	242
Zell's Café	SE/Belmont	256
Original Hotcake & Steak House	SE/Inner	176
Bertie Lou's Cafe	SE/Sellwood	42
Fat Albert's	SE/Sellwood	92
Fat City Breakfast Cafe	SW/Outer	94

EARLY-BIRD PLACES

Marco's Cafe	SW/Inner	152
Original Pancake House	SW/Inner	178
Cup & Saucer	Several	76

BREAKFAST IN BRIDGETOWN

It's Breakfast for Dinner!

A common question over the years has been, "Where can I get late-night breakfast?"

Well, here you go. And by late-night, I mean dinner and on. They are sorted by location so you don't get lost.

Place	Location	Page
Brunch Box	Downtown	56
Kenny and Zuke's	Downtown	140
The Roxy	Downtown	212
Holman's	E Burnside	116
Old Wives' Tales	E Burnside	170
Gravy	N/Inner	102
Overlook Family Restaurant	N/Inner	180
Tasty n Sons / Tasty n Alder	N/Inner and Downtown	234
Pattie's Home Plate Café	N/Outer	188
Po'shines (weekends)	N/Outer	196
Radio Room	NE/Alberta	206
Pine State Biscuits	NE/Alberta and SE/Division	192
Kornblatt's	NW	144
Stepping Stone Cafe	NW	228
Original Hotcake & Steak House	SE/Inner	176
Marco's Cafe	SW/Inner	152
Cup & Saucer	Several	76

For me, "Parents" is a category like vegetarians and vegans: I am not among your number, but I try to keep you in mind, and I ask some of you for input.

I've only heard of a few places that seem to actually not dig kids, but these make a particular effort to welcome our littlest friends. I've sorted them by location.

Place	Location	Page
Portland Farmers Market	Downtown	194
Mama Mia Trattoria	Downtown	150
Mother's Bistro	Downtown	160
East Burn	E Burnside	86
Old Wives' Tales	E Burnside	170
Muddy's	N/Inner	162
Pattie's Home Plate Café	N/Outer	188
Po'shines	N/Outer	196
Vita Cafe	NE/Alberta	248
Alameda Cafe	NE/Fremont	26
New Deal Café	NE/Hollywod	168
Slappy Cakes	SE/Belmont	226
Sckavonc's	SE/Division	216

BEST FOR LARGE GROUPS

Each place in the book is rated for how it would handle large groups, if it would. Many places can handle groups of, say, six to eight; most of them will require at least a heads-up, if they don't take reservations. But if you want to be sure, or if there are more than six of you, these are your best bets.

All of these places take (or even require) reservations for groups of six or more.

For you noncarnivores out there in Portland, congratulations. You live in a great place for breakfast.

While I am not one of you, I've tried to keep you in mind as I checked out all these restaurants. Each place in the book has its own little listing at the end for how I think you'll do there, but these particularly stand out as places where vegetarians and/or vegans would have more options than the ol' Spinach Omelet.

Am I full of it? Get in touch and let me know.

Be sure to read through the carts section on page 264, as well. There are some good ones there.

Place	Category	Location	Page
Portland Farmers Market	Weekend/Veggie	Downtown	194
West Cafe	Weekend/Classy	Downtown	250
City State Diner	Hip/Old School	E Burnside	68
East Burn	Hip/Weekend	E Burnside	86
Old Wives' Tales	New/Kiddie	E Burnside	170
Beaterville Cafe	Hip/Mom & Pop	N/Inner	40
Equinox	New/Weekend	N/Inner	90
Mextiza	Weekend/New	N/Inner	156
Muddy's	Hip/Veggie	N/Inner	162
Vita Cafe	Hip/Kiddie	NE/Alberta	248
Din Din	Weekend/New/Hip	NE/Inner	82
Verde Cocina	New/Weekend	Pearl and SW/Inner	244
Cricket Café	Hip	SE/Belmont	74
Paradox Café	Hip	SE/Belmont	186
Slappy Cakes	Kiddie	SE/Belmont	226
Utopia Cafe	New/Hip	SE/Belmont	242
Wild Abandon	Hip	SE/Belmont	252
Xico	Weekend/New	SE/Division	254
Harlow	Hip/New/Veggie	SE/Hawthorne	106
Hawthorne Street Café	New/Hip	SE/Hawthorne	108
Jam on Hawthorne	New/Hip	SE/Hawthorne	126

VEGGIE-FRIENDLY PLACES

J&M Cafe	New/Classy	SE/Hawthorne	124
Junior's Cafe	Hip	SE/Inner	138
Bar Carlo	New/Hip	SE/Outer	36
Delta Cafe Bar	Hip/Weekend	SE/Outer	78
Cup & Saucer Cafe	Hip	Several	76

LET'S EAT OUT(SIDE)!

Feel like dining under the, um, legendary Portland sun? Here are your options for outdoor seating among the places covered in the book.

Place	Location	Scene	Page
Brasserie Montmartre	Downtown	Sidewalk tables, quiet street	48
Portland Farmers Market	Downtown	The whole thing!	194
Kenny and Zuke's	Downtown	Uncovered sidewalk tables	140
Raven & Rose	Downtown	Uncovered sidewalk tables	208
Veritable Quandary	Downtown	Garden patio, no cover	246
Holman's	E Burnside	Private patio	116
Screen Door	E Burnside	Uncovered patio near Burnside	218
EaT: An Oyster Bar	N/Inner	Covered patio	88
Equinox	N/Inner	Uncovered patio	90
Mextiza	N/Inner	Patio on semibusy street	156
John Street Cafe	N/Outer	Shady, quiet garden patio	132
Pattie's Home Plate Café	N/Outer	Uncovered sidewalk tables	188
Helser's	NE/Alberta	Uncovered sidewalk tables	110
Petite Provence	NE/Alberta	Uncovered sidewalk tables	190
Podnah's Pit	NE/Alberta	Uncovered sidewalk tables	198
Radio Room	NE/Alberta	Upper/lower private patio with umbrellas	206
Tin Shed Garden Café	NE/Alberta	Shady patio and big fireplace	236
Vita Cafe	NE/Alberta	Big patio with some shade	248
Pambiche	NE/Burnside	Covered tables, heat lamps	182
Alameda Cafe	NE/Fremont	Umbrella sidewalk tables	26
New Deal Café	NE/Hollywood	Open tables on the street	168
Bridges Cafe	NE/MLK	Uncovered tables near MLK	52
Cameo Cafe East	NE/Outer	Deck with some cover	64
23 Hoyt	NW	Sidewalk tables	22
Besaw's	NW	Covered patio	44
Cafe Nell	NW	Sidewalk tables, no cover	64

LET'S EAT OUT(SIDE)!

Industrial Café and Saloon	NW	Uncovered patio	118
Kornblatt's	NW	Uncovered sidewalk tables	142
Meriwether's	NW	Quiet patio with some cover	154
Papa Haydn	NW and Sellwood	Sidewalk tables	184
Fuller's Coffee Shop	Pearl	Open tables on the street	96
Irving Street Kitchen	Pearl	Patio above semibusy street	120
Isabel	Pearl	Uncovered patio	122
Jamison	Pearl	Patio by a park	130
Cricket Café	SE/Belmont	Uncovered sidewalk tables	74
Wild Abandon	SE/Belmont	Big patio with some shade	252
Detour Cafe	SE/Division	Shady, covered patio	80
Lauretta Jean's	SE/Division	Uncovered sidewalk tables	144
Xico	SE/Division	Private patio	254
Hawthorne Stret Cafe	SE/Hawthorne	Patio above Hawthorne	108
Bertie Lou's Cafe	SE/Sellwood	Picnic tables on the street	42
Aquariva	SW/Inner	Beautiful riverside patio	28
Hands On Café	SW/Inner	Lovely garden patio	104
Seasons and Regions	SW/Outer	Patio, covered and heated in winter	220
Cup & Saucer Cafe	Several	Uncovered sidewalk tables	76

Instead of cluttering up the book with restaurants' Facebook links and Twitter @nonsense, I instead offer all the Facebook and Twitter and website links you can stand on my website, breakfastinbridgetown.com. Go there, click "Restaurants Online," and find what you need.

I do have a Facebook page just for my breakfast exploits; it's facebook.com/pdxbreakfast.

And there's a Twitter feed: @pdxbreakfastguy. You can subscribe there to my "PDX Breakfast Places" list, as well.

And finally, I am on Google+ as well as at PaulGerald.com, where I discuss hikes and travel exploits and Portland Heritage Trees and English soccer and spiritual wanderings. You can also go there and subscribe to my "Breakfast Bulletin" newsletter to keep up with all of it.

Other web pages of note—and usefulness in writing a breakfast book:

- foodcartsortland.com: The hub of food cart world
- goodstuffnw.com: Food writer Kathleen Bauer specializes in farmers markets
- lizcrain.com: Local food writer and author of *Food Lover's Guide to Portland*
- pdx.eater.com: News and commentary
- portlandfood.org: A sprawling discussion of all things Portland food
- portlandfoodanddrink.com: The Food Dude's great news and review site
- stumptownvegans.com: Terrific site for vegans, occasionally talks breakfast
- eatingmywaythruportland.com: a fun blog by the amazing Amy.
- bestplacestostuffyourfaces.com: Online home of super eater Jen Stevenson.

RECOMMENDED BOOKS

There are plenty of fine books about Portland, in particular its food scene. Here are some of my favorites, which I encourage you to go get a copy of. In fact, if you catch me at various markets, fairs and festivals around town (see paulgerald.com/trips-and-talks), you'll probably see some of these for sale, in addition to all of mine.

Portland Happy Hour Guidebook by Cindy Anderson
    See happyhourguidebook.com
Portland's 100 Best Places to Stuff Your Faces by Jen Stevenson
    See bestplacestostuffyourfaces.com
A Food Lover's Guide to Portland by Liz Crain
    See lizcrain.com/foodloversguidetoportlandblog
The Best Places to Pee: A Guide to the Funky and Fabulous Bathrooms of Portland by Kelly Melillo
    See thebestplacestopee.com
Portland Hill Walks, Portland City Walks, and *The Portland Stairs Book,* all by Laura Foster
Bloody Marys: Sanguine Solutions for a Slew of Situations by Judy Bennett.
    See bloodymarybook.com
Left Coast Roast by Hanna Neuschwander

OTHER BOOKS BY ME

I guess I wouldn't be doing my self-promotion job if I didn't pimp my other books, right? Look for all of these at paulgerald.com.

60 Hikes Within 60 Miles of Portland
Day and Section Hikes on the Oregon PCT
Peaceful Places: Portland
Best Tent Camping: Oregon
The Portland Heritage Trees (Fall 2014)
An American's Guide to English Soccer (Spring 2015)

My first addiction, of many, was travel. Then sports. Then walking around in the mountains. Then, well, a few other things. Then food. Put that together, and I became a guy who wrote about sports for newspapers, travel for all sorts of people, hiking and camping books, and now this weird breakfast idea. And I'm already moving on to other combinations.

I don't know how much you really want to know about me, but in case you care: I grew up in Memphis, went to school in Texas, worked for some newspapers here and there, freelanced, cooked on fishing boats in Alaska, had some other cool and crappy jobs, and moved to Portland in 1996 because it had good coffee and beer. Also, it didn't get hot like Memphis, and there were mountains nearby.

The best things to happen to me were being born into a cool family, discovering the magic of the forest, following the Grateful Dead around the country, getting sober, meeting my current girlfriend, and along the way occasionally getting paid to do what I was doing anyway: writing, eating, camping, hiking, and traveling.

In addition to this book, which was the first one I published myself, I have also written four for a company called Keen Communications in Birmingham, Alabama. Those titles are *60 Hikes Within 60 Miles of Portland, Day and Overnight Hikes on Oregon's Pacific Crest Trail, Best in Tent Camping: Oregon*, and *Peaceful Places: Portland*.

I also lead hiking trips for the Mazamas, a hiking and climbing club in Portland, to places like Tuscany and the Alps. I'm working on a book for the fall of 2014 about the Portland Heritage Trees (see portlandheritagetrees.com). And I'm going to England several times this year and next so I can write a travel guide to English soccer, which will come out in the summer of 2015.

In other words, my life is one big ball of blessings. And I appreciate your playing a part—not just by buying the book (though that helps) but by actually reading it and being a part of the process. See, I always wanted to go to interesting places, do interesting things, and then tell people about it. So I thank you for your kind attention.

You can find me online at paulgerald.com.

THE AUTHOR'S FAVORITES

There is one question *everybody* asks me: "What's your favorite place?" Or "What's the best place?"

But for me, those are the same question, and there really is no such thing. I have favorite diners, favorite fancy places, favorite dishes, favorite ways to show off Portland…you get the idea. Plus, my mood changes, and after eating in close to 200 restaurants, I honestly sometimes forget about places. And I don't do ratings in the book anyway.

Still, everyone asks, so I forced myself to list my 12 favorites. Note that I didn't say "the 12 best in town." These places (listed alphabetically, by the way) all have some combination of good food, good memories, a vibe that I dig, and cute waitresses.

Two disclaimers: I invested exactly four minutes in putting together this list, and if you ask me in person, I probably won't remember what's on here.

Ataula because it's just straight awesome.

Bijou Café for the oyster hash and Portland class.

Clyde Common for the style, cuisine, and scenery.

Harlow for my healthy, beautiful sweetie.

Helser's because it still feels just right.

Kenny and Zuke's for the pastrami and sodas.

Olympic Provisions for the kielbasa hash.

Original Pancake House because it's eternal.

Po'shines for blackened catfish and a Southern groove.

Sanborn's for that zingy hollandaise…and German pancakes.

Simpatica for whatever they want to cook.

Zell's for being my Perfect Portland Breakfast.

Hashcapades
The Art of the Perfect Hash Adventure

CLARK HAASS

Nobody knows hash like my buddy Clark Haass, author and publisher of the cookbook *Hashcapades: The Art of the Perfect Hash Adventure*. Clark has been hashing it up around town for years, and I've had the pleasure of going on a few of the events. Here is his Top 10 list, all of which are from places you can read about elsewhere in this book.

For more on Clark, and to order his book, see hashcapades.com. There, you will also find his fantastic Hash Finder, which will help you find restaurants serving yummy hashes wherever you are.

TOP 10 HASHCAPADES

NUMBER 1 – Beast – See page 38

A view of the kitchen and two large communal tables let you share the extravaganza with other foodies. My Beast hashcapade was a Tails and Trotters Braised Pork Shoulder, Market Potatoes, Garnet Yams, Leeks, Brussel Sprouts, Poached Farm Egg & Truffled Hollandaise with an artistic swirl of sweet balsamic reduction. It's a must!

NUMBER 2 – Clyde Common – See page 70

The Smoked Lamb Hash with Parsnips & Calabrian Chili Sauce and a poached egg arrived on large, dark wooden slabs. I can only describe the flavor profile as extreme comfort food – rustic smokiness in the tender lamb, sweet roasted parsnips, luscious yolk, herbs and a kick at the end.

NUMBER 3 – Mother's Bistro – See page 160

I have it on good authority that Robert Plant enjoyed the very same hash that I enthusiastically devoured in record time. Fresh wild salmon, chives, a light creamy sauce and roasted potatoes make the perfect combination. With or without an egg, this hash is an instant classic!

NUMBER 4 – Urban Farmer – See page 263

This clever treatment was a small tin can place upside down. Our waiter lifted the can for the reveal – Corned Beef Tongue, Potatoes, Onions and fresh herbs. Perched on top was a perfectly basted egg. A hollandaise sauce was expertly drizzled all over the cylinder of hash goodness. I gained a few pounds just staring at this delightful, innovative hash!

NUMBER 5 – Broder – See page 54

Broder's Swedish heritage offers the classic Pytt i Panna, a Swedish version of hash with potatoes and beets, and a version with Smoked Trout. Our hash was served in a small cast iron pan and topped with a baked egg. One bite and you'll be hooked on the smokey, robust flavor of trout balanced with roasted beets and potatoes. Fantastic!

TOP 10 HASHCAPADES

NUMBER 6 – Gracie's – See page 258

Gracie's Cold Smoked Salmon Hash with capers, red onions, hash browns and crème fraîche is a game changer – silky yolk and crème fraîche balanced the salty salmon and capers perfectly. The shredded potatoes and onion anchored the heavenly hash in an understated, earthy way that made the whole greater than the sum of the parts!

NUMBER 7 – Cafe Nell – See page 64

Three outstanding hashes were served by Cafe Nell to my hashcapade posse: Trout, Vegan, and Sausage & Sage. I got the fresh Idaho trout grilled to perfection, which hid the southwestern style potatoes, green pepper, corn and bits of jalapeño. A sunny-side-up egg and hollandaise sauce with smoked paprika completed the remarkable presentation.

NUMBER 8 – Toast – See page 238

Lamb, rabbit, sausage, veggies, bacon, pork belly: Toast is the spice of life for hash lovers. My sausage hash had Brussels sprout leaves adorning the plate with bright green. The house-ground sausage had a slight crispness that was superb. The pièce de résistance, caramelized onion and parmesan cheese, anchored yet another sublime creation.

NUMBER 9 – Petite Provence Alberta – See page 190

Their Corned Beef Hash was stunningly yummy with multi-colored peppers, a creamy horseradish sauce and house-cured corned beef. Had I opted for the decadent patisseries in their display cases, I would have gone into food coma of epic proportions. Bon appetit!

NUMBER 10 – Olympic Provisions – See page 174

Olympic, winners of America's Best Charcuterie for their Chorizo Navarre by *Bon Appetit,* brings artisanal meats to the masses. Their kielbasa hash was delicious and spicy. Bits of lardon anchored the salty & smoky notes while the poached egg's silky ooze tempered the dish, forging an instant masterpiece – huzzah!

Quick. Where can you find a restaurant that serves hash in Portland, Oregon? What about in New York City? What? You live in Nashville? Check out the only Hash Finder on the planet—http://hashcapades .com/hash-finder! With advanced search capabilities, you can search by city, state, zip, or country and more. Check it out!